Acclaim for Travelers' Tales Books By and For Women

The Best Women's Travel Writing 2010
Gold Medal Winner, Independent Publisher Book Awards. "A funny, touching and impressive read." —Eva Holland, *World Hum*

100 Places Every Woman Should Go
"Will ignite the wanderlust in any woman…inspiring and delightful."
—Lowell Thomas Awards judges' citation, Best Travel Book 2007

100 Places in Italy Every Woman Should Go
"Reveals an intimacy with Italy and a honed sense of adventure. *Andiamo!*"
—Frances Mayes

Women in the Wild
"A spiritual, moving and totally female book to take you around the world and back." —*Mademoiselle*

A Woman's Path
"A sensitive exploration of women's lives that have been unexpectedly and spiritually touched by travel experiences . . . highly recommended."
—*Library Journal*

A Woman's World
"Packed with stories of courage and confidence, independence and introspection." —*Self Magazine*

A Woman's Passion for Travel
"Sometimes sexy, sometimes scary, sometimes philosophical and always entertaining." —*San Francisco Examiner*

Sand in My Bra
"Bursting with exuberant candor and crackling humor." —*Publishers Weekly*

A Woman's Europe
"These stories will inspire women to find a way to visit places they've only dreamed of." —*The Globe and Mail*

The World Is a Kitch-
"A vicarious delight for the virtual to~~~   r the most
seasoned culinary voyager."   'e Katzen

"Should give courage to any w   ıp on
her love of travel when she giv   *Chicago Herald*

"A witty, profound, and accessible exploration of journal-keeping."
—Anthony Weller

WOMEN'S TRAVEL LITERATURE FROM
TRAVELERS' TALES

THE BEST WOMEN'S TRAVEL WRITING

Volume 8

TRUE STORIES FROM AROUND THE WORLD

THE BEST WOMEN'S TRAVEL WRITING

Volume 8

TRUE STORIES FROM AROUND THE WORLD

Edited by
LAVINIA SPALDING

Travelers' Tales
an imprint of Solas House, Inc.
Palo Alto

Art direction: Kimberly Nelson
Cover photograph: © Ralph Lee Hopkins
Page layout: Scribe Inc.
Interior design: Scribe Inc., using the fonts Granjon, Nicolas Cochin and
Ex Ponto
Author photo: Erica Hilton
Production: Natalie Baszile

ISBN 1-60952-059-5
ISSN 1553-054X

First Edition
Printed in the United States
10 9 8 7 6 5 4 3 2 1

Whoever you are, no matter how lonely,
the world offers itself to your imagination,
calls to you like the wild geese, harsh
and exciting—
over and over announcing your place
in the family of things.

—Mary Oliver, "Wild Geese"

For my family

Table of Contents

Introduction

*W*hen I was little, we didn't travel. My parents couldn't afford airplane tickets, and we were never one of those road-tripping-skiing-camping-fishing-s'mores-by-the-bonfire families. We were a stay-indoors-play-monopoly-read-politely-on-the-sofa people. I do recall one big international trip, however, to Madrid, Spain.

What I remember is that I didn't get to go. My parents took my older brother and sister, while I stayed home with my Nana. Although I have no memory of their departure or return, I can still vividly recall the resulting 8 x 10 framed photo of my siblings, ages five and eight, posing with a statuesque flamenco dancer. All three subjects beamed widely into the camera as they held castanets above their heads, wrists turned elegantly inward. That grainy photograph hung on our living room wall every day of my childhood, taunting me.

"You wouldn't have even remembered the trip!" my mom protested whenever I complained about my missed opportunity. "You were two! And in diapers!"

None of that mattered. All I knew was that something rare and magical existed within that photo, and I wanted in.

The summer after I turned ten, I finally got the family trip I'd longed for. My parents moved us from New Hampshire to Arizona, and we spent three glorious weeks on the road. My brother Nathanael and I rode with my parents in a yellow 1965 school bus they'd converted into a camper van and named Gillie Rom ("Song of the road" in Romany, the Gypsy language) while my sister and a friend caravanned in the U-Haul. Nathanael and I spent most of our time at a foldout card table in the back, playing poker for pennies and encouraging passing truckers to honk their horns. I devoted entire days to reading Nancy Drew books, scribbling in my journal, and staring dreamily out the window at cornfields and cows.

My parents braked for all major landmarks: the Hershey chocolate factory in Pennsylvania, the Luray Caverns in Virginia, the American Museum of Science and Energy in Tennessee. I remember a Fourth of July barbecue in Memphis with pulled pork cooked for twenty-four hours, and a late-night bluegrass jam session around a campfire in Kentucky. One night at a KOA in Arkansas, my father jimmied the lock of a rental paddleboat and we all floated on a moonlit lake while he serenaded us with his classical guitar.

I had never been happier or more awakened to the promise of the world and the possibilities that exist within a family. And I've probably spent my adult life trying to prolong the experience.

There's something tremendously potent about family travel, and this fact struck me again while editing *The Best Women's Travel Writing Volume 8*. As I reviewed the stories that make up this year's collection, an unexpected theme began rising from the ink: among the cast of characters were two grandfathers, a grandmother, two mothers, a father, a brother, a couple of daughters, a son, some ancestors, a friend's parents, and two sisters-in-law.

Likewise, there's something singularly powerful about the *stories* that come from family travel. I find them fascinating, and not strictly because of an unchecked childhood obsession with a photo, or even three weeks spent in a school bus with foldout cots. What excites me in a piece of travel writing is the same quality that makes travel itself meaningful: genuine human connection. When a story involves family, this is nearly always present—often paired with some complicated and long-awaited flash of understanding, the reinterpreting of a shared history, a healthy dose of ambiguity, a deepening of ties, and in the end, a sense of renewal, perhaps even redemption.

To me, that makes for good reading.

In this year's collection, we have Amber Kelly-Anderson climbing the Great Wall of China in torrential rain with her ninety-one-year-old grandfather who yearns for nothing more than one final journey, and Carol Reichert accompanying her brother to a stem-cell clinic in the Dominican Republic on a desperate mission to find a miracle cure for his disease. There's Ann Hood's stunning memoir of seeking a little solace in Tibet after a devastating family tragedy, and Molly Beer's recognition, on a bridge between El Salvador and Guatemala, that the paths she and her father have taken in life are peacefully intersecting.

In Marcy Gordon's "Root-Bound," she recalls a trip to Sicily with her mother to research their ancestry, during which they end up finding more *famiglia* than they anticipated. Root-bound, a gardening term, refers to the point when plant roots exceed the limits of their container and grow all together in one big, tangled mass.

To me, these are the perfect words to describe the uncommon kinship that emerges from travel.

Thirty-some years have passed since the summer I spent on the road with my family. Since then I've traveled to thirty-some countries and inhabited thirty-some homes. I've lived in seven states, and for six years I called South Korea home. I've gone hang gliding in Australia and horseback riding in Costa Rica, driven a Fiat 500 across Sicily, and danced the *sevillana* on a rooftop in Spain. I've hidden from Chinese police in a hillside monastery in Tibet, outrun a typhoon in the Philippines, and lain on a dirt road by a rice field in Bali watching fireflies light up the dark. I've trekked with hill-tribe Hmong girls in Vietnam, learned to salsa in a tiny Cuban living room, ridden an elephant through a jungle in Thailand, and meditated at dusk in an ancient, deserted temple in Cambodia.

I've nursed a lifelong love affair with movement, straying ever farther from those I love most. But somewhere along the way, it dawned on me that I was always traveling with family—because the act of travel, to the extent that it separates us from our relatives, also extends, manifests, multiplies, and completes family.

Travelers' Tales' editor-at-large James O'Reilly once wrote, "It is a cliché to say that we are all kin, but it is true. Even if we hail from different clans, travel makes you certain that kinship is true not only in sentiment but in fact."

On the road, how quickly strangers become our sisters, sharing stories, tips, meals, and maps; how seamlessly our guides morph into overprotective brothers, herding us through crowds and shielding us from mysterious dangers. Our hosts become self-appointed parental figures who insist we're not eating enough. And if we aren't careful, our travel companion can turn into something resembling a conjoined twin.

Many stories in this year's collection illustrate this category of "family." Bridget Crocker learns about the enduring power of sisterhood in a river community in Zambia, while Abbie Kozolchyk forms "a funny little family" on an island in Vietnam with locals who don't speak a word of her language. Jocelyn Edelstein finds a home in a slum in Brazil with three generations of women who teach her about survival. And Jessica Wilson joins a "pilgrim corps" to walk the Camino de Santiago from France to Spain—and becomes part of what she calls "an unmistakable *we*."

There's something profoundly intense and intoxicating about friendship found en route. It's the bond that arises from being thrust into uncomfortable circumstances, and the vulnerability in trusting others to help navigate those situations. It's the exhilaration of meeting someone when we are our most alive selves, breathing new air, high on life-altering moments. It's the discovery of the commonality of the world's people and the attendant rejection of prejudices. It's the humbling experience of being suspicious of a stranger who then extends a great kindness. It's the astonishment of learning from those whom we set out to teach. It's the intimacy of sharing small spaces, the recognition of a kindred soul across the globe.

It's the travel relationship, and it can only call itself family.

For years, Travelers' Tales has brought together tribes of travel writers whose stories make the world a more familiar place and tribes of travel readers who connect to the storytellers, making it a more *familial* place. With each tale, we move closer to one another, and closer to someone in a faraway part of the world, and it seems a new leaf sprouts on a branch of our extended family tree.

This book will take you from Afghanistan to Brazil, from Cambodia to the Dominican Republic, from England to France and Guatemala, and all the way to Zambia, with umpteen points in between. The women in this book will take you on inner journeys as distinct as each destination. As you read, you may find your paths crossing, your lives colliding, and your stories becoming inexorably intertwined—perhaps even root-bound. You might develop a feeling of affinity for not only the authors, but also the amazing characters they'll introduce you to.

You'll meet a beautiful boatman in Belize, a blundering bicycling guide in Kyrgyzstan, a cocky cab driver in Argentina, and a puzzling palm reader in India. In France, you'll learn a thing or two about marriage from a famous restaurateur and find your preconceptions challenged by a village ice cream maker. You might even fall for a stubborn Brit in Oman, a butterfly photographer in Mexico, a dreadlocked soccer coach in Kenya, a long-lashed Muslim in Afghanistan, or a quiet, pancake-making bird researcher in New Zealand.

After all, anything can happen on the road—especially when you're traveling with family.

—Lavinia Spalding
San Francisco, CA

$\mathcal{S}$ $\mathcal{S}$ $\mathcal{S}$

Lost and Liberated

In a French village, their preconceptions melted away.

"*I*'m lost. I'm late. I'm sorry," I blurted into the phone, in French.

Silence.

"So, Monsieur Manouvrier, if it's O.K. I would still like to meet you today."

"You are an hour late. Do you think I have nothing better to do? You Americans think you are so important?" he bellowed, barely breathing between salvos. "Do you think we are so honored to speak to an American that we will stop everything else in our lives?"

I wanted to shout, "You know nothing about me!" But since it was my last day in the Dordogne, and I wanted to meet this man before I left, I begged. "Please, may I still come?"

"Fine," he replied. The slam of the receiver reverberated in my ear before I could ask him for better directions.

As an American who had spent many years traveling in France, I sometimes felt like the honorary town piñata, enduring swing upon jab about my accent, my nationality, and the political leanings of our president who, I had constantly to remind people, was not a personal friend of mine. But despite the occasional bashing, I'd also become a defender of the French, charmed by the generosity of those who welcomed me, a stranger, into their homes, and seduced by their pervasive and earnest *joie de vivre*.

So, alone in a three-chimney village somewhere in southwestern France, at a crossroads, literally and figuratively, I had two choices: I could abandon this meeting altogether or I could exemplify American perseverance. I folded up my map and set out, knowing that the long road ahead was more than just the one I was lost on.

In France, as in many parts of the world, the best information arrives by word of mouth, or *de bouche à oreille* as they say, from mouth to ear. This is how I had learned of Roland Manouvrier, an artisanal ice cream maker—and the source of my navigational woes.

I'd been in the Dordogne for nearly a month researching a culinary travel book. Having amassed a stockpile of classic recipes from local chefs and home cooks, I was in search of something—and someone—a little different. One of these people was Chef Nicolas De Visch, who had taken over his parents' restaurant in the medieval village of Issigeac, and whose menu did not include a single serving of duck or *foie gras*— two mainstays of the regional cuisine. Nicolas had invited me to dinner and after several courses of his unconventional cooking, plunked a tub of ice cream down on the table, handed me an espresso spoon, and motioned for me to dig into the creamy white contents. Preparing my taste buds for vanilla or coconut, or some other sweet savor, I closed my lips around the mouthful. The cold burned my tongue, then melted down the back of my throat. Nicolas's eyebrows arched in question.

"Goat cheese?" I guessed.

"Yes, from the village of Rocamadour," he confirmed. "And you really must meet this guy before you go."

After crisscrossing the Dordogne countryside for nearly two hours, I had pulled off the road to make that call to Roland.

My otherwise trusty GPS had been no match for rural French addresses without street names or numbers, only titles like "The Sheep Barn" and "The Old Mill." Finally, thanks to a helpful barista, I zeroed in on Roland's address, given simply as "The Industrial Zone" in the village of Saint-Geniès.

When I arrived twenty minutes later, Roland met me at his office door wearing a white lab coat, a plastic hair net set askew atop his wavy brown hair, and a scowl. The archetypal mad scientist, I thought. For a second the story of "Hansel and Gretel" popped into my head. I wondered if anyone would hear me scream as Roland shoved me into a cauldron over a hot fire. Would I be his next flavor—*Glacé à l'Américaine?*

"How much time do you need?" he barked, interrupting my reverie.

"As much as you'll give me," I answered. He corrected my French.

"Because you're late, I'm late, and I must make deliveries."

"How about I help you? We can talk on the road," I offered.

"Pppfff . . ." Roland produced the classic French noise made by blowing air through one's relaxed lips, often done to dismiss something just said.

I followed him through his stainless-steel kitchen and helped him load frozen cases of ice cream into his delivery van. As I moved them into place, I noticed the flavors penned in black ink on the lid of each container: Tomato-Basil. Szechwan. Rose. Violet. Calvados. I asked Roland if I could include one of his unusual recipes in my book.

"What do you think? I have a formula like at McDonald's? I don't write my recipes down. They are not exact, and depend on many influences."

"Pppfff . . ." he added.

We coursed the serpentine Dordogne roads, past fields of lemon-yellow flowers and over oak-encrusted hills, delivering the frozen parcels every fifteen to twenty minutes. Each time Roland got back in the car, he shelled me with questions: Do you like Andy Warhol? Have you been to New York? Have you ever seen a real cowboy? How about a real Indian? What is the point of baseball? Each time I answered, he corrected my French.

"Would you like to drink something?" Roland eventually asked.

Finally, I thought. *A question that isn't about America and cultural icons.* Hoping to demonstrate my language prowess and keep his corrections at bay, I came up with the perfect response, an idiomatic expression I'd recently learned.

"*Oui. Les grands esprits se rencontrent,*" I replied. Yes. Great minds think alike. "*J'aimerais une boisson froide.*" I would love a cold drink.

"*Une boisson FRAICHE,*" Roland said, emphasizing the correct adjective. "*Pas froide.*" He added in a verb suggestion while he was at it, and didn't even mention the expression I'd whipped out to impress him.

I didn't mind being corrected. It was part of learning a new language. But after an hour of the question-response-correction routine—and what felt like nitpicking at what was, in fact, intelligible French—my patience had eroded.

I finally took a swing back at him. "If you prefer, we could speak in English. Would *that* be easier for you?"

"Why would I speak in English? I am in France and French is my language!" he bellowed. The sarcasm was lost on him.

My face flushed and my jaw tightened. Short fused and aching from the smile I'd been faking for the last hour, I was ready to abandon this day and this ill-mannered ice cream man. I blew up.

"You know what?" I hollered, "It's people like YOU who give the French a bad reputation in my country. And in case YOU haven't noticed, I am in YOUR country speaking YOUR language because YOU can't speak mine."

I braced myself for retaliation. Roland stared straight ahead, his hands clenching the steering wheel. After a tense ten-second interlude, he asked me about the reputation the French have in America. I quietly listened to the advice of the voices in my head. One said, "Be diplomatic, you're a professional." The other said, "Be honest, he's an asshole." I cleared my throat.

"Though generalizing," I began, "we find you rude, arrogant, and hateful toward Americans." A good synthesis of both voices, I thought.

Roland's belly-bouncing chuckle filled the air, but he said nothing more, not even to correct me.

We crossed a bridge and puttered down the main two-lane street of Saint-Léon-sur-Vézère, our final stop for the day. The sun was low in the summer sky and cast an ochre glow on the stone buildings. Garlands of yellow and orange paper flowers strung between the steeply pitched rooftops swayed overhead, remnants of a recent festival. We parked and found a table in the sun at the town's only café. Roland ordered me to wait while he delivered ice cream to his brother down the street. I watched him shake hands and kiss-kiss the cheeks of a few people along the way before disappearing into a doorway. When I saw him again, he was back on the street, handing out ice cream cones from the back of his van to lucky passersby. He waved me over.

I asked him if he lived in Saint-Leon-sur-Vézère.

"No. This is where I was born," he said.

Roland pulled out another familiar white container, scooped the bright orange ice cream into two cones, and handed me one. The mandarin orange flavor couldn't have tasted better if I'd plucked it from a tree.

We wandered through the cobblestone streets of the riverside village, and as I savored my frozen treat, Roland unlatched his memories. He pointed out the window he'd broken while trying to master a yo-yo; the home of a girl he once had a crush on; the church where he got married. We stopped in front of the brown wooden door of a village house, and Roland told me the lady who once lived there had found a rusted American G.I. helmet in her garden.

"She gave the helmet to my father, and we kept it displayed on top of an armoire in our dining room for many years," Roland said.

"Why?" I asked. "What interest did your father have in it?"

"We didn't know anything about the soldier. Did he come from Oklahoma? Wyoming? Did he have a family?" Roland said. Then he raised his finger in the air. "The only thing we knew for certain was that this anonymous American came here to liberate France. For that we are grateful."

Tears pricked my eyes, and I silently blinked them away. It wasn't just the unexpected provenance of Roland's story, or the softening of his voice. His words had conjured an image in my head of a framed black-and-white photograph hanging in my dining room back home: my nineteen-year-old grand-father—my own hero—in his G.I. helmet.

We sat, wordless, atop a low rock wall for several minutes, feet dangling over the Vézère River.

"Thank you for sharing that story," I eventually said.

"Thank you for come today," Roland replied, in English.

I didn't correct him.

Kimberley Lovato is a freelance writer based in San Francisco. Her writing has appeared in National Geographic Traveler, Afar, Delta Sky Magazine, Executive Travel, *and in other print and online media. Roland's recipe for tomato-basil sorbet appeared in her mailbox a month after their meeting and can be found on page 123 of her culinary travel book,* Walnut Wine &Truffle Groves, *which won two awards in the category of Culinary Travel: the 2010 Cordon d'Or International Culinary Academy Award, and the 2010 Gourmand International World Cookbook Award. Her website is www.kimberleylovato.com.*

ANN HOOD

☙ ☙ ☙

The Runaway

Can grief be outrun?

When the SUV I took from the train station to my hotel in Lhasa last January got blocked by two men haggling over a yak's head, I had one thought: *I could not be farther away from my little red house in Providence, Rhode Island*. I'd had that thought before—on a starlit night on an island in the middle of Lake Titicaca; on a crowded street in Phnom Penh as a man clutching an AK-47 strolled past me; on a boat in the Mekong River bumping against other boats loaded with jackfruit, mangosteen, and durian. The realization that I am somewhere removed from life as I know it, somewhere no one can reach me, where I can't read menus or street signs and where the very air I breathe smells different, brings me a strange comfort.

Ever since 2002, when my daughter Grace died suddenly at the age of five from a virulent form of strep, I have had the desire to flee. At first, I wanted to sell our house and move—to Oregon, to Italy, to the moon. It didn't matter where. What mattered was that I leave the familiar rooms and streets where Grace's footsteps now echoed louder than they had when she was alive. Our kitchen floor still had glitter on it from the art project she never finished. In the corner of one room I found her ballet tights rolled into a ball, still smelling of the mild stink of her feet. In her bedroom, wrappers from forbidden candy she had sneaked nestled in drawers. When I stepped out the front door, when I walked down the street, I could still see her dashing ahead of me in her metallic purple sneakers, her big brother, Sam, at her side. "Stop at the corner!" I could hear myself shout. I had worried about a speeding car careening down one of the alleys that line our neighborhood when I should have been dreading a microscopic, deadly bacterium. How foolish the panic in my voice seemed now.

After Grace died, I wanted to run away, to go somewhere mysterious and distant. Surely, I thought, there were places in the world where I would not be haunted. I had been a nomad of sorts for most of my adult life. Looking back, perhaps I have always been running away. From a small-town childhood. From broken hearts—my own and those I broke. From loneliness and a restlessness that has bubbled in me for as long as I can remember.

My father used to tell me stories about his years in Peking (Beijing) in the late 1940s. People dropped dead from starvation right at his feet, he said. There were dark rooms where men gambled. Women still had bound feet and limped down the street behind their husbands. He told me how he'd skied in Greece and scuba dived off the coast of Haiti. He ate dog in Morocco and got bit by a mongoose in Cuba. Perhaps it is no surprise then that at the age of sixteen, I took the $500 I'd earned in two years of modeling for the local department store, Jordan Marsh, and flew to Bermuda, where I snorkeled and drank rum swizzles and lay on a beach of pink sand. With the next year's savings, I flew to Nassau in the Bahamas to eat conch chowder and dance to steel drums. And so it went through college: a voodoo ceremony in Brazil, a double rainbow on Maui, Mardi Gras in New Orleans.

When I graduated, the only job I wanted was as a flight attendant with an international airline. I studied route maps the way my friends studied Kaplan books for the LSATs and GREs. I memorized codes for airports—LHR, CDG, MIL—intending to visit every one. In eight years at the airline, I flew more than a million miles. When not in the air, I sailed down the Nile and climbed the Acropolis; I bought knockoff handbags in Rome and watches in Zurich; I wore out dozens of shoes on cobblestone streets. Even after my job ended, I planned getaways. When Sam was born, and then Grace, I kept going, breaking umbrella strollers on the bumpy sidewalks of Warsaw. Three years after Grace died, my husband, Lorne, and I adopted a little girl, Annabelle, and within three weeks she was on my lap in a boat on Lake Titicaca.

The advice commonly given to grieving people is to stay put. Don't move, don't quit your job or leave your spouse. Yet my instinct was to go, to run away as far and as fast as I could. "You can go away," I was told, "but when you get home, nothing will be better." Didn't they understand that in those months after Grace died, I thought nothing would ever be better? Simple tasks became impossible, but when friends invited us to visit them in France that summer, I said yes. It took me an entire afternoon to book three tickets to Paris over the telephone. Reading the numbers off my American Express card proved daunting. They jumped and reversed until I cried. "My daughter is dead!" I sobbed to the frustrated ticket agent. "I still need a valid credit card," she said.

Finally I had tickets, a travel plan, an escape. Lorne and Sam and I cried our way through Provence, following van Gogh's footsteps in Arles and shopping the market in Aix-en-Provence. At our friends' house, I gratefully slept the deep, numbing sleep of jet lag and woke to cold wine, crashing waves, and jaw-dropping views. In the fog of grief, I visited Marseille and ate bouillabaisse. Well-wishers were right: when I got home, nothing had changed. But while I was away, I was distracted and off-kilter in a different way. I struggled with unfamiliar, twisting streets and menus I couldn't decipher, while at home I struggled with the familiar and I still could decipher nothing. Better, I thought on my first grief-struck night back home, to navigate the foreign and exotic than to fail to navigate what I used to manage so easily.

That was how I found myself in Lhasa, stuck behind the head of a yak. As years passed and the grief continued, I traveled to more remote locations. The farther or higher or more isolated, the better I felt. The unknown brought a strange safety. The vaccinations, the visas, the curve of alphabets I could not read reminded me that the world holds mystery and danger side by side with joy and wonder. These were the same contradictions I'd grappled with every day since Grace died.

On a snowy night eight years after her death, Lorne, Annabelle and I boarded a train in Beijing at midnight, headed for Tibet. The journey would take forty-eight hours, which seemed to horrify people when I told them. But to me, the long trip sounded divine. With my French press coffeepot and a pound of Peet's French Roast, my knitting and a bag of old *New Yorkers*, as well as crayons and paper for Annabelle and a dog-eared copy of *Charlie and the Chocolate Factory*, I set up our little train compartment as if it were our home. In many ways it was. My comfort came not just from the places I was going but also from the journey to them. Even after so many years, opening curtains and finding a herd of yaks, or sitting at a table in a crowded dining car eating spicy noodles, brings wonder back into my still-broken heart. As the train slowed on its approach into Lhasa, I whispered to my husband, "I wish we didn't have to get off. I could just go and go on this train."

Moments later, we stepped into the thin air of Lhasa, its sky bluer than anything has a right to be. Everywhere we looked, ragged faded prayer flags blew in the breeze. The smell of yak butter permeated our hair and clothes, mixing with the scent of burning juniper. On the road to our hotel, we passed scores of pilgrims moving in synchronized motions, dropping from knees to stomach along the crowded roads.

I took a deep breath. For oxygen, yes. But also to renew myself. Days of travel, by air and train and now car, had brought me here. I was tired and achy and overwhelmed by sights and sounds. And in this way, I moved along a different journey, the one that began eight Aprils before in an intensive care unit, when I stood by my dead daughter's side and wanted to run. In that moment, I imagined running out of that hospital, away from its smell of death and the sounds of machines stopping and the stillness of my little girl. I wanted to run through the streets of my hometown of Providence, screaming and screaming into the night. But of course I couldn't. I stood in that room and signed papers and answered questions and held my hand out to the nurse who gave me Grace's brightly colored clothes in a Ziploc bag. Later, at home in the bed where I had slept for ten years, I heard the familiar sounds of neighbors going to work, college students on their skateboards, *The New York Times* dropping on my front stoop. Once so soothing, they all felt like an assault. *Run*, my brain ordered. *Run*.

Finally, the yak head is tossed into a truck, and the small street opens up. The SUV squeezes between mountains of pale-yellow yak butter and Chinese soldiers carrying rifles. Inside our hotel, yak-butter tea waits for us; orange and pink silk cushions line the floor. Venturing out again, I join a crowd of people in colorful ethnic clothes and monks in yellow robes, jostling through a dark temple. They mumble prayers. They reach out to touch the toe of a statue. They light offerings of incense and butter. I have no prayers, no religion, no ritual except this act of throwing myself into the unknown.

That first night, we climb narrow stone steps to the roof of the hotel. A crooked handwritten sign says WELCOME TO THE ROOFTOP OF THE WORLD. I am gasping by the time I reach the top. The altitude makes my heart pound against my ribs and my head ache. It's hard to breathe here.

Leaning against the sign, I return to that hospital, that ICU. That night when Grace died, I couldn't catch my breath. The foreign world of death overwhelmed me, sucked the air from me. I remember my hands flailing like a drowning person's. I remember drowning in grief.

People think grief ends as time passes, when really it just changes shape. You should, they believe, be over it. Although it is true that sometimes days pass without me thinking about Grace, or losing her, it is also true that I can hear a song or glimpse a little blond-haired girl, and my knees will still buckle. When I am housebound for too long, when I must stay put, grief intrudes more often. Over time I have learned to see it coming, to recognize its early signs: the inability to concentrate, the jangling nerves and short temper, too many hours staring at daytime TV. I've learned that planning my next escape can ease the pain. I turn off *The Barefoot Contessa* and pick up a travel guide, mapping out the best flights to Entebbe or Vientiane, the routes I can follow to disappear into a different world. Perhaps I will always be looking for these routes out of grief, for these places that can shake me up, that can remind me that this big world is beautiful after all.

Slowly, my heart calms on that rooftop in Lhasa. I take a long, slow breath and look up at the sky, still so blue it almost hurts. I feel my heart swell with wonder. In the years I have been trying to outrun grief, I've learned that escaping makes me grateful to be here, to be alive. In a moment I will be drinking Lhasa beer, eating yak ribs and samosas. But first I stretch my hands upward, reaching toward that sky, as if I can actually touch it.

$$\approx \quad \approx \quad \approx$$

Ann Hood is the author, most recently, of the novels The Knitting Circle *and* The Red Thread, *and the memoir,* Comfort:

A Journey Through Grief. *Her short stories and essays have appeared in many publications, including* The New York Times, The Atlantic Monthly, Tin House, *and* The Paris Review. *She has recently launched a series for middle readers,* The Treasure Chest, *and her novel,* The Obituary Writer, *will be published in 2013.*

❧ ❧ ❧

Bridge on the Border

A father-daughter trip to nowhere and everywhere.

On Christmas Eve day, I stood with my father on the bridge over the Rio Paz. It was no-man's land—a gap between two nations—but children swam in the glittering brown river, and birds flitted back and forth, from El Salvador, to Guatemala, back again. We were nowhere and everywhere.

Actually, my whole family was visiting, my parents and my two younger siblings, both still in college, and my best friend. I had been finagled into hosting the holidays.

"I'm picturing a quaint little white church," my mother had imagined aloud. "For midnight Mass?"

My mother never goes to Mass, midnight or otherwise, and she had never been to El Salvador. I tried to stifle my exasperation. What was white was the wall outside my window: two stories tall and trimmed in razor wire. She might as well have been asking for a chance to dance around a ten-gallon sombrero.

Exhausted merely by the idea of their visit, I had decided to resolve the problem of what to do with my flock in El Salvador-of-all-places by whisking them out of the country as quickly as I could. Maybe it was a cop-out, but at least pretty, touristy Antigua with all its quintessential bougainvillea and

14

tejas roofs might have something that could pass for a quaint little white church.

This is why, on Christmas Eve, my family saw most of what they would of El Salvador—volcanoes, burning cane fields, tin-roofed shanties, pickups buckling under loads of standing passengers—from the surreal vantage point of an overly air-conditioned first class bus, while a stewardess offered them juice boxes and potato chips.

When the impasse came, we were halfway between San Salvador and Guatemala City, at the Las Chinamas border, which straddles the Rio Paz. El Salvador and Guatemala were working to expedite crossings, so we went straight to the Guatemala station, where the stewardess on the bus recited the strict no-wait policy—rumor had it there was nothing so punctual in Central America as a bus leaving you behind.

I suppose it was an oversight—especially with all the time we spent being cut in front of in line—not to notice I had no entrance stamp in my passport from the last time I'd crossed into El Salvador. According to the stamps, I had either stood on that bridge between the countries for three weeks, or I had been in El Salvador illegally.

This border officer was more thorough. To prove this, he flipped through my battered passport page by page.

When I just stood there looking at him, waiting for him to tell me what to do, he turned my pages a second time.

Eventually I would resort to the old standard: I began to cry, loudly, sniffling.

At last, if only to get rid of me, the border patrol officer sent me back across to the Salvadoran side to see someone called El Delegado. I turned off the taps, snatched my offending passport, and rushed out the door.

I planned to cross back alone, to hurry, but my father volunteered to accompany me. Granted, my father had been to

Central America before, and under more frightening circumstances than these, but he wasn't the most obvious ally. He didn't speak Spanish, and although my father is a farmer and accordingly strong, he is slim and not very tall (in those days I was frequently guilty of making off with his blue jeans). He is neither imposing nor forceful, not the way that my implacable mother can be. After months handling problems like this one by myself, however, I found I was relieved to have my father beside me. I batted away tears that I pretended were still related to the face-off in the station behind us while my father hailed a *torito*, or tricycle taxi. As we zoomed down the swoop of pitted road across the bridge over the river that was the border, the rest of my family, their crisp passports in order, returned to the bus to wait for us or the bus's departure, whichever came first.

"Thirty minutes," the bus stewardess had warned. And thirty minutes were well up already.

Seventeen years had passed since my father was briefly an observer in Central America, during the wars. It was the only time he'd ever been in a country that wasn't directly adjacent to our own. He'd met with grassroots organizers working to improve the quality of life for the poor through means other than violence. He visited cooperatives and met with economists and government officials. I know from my father's Kodak slides that they visited clinics and small businesses and shantytowns full of war refugees.

I was in first grade, but I remember my father's absence. Or, rather, I remember my mother spinning that fascinating globe with its bumps for mountains and so much blue. I spotted the Great Lakes where I knew my home was and put my finger there. Then my mother pointed out that thin, multicolored strip of land.

"Here," she said. "In El Salvador." Or: "In Honduras." Or: "In Nicaragua."

I put my other finger on that skinny place where my father was and stretched to touch my thumbs together.

I somehow knew to ask: "Is that one safe?"

I could not have known at six what "safe" meant in the context of those places in that time. I still don't know.

"Here," my mother told me because I was the oldest and the only one she could tell. She was still reeling from a phone call, her eyes not quite on me but thinking, remembering my father's crackling words in her ears. "He is right here. El Salvador. And everything is okay."

Her pointer finger covered that whole country.

Working backwards, I can remember my father's preparations for the trip. I can hear him repeating awkwardly after overly loud voices on the cassette player. Surely it was standard stuff:

" *¿Dondé esta el mercado?* "

" *La cuenta, por favor.* "

There was a vent in the kitchen ceiling that allowed the heat from the woodstove, and with it sounds of the house below, to rise up into my bedroom. I often went to sleep to the sound of my father singing at the sink, but the Spanish-on-tape was different. I must have gone down to investigate because I can see him washing dishes in felt bootliners, long underwear showing through the frays in his grease-streaked dungarees. I see him concentrating on his tape. In the memory, he does not turn around. He doesn't know that I am there imagining, as he is, another world.

As my father and I approached the Salvadoran immigration station I began rehearsing my own Spanish words, bringing vocabulary forward in my mind. Slang words were the most important: *puchica, va, que paja.* Slang was the next best thing to knowing somebody's cousin. I didn't expect to know any of the right cousins that day.

" *¿El Delegado?* " I asked an armed man in uniform.

He gestured with the gun.

"*Allá.*"

I turned to face a group of men in combat boots and bul-
letproof vests who stared back at me. I took a deep breath
and charged forward, wondering bleakly whether my father
was picking up the low hissing sound one of them was making at me.

"*Estoy buscando El Delegado,*" I announced to the group.
The man who stepped forward had a thick mustache and his
eyes glittered at me with what I hoped was just amusement.

"*¿En que puedo servirle?*" the official asked in a voice that
suggested he did not serve anyone for free.

"*Señor,*" I began, glancing at our armed-and-armored
audience. I touched my almost-blond hair. Then I let loose
the story in one much interrupted garble of unconjugated
Spanish. My family. Of the U.S.—where in the U.S.?—
Nueva York. They sit on the bus. There is exit stamp from
Guatemala and no entrance to El Salvador—same place,
same immigration, one stamp and not the other—when I go
for a trip to Tikal—Yes, pretty ruins. I like Central America
very much—I am a teacher—today I take my family to show
Guatemala—For truth? I be illegal in the country? I must to
spend Christmas in handcuffs?

I smiled up at El Delegado, and he beamed before his sub-
ordinates, drawing out the show with great flourishes. My
father, eager to please, nodded and grinned as if he too understood the joke. Which, of course, was me.

At last El Delegado finished toying with us and pointed
out the cashier's office where we paid a ten-dollar fine. With
receipt in hand, my father and I set off on foot for Guatemala
(the *toritos* go downhill only), waving goodbye to El Delegado's posse as they shouted their good wishes for our travels.

After our little dance with this border policeman, the urgency
of our project fizzled out. No doubt, the bus had left or would

leave soon, but my father and I strolled across the bridge and then stopped to look over the rail. Below us, slow brown water flowed. The air was warm and smelled like urine baking on the concrete, like overripe fruit, like dust and diesel, like *pupusas* frying in the distance under some blue plastic tarp roof by one of the two immigration stations. There were children playing in the river. From the looks of it they were supposed to be sifting sand from stones through screens but had abandoned their work, along with their clothing, on the rocky shore. Their voices chimed upward, mixed with the sounds of water splashing.

On that bridge over the Rio Paz, the place that my little-girl finger once covered came alive, my father's Kodak slides turned 3-D, green and vivid and ripe-smelling all around us. Even the Spanish language words on tape had turned silvery and sensible. Suddenly, hitchhiking to Guatemala City sounded fun. We'd ride in the back of a pickup truck, our faces to the wind, just my dad and me. We could do anything.

Eventually, my father and I would hike up the hill to the Guatemalan border station. I would kick rocks and my father would whistle. We would cross into Guatemala, my passport properly stamped, and a Christmas miracle would be awaiting us with KING QUALITY BUS emblazoned across its side and my mother standing in its open doorway, one foot on the ground and one on the step. Later that night, my mother would hear the Christmas Eve service in a yellow church, which was close enough, and see *santeros* parade through the street. Then Guatemala would set her straight with an all-night, tooth-rattling fireworks extravaganza.

But in that moment, resting above the Rio Paz, I was leading my father in his own footsteps, bridging a farm in New York and a country too tiny to see clearly on a globe, my father's past and my present, like a not-so-little girl connecting dots. But it was really the stillness that mattered, not the disastrous history or the potential disasters ahead, not where we were from or where we were going, but where we were, right at that moment.

Molly Beer is a terrible traveler. She reads books about Africa while camping in Tibet, cooks Italian food in her Mexican kitchen, or writes obsessively about El Salvador while living on a rooftop in Ecuador. Worse still, she can't pack, she suffers from motion sickness, she is terrified of volcanoes, and she once (three days into the Aldo Leopold wilderness) tore up the map. If she couldn't write her way to the sense of things, she would probably just stay home. Currently an Olive O'Connor Fellow in Creative Writing at Colgate University, Molly Beer's most recent travel writing appears in Vela, Salon, Guernica, Perceptive Travel, *and* Glimpse, *where she was a 2010 Correspondent. She is also the co-author of* Singing Out, *published in 2010.*

🐚 🐚 🐚

Twenty Years and Counting

On the things we set in motion.

Since 1784, Le Grand Véfour has occupied the north-west corner of the Jardins du Palais Royal in Paris. The restaurant seems forever married to the phrase "venerable institution," because if only for the roster of French luminaries—from Napoleon to Victor Hugo to Jean-Paul Sartre—who have warmed its velvet banquettes over the years. And then there's me. One fall afternoon twenty years ago, I had my wedding dinner there.

Just weeks later, a young Savoyard chef named Guy Martin was plucked from the Hotel Château de Divonne in the tiny Lake Geneva spa town of Divonne-les-Bains to lead Le Grand Véfour into the twenty-first century. I had never met Guy Martin, but this year, at both of our two-decade marks, I wondered if there might be parallels between the life of a restaurant and the course of a marriage. So I returned to Le Grand Véfour to raise a glass to history—France's, the restaurant's, and my own.

I first ate at Le Grand Véfour in the summer of 1983 with a sporty count named Nicolas who squired me around Paris in a Fiat Spider, but whose diminished circumstances became obvious when the bill arrived. He was a couple hundred francs short. But what did I care who paid the check? Champagne was coursing through our veins, and the restaurant's gilded opulence gave us the sensation that we were tucked inside a fancy chocolate box. Despite its age, Le Grand Véfour had the order and polish of something new and, for me, uncharted. Glass panels lined the dining room, along with portraits of fleshy, bare-breasted goddesses bearing peaches or colored ices—paintings 200 years old, but with hues and sentiments as fresh as that July morning. All around me, the thrill of seduction mingled with the tranquility of permanence.

The scent of tarragon wafted up from my lamb chops, and cassis ice cream added another layer of pleasure, which—along with Nicolas's hand intermittently grazing my thigh under the table—heightened the anticipation in all my senses. The bubbly, his lips on my bare shoulder, a warm summer night—Le Grand Véfour was promise itself and the pure essence of Paris. I never forgot it.

Eight years later I was back, living in Paris and working as a journalist, traveling for stories in Eastern Europe and the Middle East. When I got engaged to Mark, an American sculptor, there seemed no question that we would forego the big to-do stateside and get married in the city we now called home. He had bought my engagement ring—a gorgeous and well-worn platinum, diamond, and sapphire band—at an upscale pawnshop on the rue de Turenne for 1,200 francs, or about $200 at the time. Our rented apartment had a fancy Marais address, but I'd spent the better part of the previous year steaming off the stained brown wallpaper that covered every inch of the place, substituting the bare light bulbs on the ceiling with fixtures from the market at Clignancourt, and hiding the prewar linoleum under carpets I bought at souks from Istanbul to Fez.

In France, no one cared where we had gone to college or what our fathers did back home. We worked hard, scraped by, consorted with journalists and artists, and weren't on any regular family dole that propped up our lifestyle. Still, I was the youngest of four unmarried daughters, so my parents were eager to foot the bill for whatever I chose for the fifty people we planned to invite—family, a few good friends from the States and, mostly, those who comprised our life in France.

I had already lived in Paris long enough to dress the part, but some other things remained difficult for a young American woman. Like finding a wedding venue. I aimed high, but Paris was shutting me out. I inquired at what seemed like the city's entire varsity restaurant line-up: L'Orangerie and l'Amboiserie, Taillevent and Maison Blanche. In each dining room, the gatekeeper shook his head, topped it off with a puckered expression of Gallic scorn, and sent me packing. They seemed to be telling me what I suspected: we had no business getting married in such a place. Yankee, go home.

I hadn't dared approach Le Grand Véfour; it was considered a sanctum, impenetrable and holy, despite a perceived decline I'd read about following the recent death of its chef of thirty-six years. But one day, while getting a haircut at a salon in the Galerie Vivienne, I realized I was a stone's throw from the restaurant.

"Your hair looks very sad," my coiffeuse, Monique, told me flatly, referring to my brunette locks.

"Really?" I asked. Two hours later I walked out a blonde—and not a classy-looking one.

Maybe it was the hair that made me lose my guile, because something marched me straight over to Le Grand Véfour. I stopped to read the placard in memory of Colette, who had lived upstairs and who, at the end of her life, was carried down each day for lunch at her lavish personal canteen. I turned the corner on the rue de Beaujolais and walked inside, where I was greeted by an imposing woman with a spray of silk ruffles at her neck.

"Hello," I said. "I'm getting married on September 7th at the *mairie* of the 3rd arrondissement, and afterwards, I would like to have my dinner here."

To my astonishment, her face lit up.

"I'm Madame Ruggieri," she said. "Congratulations. We would be delighted to host your celebration."

When our wedding party arrived at Le Grand Véfour on an unusually sultry Saturday in September, waiters greeted us beneath the colonnade with flutes of pink Champagne on silver trays. At the time, the wine giant Taittinger owned the restaurant, and it had been closed for a month—officially, this was the final day of its summer hiatus, during which it had been buffed, shined, and spruced up. Tomorrow it would open to the public again, but today it was ours. With the sun pouring in and reflecting off its many mirrors, the room shimmered. A solo cellist played a Bach suite as we trickled inside.

Above the tables in Le Grand Véfour are small plaques in memoriam to those who occupied them. Mark and I sat side by side on Napoleon and Josephine's banquette. Our lamb medallions were drizzled with basil sauce this time, and our wedding cake was topped with pulled sugar roses. The freesia and lilies that Madame Ruggieri and I had chosen for the tables were almost unnecessary, upstaged by the room itself.

"I'm your wife," I whispered to Mark at some point during dinner. He reached around me on the banquette, grasped my hip and pulled me toward him, sensing my incredulity at the pronouncement. I wasn't thinking about how long, or if, we'd last. I simply needed to name what I had become, as if saying the word meant I had simultaneously transformed into a more true and worthy soul. But I didn't feel the least bit changed. Instead, I sensed I had boarded the finest and sturdiest of ships but was terrified of water, and furthermore, it was too late for me to disembark. Now, my destiny was choosing me.

"I guess that makes me your husband," he whispered.

"Forever," I said, and shrugged, punctuating the word with finality, rather than doubt.

"I'm sure of it," he said, and we toasted each other, almost silently.

The dining room was brightly illuminated, but white curtains covered the lower half of the windows, blocking the view. Mark and I, my family, my friends—we were safely contained on an island in the middle of Paris. All that was visible from our table was the sky, the green tops of the linden trees, and the limestone columns that have framed the gardens for over two centuries.

Within a few weeks, after our honeymoon, I was back in Paris, sorting through gifts of crystal and china, and I read in the paper about Guy Martin, the thirty-three-year-old chef who had taken over at Le Grand Véfour. Such things made headlines in France.

Two decades later, while planning the trip to Paris to commemorate our anniversary, I remembered that news story and was stunned to learn that not only was Martin still there, but in 2010 he'd bought the restaurant outright. Whether it was fate or choice or some kind of compromise that had carried him to this point, Guy Martin—like Mark and I—had remained devoted to the decision he made all those years ago. I was intrigued. I wanted to meet him and hear what he might have to say on the subject.

As I left for Paris, I was uncertain what awaited me. I suppose I wanted to recall the promise of my wedding day, to experience anew the splendid room, and to peer back on my less-weary self with eyes that were now two decades older and two decades more married. It was a sensation I sought, an assurance that longevity, whether in a restaurant or a relationship, does not have to equal decrepitude. I wondered whether my marriage had measured up to the place where it began, or vice-versa.

I hadn't expected to make it this far. Three years earlier, my relationship and all my beliefs had been shattered when I fell, briefly, for another man. Had the object of my obsession wished it, I would have walked across the ocean to Africa, where he lived, to start a new life with him. But he didn't, and my heart splintered in the aftermath. Agonized, I broke down, unable to move from my bed for weeks and then months as I stared out the window and flooded my pillow with tears for another man.

I reached to Mark to rescue me, and incredibly, he did. My husband saw me as more deserving of pity—or at least compassion—than punishment and forgave me for what was certainly a betrayal, but also, in his eyes, a most human transgression. In retrospect, I chock it up to midlife and hormones and the insane need to try and stop the mirthless passage of years. We were quite roughed up by the episode, but once I emerged on the other side—alive, first of all, and stronger—there were no more doubts that we would stay together. Forget about people changing, moving apart, growing in opposite directions. For Mark, to fail would have been to acknowledge a twenty-year mistake, and he couldn't brook such a waste of his time and judgment. Plus, we had never stopped loving each other.

But Mark and I would have to celebrate that victory—and our milestone—together, later, at home. He was stuck stateside with a pressing deadline, and besides, we were broke again and couldn't justify two tickets to France. So I would be dining solo at Le Grand Véfour. It wasn't at all what I'd hoped, but I was curious nonetheless and even excited, for both that transcendent realm of my six-course lunch and the fact-finding mission with Guy Martin that would accompany it.

The day before my reservation at Le Grand Véfour, I retraced the path I took on my wedding day. I visited the palatial *mairie* off the rue de Bretagne where, after the ceremony, the mayor of the 3rd arrondissement handed us our official *livre de famille*, with blank pages for up to eight kids. Had the playground across the street been there on our wedding day? If so, I never noticed. Before I had my children, now fourteen and seventeen, a sandbox and jungle gym were all but invisible to me. Now I stood near the playground trying to remember how Mark and I had traveled the meaningful distance from the *mairie* to Le Grand Véfour. Had a car taken us? How did my friends get there? I didn't recall being a jittery bride, but I was surprised to have erased that detail as well.

This time I took the metro to Bourse and walked over to the gardens, where I lingered over an alfresco breakfast of café crème and a brioche. It was an April day erupting with color and heat, and I tried to imagine how the courtyard must have appeared long ago at this time of year, from up above in Colette's salon. "The Palais-Royal stirs at once under the influence of humidity, of light filtered through soft clouds, of warmth," she wrote. "The green mist hanging over the elms is no longer a mist, it is tomorrow's foliage."

After my coffee and stroll, I took the long ride back to my old neighborhood near Père Lachaise, where I was staying in a hotel. At the front desk I felt the ions shift in a blast of sensory memory; to my disbelief, standing beside me was one of my husband's dear friends who had been a witness at our wedding. We were utterly stunned into silence and then, laughter. An Australian artist, he was living in Arles and had done the paintings in the hotel. I hadn't seen him in eight years, and his wife had recently passed away. Mark and I weren't able to attend her funeral service, and I still felt awful about it. We hugged, caught up on all our children, had a drink, and wondered where the time had gone.

The following day, upstairs at Le Grand Véfour, I met Guy Martin and told him about the strange coincidence and how pleased I was that my friend would be joining me for lunch. He wasn't surprised.

"This is a magical place in a magical setting," Martin told me. "There's nowhere else in the world like it. When you do an important celebration here—no matter what happens down the line—it will always lead to exceptional things."

When I walked into the restaurant, it enveloped me in the familiar. Twenty years seemed utterly insignificant—both the vestibule and dining room appeared untouched by the passing decades. But incredibly, nothing felt stale or neglected. It was there still, that gleaming lightness that made me feel like I was swimming in soda and that heady sensation of being instantly transformed into someone of consequence. As I stood on the carpet in a pool of sunlight, I nearly ached with life. The room was still shiny and alive and bursting with anticipation.

Although at first it seemed unchanged, upon closer inspection I noticed subtle nods to the present day—hidden fixtures brightened the female forms painted on the wall, and the lace curtains that once ran along the perimeter had been replaced by etched glass.

But the soul of Le Grand Véfour was still there, preserved not only in the décor but also in the traditional recipes, which Martin was constantly reinterpreting and updating. The point, he said, was to allow for the inevitability of change and to let history propel you forward rather than weigh you down. Nothing stays the same, he insisted, because nothing ever can.

"I'm growing every day," he said. "The same goes for my cooking. It's not a static thing. It is always in perpetual motion."

I wondered out loud whether there was some wisdom to be gleaned here, and what I could extrapolate about life and marriage. Mark and I had survived, but I still sometimes wondered how I could wake up to the same man, every day, for the rest of my days here on earth. Martin said that in his case, the key was to remember the person he was back then and to trust the impressions that had brought him there in the first place.

"When I came here from Savoie, the Palais Royal gardens smelled like home. I couldn't believe I was in Paris," he said. "The first time I pushed in the door of the restaurant,

I gasped. It was just like that." He snapped his fingers. "It was a *coup de coeur*, like when you meet someone—you aren't certain, but you know something happened. You just know. I knew I belonged here."

In other words, I needed to envision the young man I'd fallen in love with and trust that I would feel the same way about him if we met today. I needed always to remind myself why it was Mark I'd chosen to marry. And I needed to recall the much younger woman I had been—the one who was never going to settle—and believe that even if I tended to be guided somewhat by passion, I also possessed a good dose of sense to harness the free will required for a sound decision.

I closed my eyes and saw Mark and me with our limbs entwined, never imagining that I could one day be middle-aged and scarred by an episode of doubt, looking to a Paris restaurateur to shine a light on my future while illuminating my past.

For twenty years, Martin had setbacks and dark times, and when Michelin took away his third star, it was his own version of the infidelity that nearly destroyed my marriage—and certainly my faith in the institution. But as guardian of Le Grand Véfour's culinary legacy, he also led it into the twenty-first century with the same devotion that motivates those too optimistic, or hopeful, to entertain the idea of failure: hard work, flexibility, creativity, love.

"I never thought I'd be here for twenty years," he says.

"Tell me about it," I said.

"Sometimes I'm still surprised."

"Yes, me too," I said.

"But as long as I feel good here, and as long as I have faith in what I do, I'll stay," he said. "Life is very short."

That, I realized, could also mean, why bother? Other adventures and other paths constantly tempt every man and woman in this life, forever posing the question of whether it takes more courage to stay put or move on. After all, in marriage—and in food—twenty years is already no small achievement.

This time I sat in Jean Cocteau's chair with my old friend, who had been here with us two decades ago. It was a strange thrill to now feel my own history in this room. The chilled bottle of pink Champagne we drank was the same kind Mark and I had served at our wedding, probably the same kind I'd shared with Nicolas, and the same I'll drink with my husband on our fortieth anniversary. Even the food managed to be revelatory: Martin's modern turn on Le Grand Véfour's classic ravioli, now prepared with the finest foie gras in the land, seemed to prove that the best use of the past is to chart the course for the path ahead.

Still, I missed Mark. He had alluded to his tenacity all those years ago, and because of it, I had something to celebrate. We had weathered what for many couples would have been insurmountable. And if I could learn anything from a restaurant that had withstood centuries and wars and misfortune—and a chef who taught me that fidelity does not have to mean compromise—then we too would last forever.

I knew that just outside in the gardens, lovers kissed, babies tumbled, and a work crew trimmed the lawn, leaving the smell of cut grass. We could see none of it above the newly etched windows, just the sky over Paris—eternal, faithful, delicious.

Marcia DeSanctis is a journalist and writer whose work has appeared in many publications, including Vogue, Departures, The New York Times Magazine, Recce, Best Women's Travel Writing 2011, Best Travel Writing 2011 *and* Town & Country. *Her story* Masha *won the Solas Grand Prize Silver Award for Travel Writing in 2011. Formerly, she was a network news producer for ABC, NBC, CBS and Dow Jones. You can visit her at www.marciadesanctis.com.*

ANGIE CHUANG

ॐ   ॐ   ॐ

Learning to Pray

In a Kabul kitchen, a journalist
discovers the secrets of sisterhood.

The yellow door looked far heavier than it was. Every time we Americans—Laila and I—swung it open, we pulled or pushed too hard, and it flailed wildly on its hinges. Back and forth, back and forth. It had a large, crooked black English letter painted on it. "What does the K stand for?" I asked, puzzling at it as if it represented a secret code. "Kabul," the city we were in? "Karzai," a show of support for the president? Nearly three years after the U.S. had overthrown the Taliban, most Afghans still spoke of him with a trace of hope.

Nafisa smiled: "It stands for kitchen." Our laughter filled the room.

This was our space, the room in the compound-style Kabul home where we four young women, American and Afghan, spent most of our waking time together. Nafisa and Nazo enjoyed our company as they did their household chores. The men had their own spaces, such as the *saloon*, or sitting room, in which they made important decisions. But the kitchen was the women's space, where we could have private conversations, sharing secrets with little worry that someone might walk in or overhear. The kitchen was where Nafisa and Nazo could be themselves.

31

Nafisa and Nazo were sisters-in-law, both in their twenties. Nafisa had moved a year before from Pakistan to marry Nazo's brother Ayub in a union arranged by their families. The two young women did all the cooking and most of the housework together, and as a result, they spent more time with each other than with anyone else in the house. Nafisa had liquid brown eyes and straight black hair, and was serene and serious. Nazo's startling green eyes had an impish glow, and her curly dark hair was always trying to escape from her *chador*, or headscarf. They chatted, bickered, and laughed with such ease that I sometimes wondered if Nafisa's marriage had been arranged for her compatibility not only with Ayub but also with his sister, Nazo.

Ayub was on a business trip in Kandahar when we arrived, so Laila, Nafisa, Nazo, and I shared the room usually occupied by the newlyweds—the only one in the house that had access to a western-style flush toilet. The room barely accommodated the double bed and the two sleeping mats.

It was May 2004. After September 11, I had begun to report on the Shirzais, an Oregon-based Afghan immigrant family, and their plans to reconnect with their country as it rebuilt post-Taliban. I first met Laila Shirzai in my official role as a journalist, but we soon became friends. She was an ideal travel companion, a hybrid between American and Afghan. She'd grown up in Pakistan's Afghan-refugee enclaves and attended high school and college in the United States. This trip had been her idea, and we stayed in the home of her aunt, who was Nazo's mother and, of course, Nafisa's mother-in-law.

Laila and I had fallen into the foreign yet comforting rhythm of the sisters-in-law's days. Shortly after the 4:30 A.M. prayer call, they would pray while we snoozed. Then they came in with a tray of bread and tea to rouse us. Many days, Laila and I helped the two young women in the kitchen as they prepared meals; we chatted as we stood side-by-side, chopping onions and tomatoes. We also went shopping together and attended a birthday party for Nazo's friend. And we visited Nazo's school, an overcrowded, slapdash attempt to restart girls' education a decade after the Taliban had banned it. (Nazo, at twenty-two, was in the tenth grade because of the time she had missed.) Often, we just sat on the edge of the concrete-covered well in the house's courtyard, leaning into each other under the fig trees.

One morning, I got up earlier than usual and lingered with a cup of tea in the kitchen as the household began its day. Nazo came in, wearing her school uniform of a black *shalwar kameez*, a traditional tunic-and-pants outfit, and a white headscarf. Her English was not as fluent as Nafisa's, so she often asked me for help with unfamiliar or forgotten words.

On this morning, she said, "I cannot remember the word that means you are sleeping but you are seeing things like you are waking."

"Dream," I said.

"Ah, yes," she said, with a sly giggle. "Drreeam."

She paused, a glint in her green eyes.

"Did you have a dream last night?" I asked.

Her pale cheeks turned pink. "Yesterday I dream about Yellow Pants." She covered her face with her hands.

"Yellow Pants" was her nickname for a black-haired young man whom she had spotted in Nafisa's wedding video, wearing bright goldenrod trousers and a black shirt. The men and women had celebrated and danced in separate rooms, so she hadn't seen him in person at the wedding—only in the video. A few days ago, Nazo had shown us the video of the men dancing in their room and told us she was having friends at her girls' school inquire about the man in the yellow pants.

There was no dating in Afghanistan, and chances were, Nazo would have an arranged marriage like Nafisa and her brother. But if she happened to spot someone, she knew how to put the wheels in motion. A vast and seemingly invisible network of women might contact Nazo's mother, and the two of them might be able to meet in a formal setting, in the presence of the two families.

"What was Yellow Pants doing in your dream?" I said, and playfully nudged Nazo.

She shrieked from behind her hands and pretended to run out of the kitchen. Then she returned, looked me in the eye, and deadpanned, "He was dancing. Just like in the video."

I wondered if she really meant that, or if "dancing" was a euphemism. It was hard to know sometimes how innocent—or not—she and Nafisa were, what they understood of relationships, love, sex. Nafisa and Nazo had asked Laila and me about our love lives, but American-style dating was unfathomable to them. I told them about my past relationships—one with a man whom I wanted to marry, others with men I had no intention of marrying—and how and why they'd failed. But Nafisa and Nazo only furrowed their brows with compassion as I described various breakups, and I started wishing I had a simpler answer for them. As for Laila, she always changed the subject quickly, not wanting to tell them about the white American boyfriend from college she was keeping a secret from her family.

They watched Hollywood movies, but even those were viewed through the lens of their experiences. After the Taliban were overthrown and movie theaters returned to Kabul, *Titanic* was a runaway hit, perhaps because romance between early-twentieth century Americans felt almost like that of early-twenty-first century Afghans. A young, upper-class woman, Rose, forced by her family to marry a man from her social class, falls in love with Jack, a poor man of whom her family disapproves. Even the unhappy outcome—the two lovers parted eternally by the shipwreck—rang truer to Afghans than the typical Hollywood fare. Love-conquers-all endings seemed unrealistic. Disaster they understood. Of course, the version that was shown in Kabul theaters was censored. Scenes American audiences came to think of as Titanic's signature moments—Jack sketching Rose in the nude, or the

two lovers fogging up the windows of her fiancé's Renault—
were unceremoniously deleted.

Nafisa showed me pictures of her and Ayub at their
wedding. He was tall, square-jawed, and handsome, with
a trimmed beard and deep-set eyes. She wore the heavily
beaded, multicolored dress of a Pashtun bride, piles of gold
jewelry, and a mournful expression. "A bride must not smile,
even if she is happy," she said. "She must act like she is sad to
leave her family." Ayub had landed a lucrative wartime job
with the United Nations and was sometimes on the road for
weeks at a time, as he was when we'd arrived in Kabul.

Their wedding was less than a year ago, and Nafisa was
now in her second trimester of pregnancy, her otherwise lithe
body just beginning to show under her *shalwar kameez*. Did
she miss her husband, I asked?

"Yes," she said, sighing. "But when he comes back it is
very nice."

A coy smile played on her face. "Very nice?" I asked.

"Very nice," she repeated, looking down and blushing.
She straightened herself up. "Now I must go do the laundry,"
and breezily took leave of me. As she swung open the kitchen
door, she glanced over her shoulder with her big brown eyes
and winked.

A couple days later, Nafisa skipped her usual afternoon
nap, took a shower, picked out a fresh outfit—a soft pink silk
shalwar kameez—put on perfume and makeup, and tried on
five different *chador* before settling on one. As we all sat in the
kitchen, watching her put the finishing touches on dinner, I
caught her eye. "You're nervous today," I said. "And pretty."

"*Inginir*," she said, using the family's nickname for her
husband—the Pashto word for "engineer" meant an educated
man—"is coming home today."

Then, turning to me so only I could see it, she took her
delicate hand, balled into a fist, and bit down on her pinky
knuckle. She gasped softly, feigning breathlessness, grinned

at me, then returned to stirring the stew. It was sexier than all the deleted scenes from *Titanic* combined.

We saw less of Nafisa after that evening, though the four of us still slept in the couple's room. She still joined us at night, only later than usual. Nazo, meanwhile, announced that she was having friends inquire about another young man she'd seen at the birthday party we'd attended.

"White Suit," she said, eyes dreamy.

I remembered him—he was, indeed, wearing an all-white suit with a bright red shirt. He had a smooth face and was a flamboyant dancer.

"What about Yellow Pants?"

She laughed. Yesterday, we had contemplated some questionable meat in the freezer after one of the city's frequent power outages. I taught her the word "expired," explaining the labels in American grocery stores that indicated when something should be discarded.

"Yellow Pants," she said, flipping the end of her *chador* dramatically over her shoulder, "has expired."

I took a temporary hiatus from Nazo's updates and Nafisa's revelations when Laila and I took a road trip to the family's rural village in the Ghazni province. We traveled with the younger brother of Nazo and Ayub, Asad, who fulfilled the essential role of escort and bodyguard.

Within the confines of his mother's house, I had kept my eyes averted from her only single son, like a proper female houseguest. But as we ventured out onto rural Afghanistan's unpaved roads, I stole glances in the rearview mirror of our hired car. Asad's dark, deep-set eyes were fringed by lashes so long they cast shadows on his brown cheeks. He passed time on the long drive by telling us Mullah Nasruddin jokes, laughing loudly at his own punchlines about the legendary Sufi wise fool.

Soon, we were back in Kabul, and our remaining time passed quickly. We spent our final days saying goodbyes, savoring last meals, exchanging gifts, and posing for pictures. By the time the four of us retired to our room together one final time, I was relieved. We were sprawled across our sleeping mats and cushions.

Nafisa looked impatient. She kept trying to catch Nazo's eye. Nazo was making a list of qualifications for her future husband—among them "a little fat" and "a lot of money"—when her sister-in-law interrupted her.

"I think it is Angie's turn," she said.

I felt my cheeks grow warm. "I don't have a list."

"O.K., Nazo and I will help you write your list," Nafisa said. "Number one: name begins with 'A.' Ends with 'D.' Do we know anyone like this?"

Nazo giggled.

"Nafisa!" I said, face growing hotter. Asad. After the roadtrip, he had been ducking into the kitchen now and then to ask me about English vocabulary, just like his sister had. I laughed a little too loudly at his jokes and tried to wipe the grin off my face after he left, all the while wondering when his next visit would be. Each time, I felt Nafisa and Nazo's eyes boring into me as they pretended to be absorbed with the cooking.

"You like my brother?" Nazo said. Her green eyes danced cartoonishly.

"He is very nice," I said carefully.

"She says he's very nice," Nazo said to Nafisa, as if she were an interpreter.

"You like him," Nafisa said, leaning close to me. "You like us. You should marry him."

Nafisa's face could look so serious, with those big eyes, that naturally downturned mouth. *But surely she's joking.* Nazo nodded, looking earnest herself. I turned to Laila for a hint, but she was keeping a close-lipped smile on her face.

"What? Marry?" I said, my voice sounding strained. "You're kidding."

"No," Nafisa said, her uncovered black ponytail flipping emphatically over her shoulder. "You marry him. You will be our sister."

"I can't marry him. I hardly know him!" I protested.

"You have known him for twelve days," Nafisa said. She had counted the days since our road trip to the village? "That is more time than I knew my husband before I decided to marry him. And look, we are happy."

They were. After her husband left again, Nafisa had moped the entire day. On the one hand, it was hard for me to imagine how this kind of attraction—and yes, love—had developed after they had married barely knowing each other. It was ludicrous to discuss Asad and marriage with his sister and sister-in-law when he and I had only had a handful of conversations, never alone. Could they be that naïve?

But then I remembered her biting down on her pinky knuckle in the kitchen. I looked at the slight swell of her pregnant belly under her *shalwar kameez*. All this, with a man she had only known from a few hours' worth of supervised meetings.

"Well?" Nafisa said.

I had no answer for her.

"We just want you to be our sister."

Nafisa had said "sister" once already, but now I began to understand. Nafisa and Nazo, their rapport so easy, like a married couple, even when they bickered. How they moved in the kitchen, never bumping into each other. Nazo told me once that she and Nafisa would have a say in whomever their remaining single brothers married, because they would be taking on a new sister as well.

"You already feel like sisters to me," I said, meaning it. I had never become so close to women in such a short time. In a culture that separated men and women, women developed an instant, easy intimacy within their inner sanctums. It had been so natural to fall into that uncomplicated closeness. But with this talk of marriage, why hadn't they brought up the obvious? "I just can't marry your brother, because I'm not Afghan and I'm not Muslim. I wouldn't be acceptable."

"It is no problem," Nafisa said. "You will not have to become Muslim right away. You can take your time. I will show you how to pray. Then you convert, and it will be O.K."

I hadn't grown up religious, nor been particularly drawn to religion, but Nafisa made it sound so simple, so essential—a foregone conclusion—and I couldn't help but feel a bit charmed by it. Learn to pray, the rest would come.

I rolled my head back on the pillow, making a playful gesture of surrender to my interrogators.

Nafisa tilted her head toward me sympathetically.

"You think about this. When you are ready, you tell us your decision. Yes or no."

Back in the States, I hardly ever cried. Not at movies. Not at weddings. Rarely over a man, and only when he wasn't watching. But I cried big, fat tears when I said goodbye to Nazo and Nafisa the next morning, before we left for the airport. Nazo nearly hugged the air out of me, which only made me cry more. The wet tears in my eyes, on my face, dampening Nazo's black and white school uniform, my breath coming hard and ragged, shocked me. And I was doubly surprised, as I pulled away, to see Nazo's own electric green eyes swimming and feel my own scarf damp with her tears. We both wiped at our runny noses and laughed.

And then she was gone, late for school as usual.

Nafisa approached next, leaning in for an embrace. Then she stopped herself, straightened up, and eyed me sternly.

"So," she said. "Did you make your decision? What is your answer: yes or no?"

My jaw dropped a bit, and I studied her face. Her gaze was unrelenting, but the corner of her mouth curved upward.

"*Nafisa*," I said, feigning exasperation. I wanted to say, "I can't marry your brother-in-law," but I didn't want that to come off as a rejection of him or, worse, of her and Nazo. And the truth was, my attraction to him was real, a constant ripple under my cool surface. "How about a first date?" I wanted to quip, but I knew the joke would be lost on her.

"Should I ask him if he wants to marry you?" Nafisa offered.

"NO!" I said, too loudly. "Please don't."

"O.K., O.K.," Nafisa said. She grabbed my hand with her slim, cool fingers. "But I would like you come back and see us, and if you married him, you could."

I promised to come back and see her and Nazo even if I didn't marry him, and I felt myself getting choked up again. Then our driver pounded at the courtyard door and yelled something in Pashto. Nafisa's eyes widened.

"Oh no," she said. "The driver was in traffic. You are late for the airport! You must go now."

We let the driver into the courtyard and rushed the luggage into the car. As I hugged Nafisa I could feel the swell of the life growing beneath her loose-fitting clothes. I hesitated, feeling tears coming on again and wanting to say something meaningful in parting. Nafisa, eyes moist, shook her head and pushed me toward the waiting car door.

A week after I returned from Afghanistan, I dreamed that Nafisa was teaching me how to pray. She appeared in my dream exactly as I remembered her in real life: heavy-lidded dark eyes, straight nose, and slightly downturned mouth. Calm elegance. Long black hair swept up into her *chador*.

Sitting on my heels at Nafisa's side, on a crimson patterned rug she had rolled out for me, I rehearsed the flow in my head—stand up, bend down, stand up, prostrate, kneel, prostate, stand up. "Don't worry," she murmured in her accented

English, words clipped just so. "You will know what to do. I told you I would teach you." Her voice comforted me.

Dawn bathed us in its soft light, and we heard the call to prayer from a distant muezzin. I turned to Nafisa, searching her face for her promise: *you will know what to do.*

I woke up, groggy in the pre-dawn gray of Portland, alone in my small apartment. It was so quiet, and so beige. Gone were the plush red carpets and the sound of Nafisa and her family padding barefoot through the house, murmuring in Pashto to each other, whispering in Arabic as they prayed.

I should have been grateful to return to American life, without daily power outages, limited clean drinking water, and NATO tanks rolling through the city. But I missed Nafisa and Nazo. And they had found their way into my dreams, which only made me miss them more.

For weeks, I mentally replayed the dream before going to sleep in hopes that it would repeat itself. It never did. Over time, all my dreams of them, and of Afghanistan, faded as I found my way back into the rhythms and comforts of American life.

It didn't occur to me until later that, in my dream, I must have already made the decision Nafisa had posed before I left Kabul. She was, after all, teaching me to pray. I must have said yes.

Angie Chuang is a writer and educator based in Washington, D.C. Her work has appeared in The Best Women's Travel Writing 2011, *Lonely Planet's travel-writing anthology* Tales From Nowhere, *the* Asian American Literary Review, Washingtonian *magazine, and other venues. She is on the journalism faculty of American University School of Communication. She is working on a nonfiction book manuscript centered on her relationship with*

an Afghan American immigrant family and travels with them in Afghanistan. The names of the Afghans and Afghan Americans have been changed to protect them and other family members in Afghanistan, who have been threatened for collaborating with an American journalist.

LUCY McCAULEY

ॐ ॐ ॐ

Beneath the Surface

Perhaps the facts most astounding and most real
are never communicated by man to man.
—Henry David Thoreau, *Walden*

*W*e drove to Walden Pond that day to escape an unseasonably humid Monday afternoon in June. I knew that Fareed and Samir weren't particularly strong swimmers, but I didn't give that much thought at the time. They had grown up in other countries and were now at MIT, working on their doctorates. I wanted to be the first to show them Walden.

We walked the path along the shore until we reached the bend that opens onto a small cove and where you can just see, if you know it is there, the trail to the site where Thoreau's cabin once stood. The late afternoon hung heavy and overcast, the evergreens a smoky-blue smudge against the sky.

When I remember that day, I think about how the place where you arrive can look so different from the place you later leave. How experience transforms the shape and color of things. The life-guarded beach and its few clusters of people lay far behind. We had this secluded shore to ourselves, watched only by pines, birches, and oaks. We spread the blanket, shed layers of clothes down to bathing suits, used a toe against each heel to coax off shoes.

I watched Fareed watching me. I watched him back: long brown legs; a smooth, ample chest; a kind face. I first met Fareed on a dance floor in a club downtown. I was captivated by his eyes, which shone with visions my eyes had never seen—of ochre-colored deserts, of marketplaces alive with mirrors and lamplight. When the dance ended, like a child Fareed took my hand and led me off the floor. So familiar it had felt from the beginning, his hand cradling mine.

In the pond, the water was cool but warmed as we moved, making our way across the cove, the three of us talking and treading water. We would pace ourselves, take this slowly. Samir had learned just that year to swim, taught by an uncle in the gulf at Beirut. At some point, surprisingly close to the shore, the water turned suddenly frigid and I knew the bottom had dropped out beneath us. After maybe twenty minutes Fareed fell behind, and I half-consciously watched his broad arms arcing as I swam, talking with Samir.

And then Fareed was gone. A rippled empty surface where his body had been. Me, treading water, not ten crawl strokes away.

Then he sprang into the air, a graceful whale breaching. Ah, I thought, he was just teasing. But then I saw his arms slapping water like the wings of a wounded bird. A still surface again, one perfect ring marking like a bull's eye where he'd been.

"Go!" Samir shouted. And as if shaken from sleep I darted toward the ring, just as Fareed resurfaced briefly. I saw the black outlines of his eyes, flung wide.

Then, empty water. Water that I grabbed but that did not contain the shoulder I reached for, the hand, finger even, the bunch of hair. Unthinkable, the idea that he could not resurface, yet that fear tore at my ear, mocking me.

Then he was there again, and this was my chance to coax him onto his back, like some fumbling magician trying to levitate a body.

Later Fareed would speak of looking up at water the color of baby moss. It was almost too easy, he told me. Just to rest at the bottom looking up at that moss-green water. His whale-like catapult in the air was his last call for help.

I grew up trusting water. We spent summers at the Carolina shore, my father teaching me to float, balancing the small of my back on his palm as the waves tossed me.

Fareed never learned to float. He told me that, growing up in Pakistan, he had learned a few strokes, but never got a chance to know what it felt like to be tired in water, to learn when it's time to get out.

These are things we discovered about each other only after that day at Walden. Until then, all the unanswered questions had still danced between us, and we'd only begun to grapple with the more difficult ones. Fareed was seven years younger than I, but most problematic for us, his family was devoutly Muslim. Although he considered himself an atheist, he told me he could never go against his family so profoundly as to marry a Westerner.

Yet early on, I think we each tried on the possibility of opening, just enough, in the direction of the other. But we always bumped up against the reality of where we were in life: he nearing the end of graduate school and ready to travel the world, while I was established in my career in publishing, thinking about having children.

Even so, during those months that led to that day at Walden, we became constant companions: hours spent browsing bookstores together, drinking tea in Harvard Square cafes, nights and nights in each other's arms. I came to know his every expression, to memorize the lines and angles of him.

That day at the pond, however, none of that seemed to help or matter. His body in my arms became a stranger.

*   *   *

I knew vaguely what to do; a boyfriend in college had been
a lifeguard and once showed me how to save a person from
drowning. But for a moment I forgot everything, and Fareed's
long-boned arms kept pulling him down like anchors.

Then, impossibly, from behind me I heard Samir splashing
around, yelling, "Help!" He too was going down. By then I had
Fareed on his back and was churning water with my free arm,
just a few feet from shore—trying for a place where he could
stand—while behind me Samir shouted "Help! Help!" in a
breathless staccato.

I took one more flaccid stroke and then shoved Fareed
away from me. We were in shallow water now. He could
stand if he just got his feet beneath him. I swam away, looking
back until I saw Fareed struggling to shore, legs buckling. I
swam hard to Samir, clawing my way to where he was dog-
paddling, a panicked look on his face. I tried to grab him but
his arms would not stop moving. Just six feet to shore, less
even, to reach a point where I could stand. I went under once,
beneath a muscular arm; I swallowed water.

I screamed to Fareed on-shore, still bent at the waist, gulp-
ing air. And like some sea creature he lumbered back into the
water that had almost swallowed him. He reached out one
long arm and Samir grasped hold.

Afterward, all of us collapsed on-shore, breathing hard. No
words. Then, after a while we stood, grabbed our clothes, and
quickly moved away from that cove.

Halfway around the pond, the view to the cove blocked by
low-hanging limbs, we all stopped and gazed at the water. It
was as if we needed to look at the pond from another angle,
where we could reclaim illusion. A good pond, a fine wood.
An ordinary day.

I think that is why they began skipping stones. Something to ground them again. Samir tossed one or two rocks, and soon they both were pelting a torrent of pebbles that leapt across the glassy surface in the late afternoon light.

Then, when we gathered our things to head for the car, Samir already ahead on the path, Fareed took my shoulders in his hands and looked at me eye to eye. "Thank you," he said.

There was no false bravado here, no denial of what had happened. Yet if I had to choose a moment when I knew without a doubt that our relationship would end, as it did a few months later, it was there at the pond, Fareed drawing me in too tightly, his voice resonating off-key in my ear.

Later I would wonder: was it all too much? Had what happened somehow tipped a balance between us that could never be set right? Fareed's voice full of relief and apprehension, thanking me as if I'd had a choice. And here's the truth: before that day, though I'd have liked to believe I would help someone in danger, secretly I doubted that I actually could.

So while Fareed was thanking me, what I couldn't articulate was the wonder I was feeling inside. Truly surprised wonder, at myself. I wouldn't have wished on anyone what Fareed had been through. But it did happen, his near-drowning, and as a result I felt something I can only describe as gratitude: that day I'd been given a chance to find out what I could do.

Still, for a long time I dreamed of drownings. One night I pulled Fareed from the water by his hair.

After he finished grad school, Fareed worked a few years for a Boston consulting firm. But then 9-11 hit, and the Patriot Act, and he began to find life in America so difficult that he returned to Pakistan well before his visa ran out. Today he's consulting again, based in London and traveling, as he'd always hoped to do. And every few months I'll get one of those international calls that sound like the person's in the very next room.

On a trip to Boston not long ago, Fareed met my husband and my small daughter, Hannah. He smiled down at her, and then like a gentle giant he scooped her up and swung her high in the air as she squealed. After awhile, as he almost never fails to do when I see him, Fareed mentioned Walden. Had I taken Hannah to the pond yet? he asked, and I said I had.

We smiled silently at each other a long moment before Hannah was asking to be lifted into the air again. He reached for her, and I found myself thinking back to that day. While trying to cross the pond we also had crossed into a place apart: a threshold experience that changed the course of things forever. A life—or two, even three—might have been taken. Fate chose otherwise. Yet in the same moment that we were spared, who we'd been to each other was lost.

I had always thought of that loss in a negative way, as something from which, I once believed, I would never quite recover. But watching Fareed lift my daughter in the air, I began to understand differently what happened. The drama of his near-drowning had simply brought to the surface an inevitable parting, the cool water of the pond slapping us awake from illusion. Until that day at Walden I had tricked myself into believing that we could traverse the barriers between us without a price.

But there was Fareed in my living room, and I looked at where his life had taken him and where mine had taken me—each of us having found our way toward what we'd wanted most deeply. And in that moment it was as if some unclosed wound I'd nursed far beneath the surface was gently and finally coming together. My daughter was laughing, and Fareed was twirling her around and around in the air, and something inside me grew whole.

፝ ፝ ፝

Lucy McCauley is a writer and editor whose essays have appeared in The Atlantic Monthly, The Los Angeles Times, The Dallas Morning News, Fast Company, Harvard Review, *and* Salon.com, *among other places. Her first documentary film,* Facing the Nazi Era: Conversations in Southern Germany, *premiered at the end of 2011 in Canada and Europe. She is the editor of eight Travelers' Tales books, including five books in the Best Women's Travel Writing series. This essay,* Beneath the Surface, *was the Gold Solas Award winner in the travel and transformation category for 2012. She lives in Dallas with her husband and daughter.*

SUSAN ORLEAN

ఞ ఞ ఞ

Storming the Castles

Was it the wine, the wheat, or the wind in her hair?

In the Loire Valley you come for the castles but you stay for the wheat. The castles are the headline event, of course—300 spectacular jewel boxes and ornate medieval confections scattered throughout the region, overlooking the meandering river. But the wheat is the richer, subtler surprise, only revealed to the more painstaking traveler. There are miles and miles of it, spread like a gigantic shag carpet— winter wheat, bleached and crisp, and early spring wheat, so fresh it is almost lime-colored, and the summer wheat, golden and bent with the weight of berries.

I first noticed it when we were just a few miles into our bike trip, on a quiet country road where our tires clicked along on the gravel. There were so many wide acres that the wheat looked almost like water rippling in the wind—a tan and gold and green grassy ocean. In a car, which is the way I usually travel, fields are just fields, an undifferentiated blurred space you whip past as you head to the main attractions. But I immediately noticed that on a bicycle, the scale is entirely different. The wheat is almost as high as your head, and it seems to keep you company, whistling and whispering and waving as you ride along.

I had never been to the Loire before, but a year earlier I'd traveled throughout the nearby Meuse Valley. I'd gone there to do some research for my book on the dog actor Rin Tin Tin, who was born there. I love being on the road, but on that trip I noticed for the first time how poorly the pace of driving suits my style. Most of both valleys are farmland, and at sixty miles an hour, that kind of landscape loses its features and you miss out on its secrets. It was only when I stopped my car that I would find something tucked away, tacked on a barn door, its narrative told in a quieter way.

I love France, and that trip to the Meuse Valley planted in me a yearning to experience it at a different pace, one that would allow me to notice it more intimately, see it more closely, but still travel a good distance. Then someone mentioned to me that the Loire Valley is an idyllic place for beginner bike trips. I consulted Google: it turns out there is a 400-plus-mile network of paths and somnolent back roads called the Loire a Velo, a route that has become a magnet for small, quirky, cycling-friendly inns. The distances between these lodgings—as few as fifteen or so miles, though you can do far more—didn't seem hugely intimidating.

Still, it was one thing to fantasize about such a trip and another to actually pull it off. Given the demands of my work schedule, I really wanted to travel with my husband, John, and son, Austin, who's six. But a first grader on a bike trip? In an unfamiliar place where we don't speak the language (or rather, where I think I speak the language but no one seems to share that opinion)? How would that work? Also, could I handle it? I'd been on a bike seat just long enough to know that if I stayed on it much longer, I could get saddle sores.

One thing seemed clear: this would either be the greatest idea ever—or we would be in over our heads from the first turn of the pedals.

For a while, it seemed the trip might dematerialize before we could even start. In the weeks before we left, I became obsessed with chafing. I think, honestly, I was transferring all my cycling-related anxieties into one identifiable problem. The fact was, the farthest I'd ever ridden was a ten-mile loop to the post office. I wasn't in bad shape, but I felt unprepared for a bike trip. In my defense, I live in an area where the topography resembles a huge sheet of bubble wrap; you can barely go a quarter mile in any direction without having to claw your way up an incline or fall off of one. So while ten miles wasn't enough to train me for France, it was a hard ten miles, right? And I would be fine. Right?

What's more, before moving to bumpy upstate New York, I had lived in Manhattan and often rode to work—three miles through Midtown that included life-flashing-before-my-eyes encounters with truck drivers and cabbies intent on viewing cyclists as targets in a roadway shooting gallery. Surely this had toughened me for the Loire Valley, the cradle of kings.

I tried talking myself into a mood of cavalier and confident anticipation, but still, for weeks before we left, I would lie in bed late at night, picturing myself twenty or thirty miles along with my thighs rubbed raw. I could hear the voices of concerned friends muttering an incantation that sounded an awful lot like "chafe, chafe, chafe." I bought tubs of Bag Balm, on the advice of people on Twitter, from whom I had solicited suggestions. (Yes, I started a hashtag called #chafingadvice. I'm not sure I'm proud of that, but I got dozens of replies.) I ordered Pearl Izumi shorts, and for good measure, a pair of Canari shorts, too—and then, as just one more good measure, I bought a pair of tiny blue Aero Tech Design shorts for Austin, in case he'd inherited my fear of chafing. I kept planning to ride a few extra miles every day to train, but somehow it never happened; I guess I was too busy ordering bike shorts.

There were other issues. My husband and I wanted to ride on our own, not as part of a group, and while there are a number of companies in France that will set up that kind of trip, we kept running into an odd sort of Continental laissez-faire: yes, we can make the trip for you, Madame, but, oh no, not that week. And not quite there. And, *oui*, we will call you back, Madame—or perhaps not, because what you wish for is simply not possible. At home, I had more troubles: Austin decided that he would come only if he could ride his own bike, because, he said, "trail-a-bikes are for babies." Since he'd just graduated from training wheels, the prospect of double-digit miles with him wobbling along was enough to take my breath away. And here I had thought chafing was the big problem.

But at last the clouds parted. Austin—bribed with the promise he could play on my iPhone during the entire flight to Paris—agreed to use the trail-a-bike, and the maddeningly pleasant but previously disobliging French travel agents suddenly, miraculously, presented us with a complete four-day itinerary.

I packed my oversupply of balms and bike shorts, and we flew to Paris then traveled by train to Blois, where we would start our trip. There we met our travel companions: Gitane Mississippis, sturdy workhorse bikes outfitted with roomy panniers and map holders attached to the handlebars.

We had only a little more than twenty-seven miles to ride, to the town of Amboise, and we were in France, after all, so we started slowly, which in France includes lingering over good food—in this case, perfect French espresso and a basket of croissants oozing almond paste, then stocking up on a dozen madeleines and a bottle of Sancerre for emergency road snacks.

Fed and provisioned, we gathered around our bikes. We were suited up, helmeted, gloved, spandexed; I felt slightly bowlegged from my bike shorts. A woman walked down the sidewalk toward us. She was one of those beautiful, sleek French women who look like they play a lot of tennis but actually just eat a lot of chocolate. She smiled when she saw our pile of gear and our outfits, and suddenly I felt ridiculously over-prepared, like a tenderfoot at a dude ranch.

As she stepped around us, she asked, in English, "Are you bicycling?"

I said we were.

"Well, it's too warm for bicycling," she said, as if she could read every bit of my apprehension. "It's much better to sit and drink wine."

I couldn't help wonder, as we set out, if maybe she was right.

The late start meant that we had to push hard the whole time we were riding, and we took only a few breaks, stopping at a bakery on the river near the village of Rilly-sur-Loire for a late lunch of sandwiches of baguettes with sweet and salty ham then for a quick dinner at a cafe not far from Amboise, where the chef had just finished roasting spring lamb with fennel and sweet peas. This was France, after all.

We arrived in Amboise in the dark, and our innkeeper met us at the door looking cross. She reminded us, with a wag of her finger and a reproachful click of her tongue, that she'd expected us earlier. Much earlier. In fact, much, much earlier, which was, evidently, when nicer guests would have arrived. She was impressively fierce for an innkeeper, so we didn't even look around; we just muttered apologies in bad high-school French and scurried to bed, hoping that when we woke up we might be transformed into nicer guests the innkeeper would be happier to see.

In the morning, we tiptoed downstairs and peeked out the front door to at last take in the view. We expected a driveway and maybe an ordinary lawn. Instead, surprise, we found ourselves practically pressing our noses up to the stone flanks of Chateau Royal d'Amboise, a massive castle built in the fifteenth century on a rock spur overlooking the Loire River. In fact, it turned out our inn was built of stone that had tumbled off the chateau over the years. (As with many of the Loire castles, a great deal of attention was paid to head chopping and dungeon banishment and boiling of miscreants in vats of oil, while castle maintenance was somewhat neglected.)

Before getting back on our bikes, we explored the marvelous, echoey pile—a castle part Renaissance, part proto-Tinker Bell's castle, furnished with just a few gargantuan log chairs and wine-toned tapestries. We roamed the stone rooms and trekked up and down the stairs, rubbed smooth by centuries of heavy treading, then we leaned out a Juliet balcony to view the gray-blue ribbon of the Loire, France's longest river and its last major wild one.

Just as we were about to leave, we discovered that the castle harbored one big surprise: the body of Leonardo da Vinci, buried in a chapel just off the entry garden. Leonardo da Vinci? Although I'd never given much thought to his final resting place, I would have pictured it being somewhere other than a chapel outside a chateau in the Loire Valley. But apparently da Vinci was a citizen of the world and spent a lot of time visiting King Francis I, who ruled here during the castle's glory years. Like the best of friends, Francis provided a permanent resting place for da Vinci when he died.

As we left Amboise, I noticed I could read every sign we passed—"*S'il vous plait aidez-nous trouver notre chien perdu Zuzu*" (please help us find our lost dog Zuzu) and "*Maison a vendre*" (house for sale)—a traveler's pleasure if ever there was one. As we coasted along, we could peek through the gates of the occasional oddball museums and attractions, like the Musee Maurice Dufresne, which appeared to be a collection of antique tractors, and my favorite, the Mini Châteaux Val de Loire. ("All of the most famous castles of the Loire Valley in miniature," the brochure proclaims. "The amazing attention to detail and incredible surroundings will enthrall the whole family!")

Pedaling onward, we stopped for a real look at the full-size castles, such as Villandry and Chambord and Azay-Le-Rideau and Chatonniere, each one insanely big and so exactly like the castles in cartoons and fairy tales that they looked almost as unreal as the models back at the museum of miniatures. The castles seemed to meet us at every turn, sitting like massive stone birthday cakes on the horizon or looming above as we went grinding up one of the valley's green hills.

There was an ancillary benefit to all of this roadside fascination: I forgot about chafing. Simply forgot. For one thing, being in France means eating and drinking so well, even on the road, that all other concerns seem trivial. But also the bike seats were comfortable, and except for a stiff climb at the beginning and end of each day, the ride was a lazy man's dream. Most of our routes were on flat bike lanes on small roads, or paths that hugged the river, close enough for us to smell the muddy water and see fish popping up now and again and, on our third afternoon, rounding the corner outside Azay-Le-Rideau, to see a family of swans with new-looking chicks out for what might have been one of their very first swims.

There were long stretches of the ride where you could fall into a humming sort of rhythm, almost as if your legs were propelling you forward without any feeling of effort, and the bike was floating; at those moments I thought, I can do this for hours! For days! For weeks! I can bike to Spain and then Russia and then—and then a scabby patch of road would jostle me and bring me back to the moment, and another castle would come into view.

Each night we stayed in a different sort of place—a bed-and-breakfast, a rustic inn that in a previous century had been an apiary, an old converted schoolhouse in a town center. The directions along the way were mostly exemplary but each night, as we closed in on our lodgings, things would go to hell and we'd cast around until we could find our way. Exasperating, but then again, none of these were big commercial hotels; they were wonderful one-off joints with kooky-shaped rooms and, in many cases, a kooky innkeeper who was running the place as a late-in-life hobby.

The balm for this frustration was often a bottle of a gorgeous local wine—a Pouilly-Fumé or a Vouvray or a sparkling Saumur—and a hunk of crottin de chavignol, the Loire Valley's famous goat cheese, shaped like a wheel and tasting of nuts. Our wrong turns really didn't seem so bad after that.

But on our third day, we rode for hours through my now-beloved wheat fields and down among some vineyards, and as the afternoon slipped into dusk we made our way through the city of Tours. We were staying in a town southwest of Tours called Ballan-Miré, at an inn called Chateau des Templiers. Easy. This particular day my husband, a more experienced rider, had gone on ahead.

The section through Tours included a patch of bad traffic and a mile or so through a grimy commercial district—the only sliver of the trip that wasn't pastoral. No matter: surely we were close to Ballan-Miré. The route circled a city park and a university campus undergoing all kinds of construction. We lost the trail there, somewhere between a backhoe loader and a tower crane. Where there should have been a golf course, we found a torn-up soccer stadium and half-built faculty housing. Austin and I rode on and reached a stream that was not supposed to be there. We backtracked. A pair of young men were jogging past, so I flagged them down. Golf course? Ballan-Miré? Smiles all around, shrugs, a few gestures to what they thought might be the right direction.

We headed the way they had indicated, but the path petered out, ending back at the edge of the stream that wasn't supposed to be there. Very few people passed, and the few who did smiled pleasantly, shrugged, pointed this way and that, then headed off. My patience was fraying. I glanced at my son, who was starting to list to the right on his trail-a-bike; I held my breath, hoping nothing would set off the question every parent dreads.

He looked over. "Mommy," he said, "when are we going to get there?"

Busted. "A few minutes," I said. "Let's go this way."

We doubled back again, tried another sidewalk, then another. Now the place was deserted. The sun tucked in behind some clouds and dimmed. We crossed one road, then another, each stretch mysteriously emptier and less marked and more confounding. I felt ridiculous. Lost here, of all places, in the exurban sprawl of a large French city? Wilderness, maybe, but here? So humiliating!

"Mommy, when will we get there?" Austin trilled. "It's more than a few minutes."

"I'll call Daddy," I said. Of course, my phone didn't work. Why had I spent so much time buying Bag Balm instead of setting up an international calling plan?

"Mommy?"

"Oh, look!" I said, "a nice man!" We had just turned a corner, and there, in this peculiarly depopulated town, was a middle-aged man running a clipper over his hedges.

"Hello, nice man!" I yelled, probably sounding a little insane and keyed up, the way you can be when you are calculating to the microsecond exactly how much time you have before your child starts an endless loop of "When are we going to get there?" in high volume. The man didn't notice us at first—that is, until I leaped off my bicycle and went running into his yard, shouting, "We're lost! We're lost! We're lost!"

Within moments, his wife emerged from the house with a kindly attitude and chocolate cookies and orange juice and a cell phone, with which they called the unattainable Shangri-la of Ballan-Miré. I asked if they could call us a taxi and let us leave our bikes in their yard until the morning, but the couple seemed tickled by their windfall of visitors and the chance to help out. They decided they wanted to drive us there, so they loaded us into their car and delivered us, then made another round-trip to bring our bikes once we were installed and debriefed. It turns out that we had been nowhere, nowhere at all, near Ballan-Mire. Even after examining the map in detail, I couldn't figure out how we'd gone wrong, or, for that matter, where we had actually been. It was as if we'd fallen into a wormhole for a while.

It was far too late to go out to eat, so our innkeeper insisted on making dinner for us; we sat around her big oak kitchen table, eating good pasta and drinking her wine, and trying to piece together how the bike path had vaporized. Out of it came a reminder of how the misfirings in travel are often what stick with you, much more than those things you think you're supposed to care about and find inspiring.

We had one more castle to go, the marvelous Forteresse Royale, a huge blocky structure on a steep hillside above Chinon. We took a few wrong turns on the way—a combination of fatigue and inattention to our itinerary, and the recklessness you feel toward the end of a journey—so we rode into Chinon not along the river, pedaling steadily and slowly along the recommended route, but slaloming down a raggedy road that pitched nearly headlong to the river. It was crazy and exhilarating, the perfect punctuation to a day that had been gently mesmerizing.

By this time, I felt like Superman, like I could ride anywhere. I was happiest on the days we rode the farthest, the days we were on the road for five or six hours, zooming along as if I had done this my whole life. I was suddenly seized with the desire to do nothing but bike trips—the intimacy of the view, the chance to see and smell and listen as part of the travel, thrilled me. And the whole notion of chafing seemed ridiculous. Could I have really been begging people via social media to help save me from this? Maybe I would start a new hashtag: #pleasesendmeanywhereonabike.

The plunge into town, into the lap of the castle, was a great payoff. For me, the day had already been full, because I felt practically melded to my bike now, almost flying through those perfect tan and golden wheat fields that had sung to us on our way to Chinon. I now knew that on a bike I could see places the way I love to, close enough to notice the odds and ends that gave it texture, at a pace that made me feel like I was truly in it—part of it—and not just passing through.

❧ ❧ ❧

Susan Orlean is the bestselling author of eight books, including My Kind of Place; The Bullfighter Checks Her Makeup; Saturday Night; *and* Lazy Little Loafers. *In 1999, she published* The Orchid Thief, *a narrative about orchid poachers in Florida, which was made into the Oscar-wining movie* Adaptation, *written by Charlie Kaufman and directed by Spike Jonze.* Rin Tin Tin: The Life and the Legend, *a sweeping account of Rin Tin Tin's journey from orphaned puppy to movie star and international icon published in 2011, was a* New York Times *bestseller and a Notable book of 2011. Orlean has written for* Vogue, Esquire, Rolling Stone, *and* Smithsonian, *and has been a staff writer for the* New Yorker *since 1992. She has covered a wide range of subjects—from umbrella inventors to origami artists to skater Tonya Harding—and she has often written about animals, including show dogs, racing pigeons, animal actors, oxen, donkeys, mules, and backyard chickens. She lives in upstate New York and Los Angeles with one dog, three cats, eight chickens, four turkeys, four guinea fowl, twelve Black Angus cattle, three ducks, and her husband and son.*

❧ ❧ ❧

Riverdance

Up a creek on a love boat in Laos.

*I*dling our boat in the deep, silty waters of the Mekong, we contemplated the mouth of the Nam Ou. It curved along a sheer limestone wall in a tight smile of translucent green, its shallow, hairpin entrance forbidding all but the smallest and lightest boats. Our riverboat, a traditional teak-hulled model with a four-cylinder Toyota engine strapped to its rear, was as long as a city bus but only four feet wide, drawing less than eighteen inches. Slightly fish-shaped and floppy with age, her tapered ends often moved independently of each other, creating a clumsy, snaking motion against the current. Flint and I had dubbed her the *Spawning Salmon* and, for better or worse, we owned her now. Planning a voyage of several days, we had just motored her gently up the Mekong, departing Luang Prabang at sunrise to avoid playing chicken with the midday barge traffic. An hour into our journey, the *Salmon* was already acting flighty. Her cooling mechanism kept seizing up, and the engine had the vapors.

Two weeks earlier, we'd hitched a ride on an empty passenger boat to explore the Nam Ou for the first time. After a few idyllic days of paddling in clear water and trekking to isolated Khmu villages in the upper valley, Flint wanted to follow the pretty river to its highest navigable point, a Chinese trading post called Hat Sa. I wanted a backstage pass to the real Laos, the land beyond the "tourist triangle." When separated from an entire culture by language, economics, and geography, local transportation often provides the quickest route through the gap—if not from A to B. An open-air river journey, surrounded by dramatic karsts and a fringe of jungle, sounded far more enticing than riding a crowded bus or dull tour van up Highway 13. We'd asked around in Luang Prabang and found it was "not possible" to hire a boat to Hat Sa—something to do with fuel costs and territory disputes among the drivers. Naturally, Flint solved this problem by purchasing his own boat.

The idea wasn't as insane as it may sound: Flint was practically born on a boat. He had built two of his own from junkyard scrap, and he could sail anything from a harbor dory to an English clipper in high seas. In fact, he had wooed me with a boat adventure when we first met in Burma, the previous year, and in spite of our many differences since then, I still told myself that any man who would buy an illegal fishing pirogue and paddle me down the Irrawaddy on a whim deserved a fighting chance. It was not the first time I'd fallen in love with a grand gesture, only to find that the moment always outshone the creator, who was after all only a man. Nonetheless, I had brought Flint to Laos, a place I found magical, hoping he would love it as I did, and I was willing to explore at least part of the country on his terms. Now the seadog in him was itching to be afloat again; he needed to be "unlocked in this landlocked nation," he said.

As for me, I'm no mariner, but an old-school Mekong riverboat is a simple machine: two long ropes run up each side and wind around the steering column, controlling the rudder. Another rope, operated by the driver's big toe, is the accelerator. There is no gearbox, so once you turn the key you're going forward: no neutral, no reverse, and no brakes. It's like driving a stretch go-cart on water. The *Salmon* was a pile of splinters and flaking mustard paint but initially, I didn't see cause for worry. Every riverboat in Asia was at least as wobbly, if not more so. The old girl looked tired, but game for one more run.

Following an engine overhaul and several trips to the market for supplies, we launched our expedition, deciding to take the established route in slow stages before sailing off the map. On our first trip upriver, Flint had crouched behind the boat pilot the whole way to Muong Noi, furiously scribbling notes. Navigating the Nam Ou on his own, he claimed, would be "not too difficult, but definitely interesting." I couldn't tell whether this little adventure was driven by diehard romanticism or his outsized ego, but either way, he seemed happy for the first time in months. My meandering style of travel did not suit Flint; he was a man who needed a mission, and at last he had one.

Now that we were circling the point of no return, the plan seemed questionable and the boat even more so. The river looked faster and fiercer than I remembered. Sandbars and boulders had somehow doubled in size since our last trip. I knew what Flint was thinking—he'd repeated it often enough: "Rivers are like women; they change with the weather." I was thinking neither of us was in top form for this—Flint had a snotty head cold, and I'd woken up with a slight fever and an ominously bloated stomach. Yet, no one suggested turning back.

Skirting the boat gingerly around the cliffs and into the Nam Ou, Flint stopped again and admitted to feeling "nervy," which turns out to be British for "woefully unprepared." During our final dash to the market, he confessed, he had lost the hand-drawn map and navigational notes from the scouting trip. *Now* I wanted to turn around, but it was too late; the Nam Ou was too narrow, and we were officially up a creek.

Immediately, we faced an "interesting" section of current. As we hesitated in the shallows, a fisherman waved us over to the bank, where he hopped effortlessly onto our boat's prow, guiding us through the first stretch of gurgling water with the precision of an air-traffic controller. We ferried him back to the side and offered to pay for his time. Smiling, the man shook his head, but his young son, who was peeking into our hold, looked up at me starry-eyed.

"Lacta-Soy?" he whispered shyly.

I handed the boy two boxes of the popular soymilk drink, and they went happily on their way. Once they were out of sight, I stopped smiling and addressed the Skipper.

"What's your plan?" I demanded.

"Believe it or not, it isn't my intention to get us killed," Flint said, looking sheepish. "I'm a complete pillock for losing those notes, I know. It's a very technical river, and I have no business driving it on the basis of watching someone else do it exactly once."

"So, now what?" I grumbled.

"Well, I think we should find a nice, calm spot to camp. In the morning, we'll wait for a passenger boat to come by. Any of those drivers could take this river blindfolded, so if we tag along behind one of those blokes, we'll be all right."

With the new plan in place, we eased our way upstream and dropped our makeshift anchor—a sandbag—on a narrow spit. Flint toyed busily with the engine, bailed out the boat, and set up our gas cooker to make dinner. Feeling increasingly unwell, I lounged in the cabin and surveyed the scene. A teenage boy wearing a castoff tie-dye shirt paddled close and stole glances at us while pretending to check his fish traps. A gaggle of children splashed in the mud against a sloping patchwork of vegetable gardens, and a few wary fishermen circled us in dugout canoes. Once they saw we weren't fishing, they relaxed, and some of the younger ones hung around to sample Flint's camp-stove spaghetti. They liked it so much he had to make a second batch for us. We turned in early and aimed to hook our little Mekong caboose to the first available passenger boat in the morning.

It was nearly midnight when I crawled out of the cabin and hinged over the side of the boat, deeply regretting the spaghetti as my stomach violently emptied itself. I spent the next hour heaped on the cold, wet sandbar, digging holes with my hands when I could and retching directly into the river when my strength was gone. On our last visit to this valley, we'd spent a night in a Khmu village, far from any purified water except the small bottles we carried with us. Waking up on a bare floor under a thatched roof full of holes, I'd accepted a cup of tea from our host, the village headman, choosing to play intestinal roulette rather than offend him by refusing his hospitality. Back in Luang Prabang, I'd picked up a course of Tinidazole at the pharmacy, just in case, but hadn't counted on being in the middle of nowhere, boat-camping, if I lost the bet. When the worst of the intestinal spasms had passed, I scrounged through my bag, gulped a pill, and fell shivering into the boat's cabin.

The next morning, moving very slowly, I helped Flint pack up. Then we sat back and waited for a boat. Hours went by, and aside from the occasional fisherman or farmer's wife passing through, the valley was still. Out of sheer boredom, we attempted a short distance on our own. The engine sputtered, and Flint kept stopping to fiddle with it. After an hour of slow progress, we pulled over again on a stretch of fine sand.

"I don't know . . ." Flint yawned, rubbing his eyes. "Perhaps we ought to call it a day. What d'ya think?"

I must have been too delirious to think, or I might have recognized what could have been a graceful exit point. Instead, I said, "I think I hear a boat coming."

The unmistakable clatter of a diesel engine echoed up the valley, followed by a half-empty passenger boat. The driver was flogging it upriver at an intimidating pace. Flint pushed us off and the *Salmon* hurtled after the other boat, swanning across the channel and then laboring to keep up.

"Can you see if we have water?" Flint shouted back at me. I was perched on the stern because the *Salmon*'s cooling pipe, an old bicycle part attached with a cheap plastic hose, demanded constant attention. Hanging on to the towrope, I leaned out over the back of the boat like some kind of displaced figurehead.

"No, we don't!" I yelled back.

"Can you try priming it? Grab a bottle and pour some water back into the pipe!"

I made an effort, but it was like trying to ride a mechanical bull and milk it at the same time. As the engine began to whine, the Skipper's pitch rose to match it.

"Can you reach that spit pipe without falling in? Suck on it and blow some air back in?"

"No," I said flatly. "I can't."

Convincing me to inhale and possibly ingest diesel fuel mixed with cholera-water would be a stretch on my best day, and I had just spent the whole night losing my guts on a sandbar. Flint noted my expression and wisely changed his tack.

"All right—can you come up here and drive for a minute?"

I ducked through the cabin, scrambled into the cockpit, and placed a tentative hand on the wheel. "Uh, O.K. . . . what should I do?" I asked.

"Follow that boat!"

Feeling like the getaway driver in a caper movie, I looped the accelerator-rope around my big toe and floored it. The boat careened upstream for a few thrilling minutes, until the engine overheated and abruptly cut out. Aiming for a sandbar, I let the *Salmon* run aground with a thud. Meanwhile, our lead boat stormed off, disappearing around a sharp bend.

"Well done," Flint nodded, his tone chagrined. "I can't get the bloody pipe to clear, either. She was going to quit on us no matter who was driving." From our awkward emergency parking spot, we could hear the other boat charging away.

"Why does he have to go so fast, anyway?" I groused.

"Not to worry," said the Skipper, "I'll have a quick tinker and we'll be off!"

Within minutes, the errant engine snarled to life; Flint gleefully kicked the boat back into the current and leapt behind the wheel. It was too late to catch our lead boat, but at least we knew which way it had gone. Lurching blindly around the bend, we found ourselves in a box canyon: a chute of whitewater enclosed by sheer cliffs on one side and stacked boulders on the other. At the bottom, wrapped around the rocks, lay a hulk of rusting metal and splintered teak—the remains of a riverboat. Even with my limited nautical experience, I knew we'd just made a very bad mistake.

Under the looming shadow of the cliff wall, the Nam Ou was stripped of its emerald hue, leaving us in a maze of seething whitecaps and black, sucking eddies. Boulders seemed to leap out of the current like gunslingers in an old Western, menacing. Flint hunched over the wheel, steering on his knees, trying to coax enough speed out of the wheezing engine to haul us up the ladder of water. Clamping his jaw in concentration, he held the *Salmon* steady, her gangly body flopping up, up, up.

"Can you see if we have water?" he shouted over the roaring engine and crashing rapids. Crouching behind him, I ducked spray and craned my neck toward the spit pipe.

"No water!" I shouted back.

"What about now?" he yelled, seconds later.

"No!"

"Keep watching!"

With the engine straining hard, the cooling pipe should have been gushing, but it produced nothing. Flint, on the other hand, spewed a constant and impressive stream of epithets, collected over a lifetime in boatyards. The boat swayed and wobbled, shuddering with effort. As I clung to the cabin's frame, training one eye on the impotent spit pipe and the other on the rapids ahead, I wondered how much time we had before the engine quit or caught fire. I wondered why life jackets couldn't be found anywhere in this country, and why I'd waited so long to learn how to swim. Between my panicked mental checklist and my pipe-watching, I barely noticed the sudden reappearance of light and color—shimmering greens and blues—along with a jump in air temperature. We were clearing the canyon. Even if the rapids were unrelenting, we now had a good chance of colliding with a mud bank rather than a rock wall. But when I glanced at the pipe again, the scrap of relief slipped away.

"Still no water!" I reported, with rising alarm. "And now there's smoke coming out!"

"Whore!" the skipper screeched at the engine. The engine screeched back, and then cut out. It took a full second to register the absence of mechanical racket, and one more to comprehend our situation. In an almost-comic moment, Flint and I both rubbernecked wildly toward the engine, then at each other. Next, Flint did something I'd never actually seen before: he turned stark white. Without four cylinders to propel her against the current, the *Salmon* had stopped moving forward and seemed to be considering a suicide run, back into the boneyard.

Flint gunned the starter a few times, then skittered out onto the prow where he pushed our sandbag into the water and jumped in after it. The rope went taut and the *Salmon* began to drag the sixty-pound bag like a fly-fishing weight, with Flint as the fly. Waist-deep in current, struggling with the lifeless riverboat, he began speaking in his "sail-training voice," the one he generally saved for coaxing inexperienced crew across the Atlantic.

"Laurie, I can't hold this boat by myself. If you can, very carefully, I need you in the water. Watch your step, now—get a good foothold."

Water cascaded around him. I moved in slow motion; the combination of adrenaline, giardia, and Tinidazole created a heavy and not unpleasant tranquilizing effect. Wearing black knit yoga pants and a tank top, I was underdressed for a ship-wreck. I had no life jacket and my feet were bare. I noted all of this as I lowered myself over the side of the boat, half-listening to Flint's nervous patter:

"Mind your feet on those rocks—careful! That's it, now just hold on to the boat and try to keep your ground!"

The *Salmon* lunged eagerly downstream. The river was only waist deep, but we were in the full force of it, stumbling and slipping on the rocks. A football field's length ahead, we could see where it broadened into a glassy pond, like a mirage. We were losing ground quickly when a fisherman waded over from the shallows to throw his weight—and unbeliev-ably buff legs—into the lineup. The boat stopped sliding. Flint and I stopped sliding, too, and we stood there panting, trying to think of what to do next. The fisherman pointed to a lee behind a cluster of rocks, and with nods of agreement, the three of us towed, shoved, and heave-ho'd the boat toward the goal, banging our shins and cutting our feet as the wicked river fought back. My clothes were soaked, and my knit pants, now twelve inches longer, threatened to wind around my feet and drag me under.

When we reached the boulders, Flint tied our towrope around the biggest one and I climbed up. Without a word, the fisherman returned to his traps, throwing us a look that clearly said, "Good luck, idiots; you'll need it."

While the Skipper made a reconnaissance trip to the near-est bank, I gripped the granite islet with my feet, held the bucking boat with both hands and considered our position. I couldn't see a way out, not without a new engine or another able body to help us. I would have gladly released the damned boat right then, but I didn't know what—or who—might be downstream. Resigned to the fate of pushing our untrustworthy vessel even farther, I stripped off my treacherous knit pants with one hand and snatched my Tevas from the steering box. The gruff fisherman passed by again and, succumbing to our frantic hand waving and panicked expressions, waded back in to help us drag the boat to the nearest bank. About halfway across the channel, Flint and I both realized that our efforts, which felt substantial, were merely guiding the boat's direction. The fisherman was forcing our fifty-foot lemon through five knots of current almost single-handedly.

"Blimey," Flint said, awestruck. "He's not even that big a chap."

As soon as we reached calm water, our fisherman-hero abruptly let go, slung his net over his shoulder, and strode off. Reaching into the hold, Flint grabbed the first thing he could lay his hands on and splashed after the man, offering meager thanks in the form of a lukewarm Heineken.

We towed the *Salmon* through the mud, waved a few ragged cows away and, with daylight fading, made camp. By now, the boat was leaking like an old wooden bucket. The Skipper had a long night of bailing ahead of him. As darkness eclipsed the river, I looked up at the dusky sky and noticed a single line of cable swooping over the opposite bank. Electric wire meant there was a road nearby, and only one major road ran through this part of Laos: Highway 13. Every southbound vehicle on it stopped in Luang Prabang. Fate was once again lighting up an exit sign with flashing lights, and this time I was going to follow it. Flint encouraged me to go and even apologized for getting me into trouble, but he refused to come with me. He was determined to push on to Nong Khiaw, the transit hub at the widest part of the river where most of the boats turned around.

"I want to finish what I started," he said.

Like the river, he confounded me with his duality: was he bold and imaginative or merely grandiose and puerile? Too exhausted to fight, I simply recounted our most recent judgment errors aloud and advised him not to confuse stubbornness with integrity.

I think he heard me, but in the end, we held dramatically different visions for the journey and for life. I had been pushing our broken boat upstream for nearly a year, against an impossible current, and as much as I treasured the picture of us dreamily afloat on the Irrawaddy, it was time to admit this river was too much for me.

For a while, the only sounds came from the whirring cicadas, grumbling cows, and the scrape-and-slosh of Flint's bailing bucket. I tucked in the mosquito net and was drifting off to sleep when I heard him say quietly, "You were magnificent out there today, in your knickers. I wouldn't have made it this far without you. I'd have lost the boat, or worse."

In the morning, Flint started the temperamental engine, and we buzzed to the opposite shore. Struggling up a sugary-soft dune, I found myself in Ban Had Kok—a small weaving village barely an hour by road from Luang Prabang. I returned to the boat with a fresh baguette for my queasy stomach and fresh intel for Flint: the bread vendor had a cell phone he could borrow. While he went to call for backup, I stayed with the boat, befriending a trio of little girls who had been spying on us from down the beach. Swiftly reaching the limits of my Lao vocabulary (about six phrases) and their English (A through G of the Alphabet Song), we moved on to charades and sand-pictures. By the time Flint came back, the girls were vaulting in and out of the boat, frolicking in the mucky water, and gleefully raiding our remaining stash of Lacta-Soy. It was the kind of afternoon I'd come for in the first place. Flint had managed to reach the fellow who'd sold him the boat and extracted his promise to send a "top mechanic." When the children wandered away, I strapped on my pack and scaled the sand dune once more to reach the road—the dull, hot, blessedly dry road. Sticking out my arm, I flagged down the first vehicle in sight. Never have I been so happy to see a tour company's mini-van.

Chastened, I returned to Luang Prabang ten pounds lighter, nursing a sprained wrist and torn rib cartilage that would never fully heal. But a hot shower, a decent meal, and another round of Tinidazole solved much of my woe. I had no regrets about walking away. For me, there would be other rivers, more reliable boats.

Flint continued up the Nam Ou alone. The trip to Nong Khiaw, less than six hours by "express boat" from Luang Prabang, took him nearly six days, even with the help of several mechanics and a local driver. He spent his final night on the boat, its keel half-submerged in mud, next to an impoverished Khmu village. Like indigenous tribes everywhere, the Khmu have genuine problems not of their own creation. I like to think it may have finally dawned on him that he was only playing castaway, an actor who had bought himself a small vanity part in a vast and complex theater of lost tribes. Like me, he suffered by choice—he had the power and the means to leave at any time. It occurred to me that he too had fallen in love with an idea, a dream that could never be fully realized in the flesh. Traveling can have that effect on people.

He later reported, Kurtz-like, that he found the Khmu village a paradise: "A howling, snorting, crying, hacking, coughing, terrible-hard paradise." At such close quarters, he could not continue to ignore their destitution, and so he gave away the *Salmon*'s inventory piece by piece. The Khmu carried away his pots and pans, buckets, utensils, food, bottled water, two new mattresses, a few tools, perhaps even some of his arrogant assumptions. The next day, a tourist boat towed him and the *Salmon* the last few miles to Nong Khiaw, where he sold her to a fisherman's son for 20,000 kip (about $2 U.S.). With that, the old boat became another boy's mechanically challenged dream, and returned to her rightful place in the world. Eventually, so did the Skipper, and so did I.

Laurie Weed is a passionate traveler and hapless romantic whose stories have appeared in four of The Best Women's Travel Writing books, in addition to magazines, guidebooks, newspapers, and on the web. She can always be found at www.laurieweed.com.

❧ ❧ ❧

What We Do After Gunfire

In Brazil, life goes on.

*J*aque sits on the porch steps that lead from her tiny house down to the basement home of her uncle. Her three children, sunburned from Rio de Janeiro's blazing February summer, hang like ornaments from her limbs and lap. I rest my elbows on the iron bar of the window and spread my fingers in the space between outside and in.

The first blast sounds like an avalanche untangling itself from the mountain. The sudden and boundless rumble shakes in my belly, echoing above my head and below my feet. From the window I see Jaque stumble down the stairs with her baby clutched to her chest and her daughter and son grasping at the hem of her skirt. She glances my way for a second, and the look on her face makes my stomach tighten. I see the warning in her eyes, and I hit the floor. My cheek presses into the dirty blue rug, and I stare at the red flashing numbers on the digital clock beside the television. It's 3:30 P.M. on a Sunday afternoon.

When I first met Jaque, she was silent and smiling, and her third child was still in her belly, waiting to enter the battleground of Falet—one of Rio de Janeiro's five hundred plus *favelas*, or slums. We pressed ice cubes against our foreheads to protest the sun that ferocious summer, and the neighbor-hood kids shouted "Teacher!" when they saw me on the street. Jaque's mother called me her white daughter, but for the first two months I lived in her home, Jaque and I barely spoke to each other. She watched me, curious yet unmoved by the strange American dance teacher who had befriended her mother and become an unexpected guest in their tiny, tin-roofed house. She refused to let me help with dinner.

But one night as I danced with her mother in the living room, overcome with the beat of my favorite Brazilian song, Jaque leapt from her seat with a wail and started shaking her hips in circles around my body, yelling, "*Eu nunca soube sobre seu coração maluco do brasileiro!*" "I never knew about your crazy Brazilian heart!"

They called Jaque *favelada*, meaning someone with the real style of the *favela*. The *favelas* of Brazil were notorious for their tangle of colorful shacks, drug trafficking rings, violent encounters with the police, and Brazilian funk music. And oh, how the *favela* could be stylish. Stylish like AK-47s slipped between the hipbones and Bermuda shorts of twenty-two-year-old drug lords. Stylish like high-heeled women stomping their feet to the rat-a-tat percussion of funk songs blasting from hand-painted boom boxes at all hours of the day and night. Stylish like the coded victory cry of three bullets released into the air while dancers chanted, "The police don't come to our parties!"

Jaque knew all the shortcuts in Falet's maze of staircases and gutters, and she knew the people who did their business there. Because she could move quickly, without bus fare, she ran all the errands for her family. She understood the *favela* like a gardener understands the geometry of her garden and is willing to touch things that have not yet become beautiful.

Jaque never looked worried when the guns fired. Her two-year-old cried loudly and her mother clucked her tongue and muttered about the end of the world, but Jaque just kept sweeping the kitchen floor in her cutoff denim skirt or tickling her baby's face. Then she'd look at me with large amber eyes and laugh: "*É malucera neh?*" "This is craziness, huh?"

My body is still flat on the floor, legs wedged under the bed, face against the scratchy carpet. Yes, I think. This is craziness. The hail of bullets has stopped and been replaced by an uncertain stillness. Twenty minutes have passed since Jaque fled down the stairs with her children, and I console myself with the thought that she's in her uncle's house taking cover in his bedroom, but the air is empty of the two-year-old's tears or the baby's giggle.

I crawl to the doorway, where I weigh the risk of standing upright to move toward the staircase that will take me outside, and to her. I wonder in this moment if we mimic our surroundings. If we yell back at bullets and bite our tongue in the ceasefire. When the kids in this neighborhood hear hip hop on the radio, they imitate the sound of machine gunfire to accompany the beat. I don't know what sound we make when we imitate death, but I'm sure I have heard it here. I'm sure that in the space between Jaque and me, there is a path from the hand that resists violence to the hand that accepts it. I silently plead with Jaque's children to make noise, but only the high-pitched wind whistles in my ear.

Jaque's favorite time of day, it seemed, was at night when all her kids were asleep and no one had come home yet. I often found her in bed covered in a blanket with her youngest baby on her chest, her four-year-old at the other end of the mattress, and her two-year-old on the bed by her side. The air echoed calmly around the breath of the children. And though her eyes were closed, she was always awake and whispered my name.

We had our most intimate conversations on these nights. Jaque didn't tell secrets to her mother because they were too much alike, and she didn't tell secrets to her sister because she was younger and more religious. But she confided in me when we were alone and her kids were asleep in the bedroom in Falet.

She told me how much she missed the father of her four-year-old daughter. He was the one she still loved, but he chose to be a trafficker. "And that," she insisted, "is not a life. Just a short existence before death."

One afternoon, months after this, I sat crying in her living room over a broken heart. She walked in and spilled a bag of rice as she waved her arms around and shouted through a beaming smile, "We deserve good men! We deserve good men!" It was the first time I'd heard her say she deserved anything good, and I nodded my head slowly with wide eyes. Because we did.

The digital clock above my head now blinks 4:15 P.M. Forty-five minutes since Jaque and her kids ran down below. The gunfire has returned, but this time it's a distant reverberation. I stand up.

When Jaque cleans the house she moves briskly, never putting anything back in place carefully, yet somehow managing not to make a sound. This is how I move downstairs now. Like a gust of wind.

In front of her uncle's door, I pause and press my ear to the splintered wood. I want Jaque to teach me how she walks through her world like a queen. I want her to show me the swiftness of her hands and the abandon of her hips. If I had a sound to mimic Jaque, it would be Rio at four in the afternoon, when the sun crackles on concrete and feet tap, preparing to dance.

The door's creaky hinge is the first sound to break the silence. Next is the whisper of my name on Jaque's lips. She is lying on her uncle's bed, eyes closed, her baby on her chest, the other two children at her feet. She grins as I curl my body into the tiny spot beside her.

"They were tired," she says, brushing a long braid off her face. "It's so peaceful when they sleep."

Jocelyn Edelstein has spent extensive time in Brazil, dancing and working on her upcoming documentary, Believe The Beat, which follows a group of hip hop dancers from Rio de Janeiro. Her documentary work has also led her to Europe where she has enjoyed the honey cake in Prague and the gelato in Florence. She currently resides on the Oregon Coast where she teaches dance to all ages, writes, and plays in the ocean. To learn more about Jocelyn, visit her website at www.danceharvest.com or to preview her upcoming documentary, visit www.urbanbodyproject.com.

ℐ℥ ℐ℥ ℐ℥

Sidecar Sally

In the Mexican jungle, her alter
ego came along for the ride.

*I*t's first light on my second day in Yelapa, Mexico, and I'm in a panga boat skimming the peaked ripples of the Banderas Bay. A dozen huddled passengers surround me on wooden benches—local Mexicans of all ages, smiling and chatting, traveling to Puerto Vallarta for the day.

"*Amigo!*" one guy yells to another, over the roar of the motor. He slaps him on the back.

I squint into the wind and chew on my thumbnail, jittery with excitement. I'm not going to Puerto Vallarta. At a tiny beach, a stop on the way to the city, I'm jumping out of the boat and meeting two to three strange men.

Tom, my landlord, called my *casita* yesterday. "We're touring the jungle back roads tomorrow," he said. "Join us?"

I paused. I thought he was calling to make sure I had hot water and a cold refrigerator. "I thought there were no roads," I said.

"There aren't."

"Uh-huh."

"We can probably make it, with the Jeep."

"Who's going?"

"Not sure. Possibly an American photographer and a crazy Australian dude who's been traveling for eight years."

I took a long, slow sip of my Pacifico. With a rare week away from my husband and two tiny kids in Colorado, I'd planned to be anti-social: write and walk and sleep. No agenda. But I love adventure, and I also tend to like photographers, and crazy people.

"In," I said.

"Great. Meet us at Boca. Wear your bikini."

In the boat, I reach behind my neck and tighten the straps of my swimsuit, under my dress. I brought two bikinis on this trip, and I'm wearing the one that's far more conservative—neutral tones, full coverage, visually boring. I know from Tom's website that in addition to renting *casas* in the village of Yelapa, he's a bikini photographer.

I am not a bikini model. I'm winter white, I have short hair, and I've birthed two children in the last four years. I love wearing bikinis—soft strings grazing skin—but the thought of being captured on film while frolicking in a jungle water-fall makes me feel self-conscious, some unflattering pose trapped forever and posted who-knows-where. If Tom photographs me, I'm hoping my suit will blend into earth, making me invisible.

I gaze out at the waves and search for the humpback whales that breed in these warm waters each winter. There's only a jagged, hazy cliff in the distance. It feels symbolic. I am a mother, bypassing typical tourist destinations for a trip into wild places with strange men, in a country that's notorious for its warring drug cartels. My father would say, "Didn't I teach you better?"

Water splashes up around the boat and grazes my eye. It feels like a tear. I wipe it away.

At the beach, Tom waves. He looks harmless enough: early forties, sandals, genuine smile. "Morning, Carrie," he says.

I babble. "Hi. I almost missed the boat. I couldn't hear my alarm clock over the sound of the waves. My neighbor knocked on my door. Ha!" I glance back toward the boat. It's gone.

He laughs. "Glad you made it." He adjusts the strap of his camera bag and leads me up a cobblestone path through a maze of haphazardly parked cars. With the discreet eye of a seasoned solo traveler, I scan Tom for anything that seems sketchy: knives, drugs, guns. Nothing. My instinct says he's trustworthy, but sometimes it's tricky to tell.

I buy a Coke Light from an open-air *tienda*. A beautiful black-eyed boy, about the age of my son, stares at me from behind the counter. "*Buenos dias*," I say, sweetly. He buries his face in his mother's skirt. Guilt stabs my belly. My own son is getting dressed for preschool right now. My daughter, age one, is probably wandering the house saying, "Mama?"

Last night, I sent my husband an email that said, "I'm touring the jungle tomorrow with Tom, my landlord. If you don't hear from me within twenty-four hours, send out a search party. XO"

Ten minutes later, he replied, "Have fun! Love you." He is eternally supportive. But I could see the concern in his eyes, even through the make-believe jungle of Cyberspace. I knew I should share his feelings.

As I exit the *tienda*, I see Tom talking to two white guys. They're near a well-worn Toyota 4-Runner and a badass motorcycle with a sidecar—flat black with a pile of spare tires, and a helmet, strapped to the back rack.

The guy with the cigarette reaches his hand out to shake mine. "Hi," he says. "I'm Joe." Three words and I know he's the Aussie. I take in his wild black hair and boots and faded jeans. *Crazy, maybe*. But he averts his eyes when he looks at me, which seems sweet and shy, respectful. He reminds me of a famous poster of James Dean.

The other guy is an ebullient American. "I'm Brian," he says. He has short clipped brown hair and a point-and-shoot camera in his hand, yet he must be the photographer. He says he's a vagabond.

Tom gives me a mischievous smile. "We've decided you're going to ride in the sidecar. We voted before you got here."

It feels like a test. *What else did they discuss before I arrived?*

"Great," I say, feigning confidence. "I love motorcycles. I used to ride a Harley."

They all look surprised. When I look down, I can see why. I look nothing like a biker chick. I'm dressed like I didn't know what to expect today, like maybe I'm going to the beach, or on a hike: brown sundress, flip flops, black fleece. I'm carrying a blue mesh bag that contains a towel, water, protein bar, and camera.

Joe looks at my painted blue toenails and half-smiles. "Do you have boots?" he asks.

"No. But I have running shoes." Really they're little Simple sneakers.

He snuffs out his cigarette with his toe. "Good. Because you might need to push, if the roads are bad."

I love riding in the sidecar. The air is brisk, blowing my hair into wild tangles. I pull the leather seat cover up to my chest, snuggle back into the cushion, and watch the palm trees of the jungle canopy morph into pines and shrubs as we climb. Not unlike the landscape of Colorado. As I peer through the trees, I look for dead bodies or surly Mexican men wielding machetes or machine guns. It's wild out there, but no blood.

Joe navigates the curves of the road. There's an instant ease between us that strikes me. He hands me his hat. I hold it. I point to an interesting sign. He nods. We don't talk, and we know almost nothing about each other, but it feels like we've been traveling together for months. I sense something awakening in me—what is it? I can't put my finger on it, but it feels important.

When we stop for a rest, I don't want to. Except that we're in the driveway of a breathtaking botanical garden, a display of color and texture and sound. There are hot pink azaleas, manicured fruit trees, frolicking dogs, a beautiful open-air restaurant containing wooden tables and benches. Birds chirp. Dishes clank in a nearby kitchen. The air smells like sunshine.

Brian saunters over. "How was the sidecar?"

"Awesome."

"You weren't cold?"

"Not really."

Tom kneels down. He snaps a photo of me stepping out of the sidecar. I giggle. He keeps shooting. I wave my hand in the air. "Take some photos of Joe," I say.

We tour the botanical gardens, which has dozens of varieties of orchids, water lilies, and tropical plants. Tom knows interesting details about the flora, like that vanilla is part of the orchid family. I snap a few photos, so I will remember.

As I climb back into the sidecar, Joe says, "You like it in there, huh?"

I smile. "I do."

He gives me a long, amused look.

Brian pipes in. "I guess we should call you Sidecar Sally."

Everyone laughs. It's not until we're rumbling out of the driveway that I realize Brian is right on. It's Sidecar Sally awakening inside of me, the part of my identity that exists opposite my role as wife and mother. She's fearless and free-spirited, a woman who takes road trips through Wyoming and Montana, or backpacks alone into the mountains with barely a plan. I'd never given her a name.

We order margaritas at a hacienda in the middle of nowhere. I choose passion fruit with *raicilla,* the local moonshine. The place is a palace, with high ceilings, dark mahogany wood-work and windows overlooking hillsides of trees and vines.

Even the women's bathroom is beautiful, with ornate sinks and elegant artwork.

We wander around individually, checking things out. Joe and I end up at the same window.

"How long are you in Yelapa, Sidecar Sally?" he asks.

I smile. "A while."

"And then where are you going?"

I pause. "Home?"

He laughs.

I give him a brotherly push. "And you?"

"Next? Copper Canyon."

I've heard of this region in Chihuahua. Some of the canyons are as deep as the Grand.

"Have you been there?" he asks.

I shake my head. "No."

Joe tells me he's traveling from Argentina to Alaska by motorcycle, and before that he bicycled across the continent of Africa.

"Wow," I say, rapt. I can imagine myself doing all of those things.

He lifts his camera and takes a photo.

"So, do you like traveling solo?" I ask. I expect him to say *hell yeah, I love it*.

"Not really," he says. "I'd like to share this experience with someone." He pauses. "But it would have to be the right woman."

My breath catches. I lean down to scratch my leg and create a subtle change in subject. I gasp. There are pinpricks of blood covering my calves, ankles, and feet. Tiny wings flutter. I spring up. "My legs!" I exclaim.

Tom looks over from the table. "Carrie! Those are No-see-um bites," he says. "Quick. Get some bug spray."

I run over to a table at the edge of the patio where I saw a tube of white cream. I slather it over my legs. But the damage is already done. Swollen welts cover my calves, ankles, and feet. I didn't even know it was happening. From the knees down, I look like I've been living in a cave in the jungle for months, like I am physically morphing into my alter ego.

The wife and mother in me would've put on insect repellent as a preventive measure. But Sidecar Sally doesn't give a shit. What's a few bug bites?

When the road becomes dirt, we go fast. It's fun and dusty and carefree, and we skid around in the sand, but I'm not scared. I can't stop smiling. In a way, this feels like a glimpse into a life I might've chosen, one without marriage and children. I'm happy with my choices—I wouldn't change them. And I think I could have been happy this way, too. World travel punctuated by longer stays in special places, a string of lovers, or sidecars, or endless dance partners.

I know there would be disadvantages: feelings of loneliness and displacement. Joe admits he wants companionship. But as much as I try to be content inside my white picket fence in Colorado, changing diapers and cooking macaroni and cheese, Sidecar Sally whispers, and sometimes screams, her need for freedom. Domesticity versus Wanderlust. It's an ongoing match.

When we reach the waterfall, I spring out of the sidecar. I trudge through the river ahead of the guys, toss my flip-flops onto the shore, and peel off my dress on a pale boulder. Tom's carrying his camera bag, but I don't even care. I don't care that my body isn't perfect, or that I'm in the jungle with three men, or that I'm not a typical mother. I hope we get stuck and that I have to push the motorcycle. I hope we're forced to park the bike above Yelapa so we can hike down at dusk into the village.

I wade into the thigh-deep cold water and stoop down to submerge my whole body. The tender skin on my chest, covering my heart, prickles. "Ooh," I say. "Yes." I walk on my hands through the pool, the sand rough under my palms, kicking my legs behind me.

Under the rush of the waterfall, I stand up. Water pummels my back and my head and my neck. It feels like a fist, or a passionate heartbeat. I squeeze my eyes shut. I breathe hard. Everything else disappears.

When I step out of the cascade and rub open my eyes, they're all there. Tom is kneeling on a rock, snapping photos of me. Joe and Brian stand on the edge of the pool in their swim trunks. They look so innocent.

"Am I the only one who's swimming?" I tease.

They stare at me like I'm crazy.

"Isn't it cold?" says Brian.

"Yeah," says Joe.

I shrug. "It's great!"

Tom looks up from his camera. His whole face lights up. "Sidecar Sally," he says, "I have never seen anyone enjoy a waterfall like that."

I throw my hands in the air. "Thank you."

We stumble upon a ranch owned by Tom's friends. The landscape is dust and brush and scattered trees. A lone azalea catches my eye, and I take in the burst of color. I feel like that right now: a bright bloom. I brush my hair from my face and do a little salsa step in the dirt.

"This town has forty people," Tom says.

I look around at the smattering of small structures. "Town?"

"Yep."

"Whoa."

We wander up onto the sweeping ranch porch. An elderly Mexican man with leathery skin hugs Tom and pours us each a shot of *raicilla*.

"Cheers!" I exclaim, clinking each glass. I shoot mine; they sip.

Tom leads us to an adjacent house with a dirt floor, where a teenaged girl is making tortillas. The air smells like smoke and earth. The girl looks up shyly when she sees all of us staring. "*Hola*," I say, trying to make eye contact. She blushes.

I watch as she mixes cornmeal with water and places a ball of dough into a ceramic hand press. She pulls down the handle—thump—and nods, satisfied. With a graceful flick of her wrist, she tosses the tortilla onto a skillet over a wood stove. It sizzles. I am amazed by so many things: her ability to keep the fire at the right temperature, the perfection of her circles, the fact that she makes tortillas twice every day.

"*Bueno*," I say, clapping my hands.

The guys goad me, so I agree to give it a try. It's way harder than it looks. I fumble around with the dough, which sticks to my fingers, creating a gooey mess in my palms. Every one of my tortillas is torn or misshapen or stuck to the press. I laugh, but it comes out sounding more uncomfortable than carefree. I look at the girl, and then the men, and something shifts deep in my gut. I have an urge to tell them: *I am a good cook. I make delicious lasagna. I take my kids to the playground and read them books.*

Instead, I wipe my hands on a towel and walk away. I wander past the painted white church, scattered wooden houses, free-range cattle. Children dart past. I smile and wave.

At the one-room schoolhouse, I stop and peer in the windows. Joe appears behind me.

"Check out those desks," I say. "They're wooden, like old times."

He laughs and points to the wall, which is covered in hand-painted pictures. I wonder if my son is painting a picture right now at his school, or practicing his letters.

Joe turns to face me. "Hey Carrie?" he asks.

"Yeah?"

"I was wondering. Do you want to see Copper Canyon?"

In my head, Sidecar Sally screams, *Yes! You do! This is a once-in-a-lifetime opportunity!*

"Do you?" asks Joe.

I itch my leg, and then look back at the children's pictures. "I would love to," I say. "But I can't."

He seems unfazed. "O.K."

I smile and try to act normal. But inside I feel raw, like fingernails are scratching my flesh. I look back toward the house where the girl is making tortillas. I imagine her holding up a ball of dough the shape of Sidecar Sally's heart. She places it on the press. The handle descends and smashes it flat. On the fire, it burns.

❧   ❧   ❧

Carrie Visintainer is a Colorado-based freelance writer. Her essays have appeared in Matter, Cahoots, Mamazina, *and* The Best Women's Travel Writing 2008. *Her travel blog, Carrie Go Wandering, can be found at carriegowandering .blogspot.com.*

❧ ❧ ❧

Taking the Oars

Sometimes a woman has to paddle against the current.

The caustic incense of mosquito coils and floor polish caught in my throat as I dropped my duffel in the foyer. Within these peeling yellow walls and barred windows, my boyfriend Greg had lived for the last several months, running a whitewater rafting company in Zambia. Although I'd just arrived for my second season, I wasn't planning to stay. I'd only flown halfway around the world to tell Greg to his face. After five years together, I owed him that much.

As I waited in the empty house, Doreen and Angela, my two best friends from the previous season, burst through the warped wooden door. Their easy smiles were almost as big as the enormous hand-woven basket they'd made for me as a returning gift.

"But, sister, why are you crying?" Angela asked. She set down the basket and touched my cheek as tears forged down my dust-coated face.

"I'm getting back on the plane for the States this afternoon," I told them. "I'm leaving Greg."

Doreen grabbed my duffel loaded with river gear and carried it into the master bedroom while Angela struck a match for the tea kettle.

"You are needing to rest," said Angela resolutely. "That is all. Sit down."

Doreen sidled onto the armrest of my chair and started petting my blond arm hairs—"fur," she called it. She wore a puzzled frown. "I think I am not understanding you," Doreen said in her throaty, rich-timbre accent. "Bleedget, why is it you will leave?"

"I'm tired of following him around," I sniffed. "I need to get a life of my own."

"But he is not hitting you," said Angela, straightening her tall, solid frame. "He has a very good job. And he does not care that you have no babies, although you have been together for some time." Angela, a single mother, smoothed thick black hair away from her dewy forehead and shook her head at me. "This is a good man."

Yes, Greg was a good man. But was he the right man for me? I wasn't convinced.

"I can't do this anymore," I told him when he turned up from the office. "I need to do my own thing."

"Well, what do you want to do?" Greg asked, setting down his paper-stuffed backpack.

I wound my long braid around my wrist. "I don't know."

"Then you might as well stay here in Africa with me," he said, looking hurt and rejected. "It's not like this is all that bad. Besides," he added, voice cracking, "we agreed together that I'd take this job. I don't want to do it alone—I need you here."

For too long, Greg and I had mistaken being in need for being in love. We sat next to each other on the couch without touching. "You promised me, Bridge. You said you'd come with me if I took the manager's position."

He was right. I pried the top off a warm Mosi Lager—wishing it was whiskey—and started unpacking my river gear out of the duffel and into the master bedroom closet. I kept my word, ignoring the promise I'd made to myself, pretending that being needed was good enough.

Over the next few months, I devoted myself to speaking Nyanja and training on the way-over-my-head Class V section of the Zambezi River known as the Boiling Pot. I abandoned myself to learning the intricacies of Victoria Falls, known locally as *Mosi-oa-Tunya*, "the smoke that thunders," and I absorbed the culture that mirrored the landscape: a deeply carved chasm cut through heat-baked savanna.

I pushed down my discontent, hiding it under endless gin and tonics and spliffs of homegrown *dagga*.

When I'd first met Doreen, last season, she was a high-sider—a porter and training guide who helped weight the rafts through the Zambezi's high-volume hydraulics. She was barely five feet tall and less than a hundred pounds, but as a highsider, Doreen carried heavy coolers, oars, and rafts in and out of the steep Batoka gorge, matching the men load for load. The other highsiders, all male, started complaining that she was taking more than her share, making it harder for them to provide for their families. Doreen didn't have a family of her own, they argued, so she didn't need the money like they did.

It was decided that Doreen must quit being a highsider and become the manager's "house girl"—and so she came to work for us, doing the washing, ironing, and floor polishing.

Doreen joined our groundskeeper, Gabriel, and guard, Mr. Amos, bringing our total number of staff to three.

"You have to do something about them," I'd told Greg. "I don't want to be the Madam—it makes me uncomfortable to have them doing all the work."

Back home, I had cleaned plenty of motel rooms for money in-between river guiding seasons. To me, having servants was an affront to my working-class ethos and Aquarian sense of global equality.

"What do you want me to do?" Greg responded. "Throw them out? Then they won't have jobs."

Obviously, that wouldn't do. "Fine, then," I proclaimed. "But I'm not going to monitor the ironing or oversee afternoon tea."

As it turned out, Doreen and I had a few things in common, besides scrubbing toilets for cash. We were both twenty-one years old and had grown up next to rivers: me in a small town next to Wyoming's Snake River and Doreen in a Tonga village outside Choma, near the upper Zambezi. Before meeting us, she'd never been around *mzungus*—white people—in her life. Before coming to Africa, I had never been around black people in my life.

We became best friends, spending afternoons swapping dance moves while playing UB40's "Red, Red Wine" over and over. We eventually broke the cassette tape, so Doreen brought in her tapes from home of Zairian *kwassa kwassa* and Lucky Dube, a South African reggae megastar.

"What's your biggest dream?" I once asked her. "If you could have any job in the world, do anything with your life, what would it be?"

She looked at the floor, and then cautiously up through thickly fringed lashes. "When I was a highsider," she said, "I was just wanting to take those oars in my own hands." She smiled earnestly. "I was wanting to steer the boat and be the one who is guiding, as you yourself are. That is my dream."

Months after unpacking my duffel bag, acquiescing to scout my life from the riverbank rather than push off shore and run it, I was sitting in the lounge with Chuck, one of the American river guides. We were stretched out on the brown velvet couch watching a pirated version of "Damned River," recorded off U.K. television and rented out by the Indian shopkeepers in downtown Livingstone.

"Bleedget," Doreen whispered, peeking around the doorway. Her face was furrowed and twisted in fear, her energy unusually frantic.

I locked onto her pulsing, fluttery eyes. Something was wrong. Really wrong.

"Come," she said, "Bring . . . your things," she motioned to my room. She meant my first aid kit—or magic, as the Zambians started calling it after I cured a highsider's cold with Benadryl.

"What's going on?" Chuck wanted to know.

Doreen looked at the polished floor.

"We'll be back," I called over my shoulder as we ran through the garden, toward the gate. The ancient Mr. Amos appeared, head swathed in a ripped up t-shirt. He pocketed his slingshot and opened the gate for us to pass.

"Yes, Yes. Hello, Mrs. Greg. Yes." Mr. Amos hunched over, looking at the ground. I'd told him to call me Bridget countless times, but he still called me Mrs. Greg, even though we weren't married.

I followed Doreen from the manager's house down Kanyanta Road in the direction of Nakatindi Village, where I assumed we were going until we cut down a small footpath leading to the guide house several blocks away.

"It's Chiluba," she told me as we sprinted from the trampled grass onto the red clay road in front of the guide house. "Her husband . . ." Doreen shook her head, unable to say the words.

Chiluba's husband was the muscled, smooth-talking Alick, one of the senior Zambian river guides. Chiluba and Alick had a one-year-old daughter together, Tandi, which means "love" in Ndebele.

Alick had recently picked up with a rich, leathery German woman—a client off a whitewater trip. She'd moved into a hotel flat in Livingstone and outfitted Alick with a new, high-dollar wardrobe.

Doreen and I passed through the guide house gate. Angela was in the dusty yard, her baby girl Mwangala jutting out from her hip, son Kachana hiding behind her legs, sucking his fingers. Angela worked as the maid at the guide house, living in the back cement lean-to with her children and her sister, Ivy.

"You have come," Angela said, relieved.

The gray walls inside the one-room shack were adorned with glossy pictures ripped out of my old Victoria's Secret catalogs and fashion magazines. Cutout vixens in black and red lingerie peered seductively at Chiluba, who was curled up knees-to-chest on a no-mattress twin bed pushed against the wall. Her head was resting on her knees as she sniffed delicately.

"Chiluba?" I said softly.

She looked up at me, tears mixed with blood spilling from her nose and cracked-open lips. There was a deep gouge above her right eyebrow. Although her doey brown eyes were bruised purple and nearly swollen all the way shut, Chiluba's pulsing gaze clung to mine, then hardened.

While I examined her she stayed motionless, silently waiting to hear my medical opinion.

"It's not so bad," I said, forcing a smile. "Don't worry, we can fix it." I touched her arm gently, then went to work, wetting some gauze with peroxide. Doreen and Angela breathed steadily behind me. Ivy had the kids outside playing in the dirt yard, distracting them.

"I do not know what I could have been thinking about," began Chiluba, "Speaking to him that way. About *her*." Jaw set, she breathed heavily out her bloody nostrils as I dabbed at her cuts with the gauze. "I just saw them together coming out of the Fairmount Hotel, and it was as if I went mad."

"Even Tandi saw them," added Angela, clucking her tongue.

"What did you say to them?" asked Doreen. Along with being incredibly shy, Doreen was terrified of marriage, which was why she remained single and childless at twenty-one—practically a spinster.

"I waited until he came home, and then I begged him to stop seeing that woman, to do it for our child's sake," Chiluba covered her mouth with her hand, holding back waves of grief before continuing. "And do you know what he told me? He said, 'Stop interfering, it is none of your concern,' and then his eyes turned a deep black. It was as if he disappeared from himself, something was taking over his body. There was nothing that could be done to stop him."

"How long has it been going on, Chiluba?" I asked quietly.

"It has been getting worse these last months. Before, I could manage, but now, you can see, it has become a burden. Everyone is seeing me this way, and I do not want my child to feel me being so weak."

I pressed her split eyebrow together and taped it shut with butterfly closures. "Why don't you leave him?"

From the doorway, Angela let out a cynical laugh and looked down, toeing the floor. "We are not like you women. We cannot just leave when the man is behaving like this. It is against the law for us to divorce our husbands. He is the one who can divorce us for any reason he likes, but we ourselves have no way to leave." Angela's husband died from cerebral malaria shortly after Mwangala's birth. She would be on her own if it weren't for her younger sister helping.

"What do you mean, *it's against the law*?"

"Yes, it is true," said Chiluba. "The only way I can leave Alick is if he divorces me, and then I must return to my family, if they will allow it. It is a very shameful thing when you are divorced, and the family most usually does not take you back."

"But you and Tandi can try to go back to the village and . . ." I started formulating a plan, an escape route to rescue her.

"No, no. *I* go back to the village. Tandi goes with Alick. Then his new wife or mistress, *she* raises Tandi." Chiluba's head reared back like a wild horse. "I would rather take a thousand beatings than see *her* raise my child."

"So what can you do?" I asked Chiluba. I had applied triple antibiotic cream to all her wounds and sealed the deep cuts with butterflies and waterproof tape until they were impenetrable.

"I must learn to keep my feelings hidden." Chiluba was finished crying. "Do you understand what I am saying?"

"Yes," I said, sliding my arm across her rounded shoulders, "I do." And then, searching for the words in Nyanja, I whispered, "*Nifuna kufa chifukwa nimvela impepo meningi.*" *I feel like dying because I am too cold.*

Chiluba nodded, and the three of us held onto her, trying to warm her cracked, frozen heart.

My third season in Zambia, I applied for and landed a job guiding on Ethiopia's Class III Omo River. Of all the rivers in the world, it was the one I most wanted to run, primarily because it was the stomping grounds of LUCY (*Australopithecus afarensis*), one of the earliest humans. Since the first descent in the early seventies, the Omo had been run sparingly, and only a handful of women guides had ever rafted it.

"Greg will let you go?" Angela was concerned. She relinquished the luxury of pursuing her dreams when she married and had two children.

"Yes, of course," I said.

Doreen helped me pack, carefully handing me carabiners, pulleys, and my river knife.

"I know you will be careful, my sister," she said, smiling proudly. "Are you afraid of the rapids?"

"Not so much the rapids," I said. By now, I had guided Class III and IV rapids in Wyoming, Idaho, and California. "I'm more scared of the hippos and crocs."

Doreen erupted in a deep, carefree laugh. "Only tell them that I have sent you. They will not harass you then."

Greg drove me to Bulawayo, Zimbabwe, to board a train for Harare, where I was to catch a flight for Addis Ababa. With time to spare before the night train departed, we ducked into a matinee of "The Power of One." We came out of the movie misty-eyed from its message of racial equality and being true to oneself, only to find we had been robbed. My bag filled with river gear was missing, as was the guard we had paid to watch our Rover.

We went to the central police station to report the crime. When it was my turn at the counter, I slid my passport over to the officer on duty.

"My duffel bag was stolen from our vehicle," I began.

"Oho," he raised his eyebrows and loudly flipped through the stamped pages of my passport. "And tell me, who is speaking for you?"

"What do you mean?" I asked.

"Who is reporting the crime for you? Who is speaking for you?"

"I'm speaking for myself," I said, bewildered.

"No, no. You must have someone to speak for you—a husband, father, or brother. Otherwise, you cannot report it."

"Here's my boyfriend . . ." I offered.

"Sorry. He is not your husband."

"But, my father and brothers are in the States."

"Well, that is truly unfortunate, then. It is Zimbabwean law that a woman must have someone speaking for her to report a crime. Next in the queue," he handed back my passport, looking over my shoulder, no longer seeing me.

Stripped of my river armor—life jacket, helmet, knife, throw bag, wrap kit—I felt vulnerable and ill-prepared for guiding a fourteen-day trip on a remote wilderness river near the Sudan border.

"What a bummer," Greg said, as we took our seats at a neighboring bar. "You were really looking forward to going."

I was tempted to numb my disappointment with a Cane and Coke, lean my head on Greg's comfortable shoulder, and head back to Livingstone. I could nearly taste the cocktail's sugary oblivion. Then I remembered Doreen beaming at me as I left, her compact, sturdy arms waving madly from the gate.

"Oh, I'm still going," I said, and ordered a Fanta.

"But you don't even have a lifejacket," Greg pointed out.

"Yeah, but I've got a ticket."

I boarded the plane as scheduled, bolstering myself with the knowledge that I had been chosen for this—been handed my dream-come-true—and there might never be another chance. I flew to Addis intent on holding those coveted oars, Doreen's proud smile nudging me forward the entire way.

When Greg asked me to marry him three years later, I began to cry. I told him they were tears of joy. The truth was that off the river, I still lacked the courage to jump into the stream of my own life.

We were married five years when I finally poured out my last bottle of whiskey, and all of my excuses along with it. I loaded my truck, leaving behind a rafting business, a house, and a good man. I packed only two things: my river gear and a very large handwoven basket.

I remembered Angela's parting words when I left Zambia for the last time: "Tell me, friend, how are we to be content, never seeing you or speaking to you again?" She didn't know that nearly a decade later, she would still be speaking to me, that the shackled aspirations of my Zambian sisters would speak clearly to me—and for me—as I headed toward the western horizon and freedom. The steering wheel firmly in my hands, I drove on, undeterred. Not because I had to, but because I could.

❧ ❧ ❧

Bridget Crocker is an adventure guide, outdoor travel writer, and mother. She has led remote river expeditions and guided first descents down many of the world's greatest river canyons in far-flung regions of Zambia, Ethiopia, the Philippines, Peru, Chile, Costa Rica, India, and the Western United States. She is a contributing author to Lonely Planet guidebooks and the outdoor clothing company, Patagonia, and her work has been featured in The Best Women's Travel Writing 2011 *and magazines such as* National Geographic Adventure, Trail Runner, Paddler, *and* Outside. *Bridget lives on the edge of the continent in Southern California with her husband and two daughters and writes about her family's adventures on her blog, The Adventures of Little Mama. Read more of her work at www.bridgetcrocker.com.*

❧ ❧ ❧

Root-Bound

Tangled in a web of roots, she is
undone by Italian hospitality.

*M*y first visit to Sicily was with my mother, when I
was fourteen—we were there to look up her Sicilian
relatives on the outskirts of Palazzolo Acreide. Although my
mother was born in New York, her older brother had lived in
Sicily until he was sixteen, so it was through his recollections
that she pieced together the location of her ancestral home and
the distant cousins who still lived there.

Palazzolo, located well off the tourist track southeast of
Siracusa, did not lend itself to casual visitors. At the time of
our visit there were no tourist offices or large hotels, just a
small square surrounded by a crumbling baroque church,
a bakery, and a few cafés. Women in black sat on benches,
and groups of men wearing vests and Borsalino hats strolled
around the square's perimeter. It appeared no one under the
age of fifty-five lived there.

Up to that point, everything I knew about Sicily I learned
from reading *The Godfather*. The book was making the
rounds at my junior high school—not for its literary merits of
course, but for the violence and raunchy sex scenes. An ambi-
tious reader before me had created a Cliff's Notes version of
the book by highlighting all the graphic sections, such as the

one in which Sonny Corleone bangs Lucy Mancini (a brides-maid) on his wedding day. *The Godfather* was set mostly in New York, but the Sicily scenes shaped my expectations of what I might find there.

Standing in the square, it felt like we were living a page right out the book.

My mother was a travel writer for our local paper back home, and this wasn't the first time I'd been dragged along on one of her crazy international escapades. As a ten-year-old I'd been smuggled into a nightclub in the Bahamas while she interviewed Peanuts Taylor, the famous bongo drum-mer, for an article about the maiden voyage of Carnival's first cruise ship, "the Mardi Gras" (although the real story was that shortly after pulling away from the dock, the ship ran aground on a sandbar just outside the Port of Miami). I'd been with her to Haiti, where we visited the Centre d'Art in Port-au-Prince and learned about Vodou symbolism in the color-ful paintings. And when I was twelve, I accompanied her to Cartagena, Colombia, where we toured a plantation that made "vitamins" from coca leaves.

Now it was the 1970s, and Alex Haley's miniseries *Roots* had turned everyone into amateur genealogists.

"We will go to the old country," she declared, "and find our Sicilian roots." She pitched the story to her editor, and off we went in search of—as she put it—"our Italian Kunta Kinte."

"*Mi scusi*," she said, trying to ask one of the men if he knew the location of the Rizza family farm outside of town. He refused to talk to her, and the women uniformly glared at us. For once, my mother's reporter charm wasn't getting us very far. It seemed we were up against a deeply ingrained suspicion of strangers and might not possess the linguistic skills to bridge the gap. Finally, a woman came out of a bakery and looked at the documents we held. As she drew a crude map and gave it to my mother, I felt like the whole town was watching.

"Should we stay here for lunch?" my mother asked.

"Are you kidding? Let's get going before they shoot us or something." I was half expecting a black sedan to come screeching around the corner and start firing bullets into the square.

She rolled her eyes and we got back in the car.

The directions led us out of town down several miles of unmaintained roads, past acres of cactus and then olive trees. After about twenty minutes, the road petered out, and my mother stopped the car in front of a modest stone farmhouse. She knocked on the door, clutching the yellowed family photos and the map. A slender young man about nineteen opened the door, and my mother thrust the documents into his face as if he were a customs agent.

"We're here from America!" she shouted.

He immediately shut the door. A minute later, a much older man in a threadbare undershirt who looked like he'd just woken from a nap emerged from the house along with a woman wearing rubber gloves and an apron splotched with red stains. They looked like Italian hillbillies, the Ma and Pa Kettle of Sicily, only more frightening. I imagined dueling banjos playing the theme from *Deliverance* in the background. For a few anxious moments we all just stared at each other. Then my mother pointed out the house in the photo she held. Aside from the trees, which had grown considerably, the house was relatively unchanged. That clinched the deal.

We were ushered into the house and despite our unexpected arrival, put up for the next three days. Their son was banished to the couch, "Ma and Pa" took his room, and we were given their bedroom.

Although my mother knew some Italian, the relatives spoke only in Sicilian dialect. I sat by silently as they struggled to communicate with each other, feeling as if I was watching a foreign film without subtitles. When we arrived, "Ma" had been in the middle of roasting and canning tomatoes, and the house smelled sweet and savory. I couldn't understand her words, but I could interpret that rich wonderful scent in any language.

I still remember the food we ate that weekend. In addition to being a travel writer, my mother also wrote a weekly food column, so I grew up eating what would have been considered exotic at the time—borscht, tagines and curries. Our family dinners were often results of research for her food column, straight out of the test kitchen and onto our plates. Admittedly, the majority of the tests proved unsuccessful.

But here, there was pasta with sardines, fennel, and pine nuts; fried eggplant with ricotta and basil; and *arancini*, the deep-fried rice balls stuffed with tomato ragu, ground beef, mozzarella, and peas—exactly the way my grandmother made them. There was wine drawn from a big glass jug that looked like an office water cooler, and I had my very first taste of grappa.

On Saturday morning I helped Ma finish putting up the tomatoes and later, in the fading afternoon light, we gathered lemons and she showed us how to make *limoncello*. My mother shadowed Ma in the kitchen and took careful notes, thrilled that our trip would yield not just a travel story, but a few food articles too.

On Sunday we all drove to town for Mass at the crumbling church off the square where we'd asked for directions. Just days before we were outsiders—strangers—but now we were celebrities. *Famiglia*! From America!

After Mass I walked in the olive groves with the son. He showed me how they spread out nets to gather the olives, and in broken English asked if he could "scratch my beautiful hair." I figured he meant touch, not scratch, but my mother and Ma were following close behind, leaving us little opportunity for further cultural exchange under the olive trees.

On the day of our departure, we stood outside the stone house, loaded down with jars of blood orange marmalade, tomato sauce, and bottles of olive oil. As a teenager, it was my job to be sullen and maintain an air of detached boredom, but as we hugged goodbye, my carefully constructed posture of aloofness began to crumble. Their hospitality had pierced me, and I was close to tears.

My mother started writing her "*Roots*" article immediately after we returned home, but it took two weeks before the film from her camera was developed and we could share our photos with my uncle. When the prints arrived, my uncle studied them carefully. He reached the last one, then slowly flipped though them again.

"Mary," he finally said to my mother, "Who are these people?"

"That's Maria and her husband and son."

"Who?"

"Cousin Maria!"

"This is not Maria," he said, shaking his head.

"But this is the house," said my mother. "Don't you recognize it?"

"I remember this house, I played there as a boy. But our house was farther down the road, past a creek."

The color drained out of my mother's face. Had we stayed with complete strangers? As she tried to recall the exact conversation with "Cousin Maria" at the door, she realized we'd never really exchanged names. Ma and Pa called each other Mario and Mama, and since she never revealed her real name, we called her Mama too. We'd just been swept up into their home and their lives, no questions asked. Our status as blood relatives was based solely on a dog-eared photo.

I found all of this completely hilarious, but my mother was horrified that the roots she thought were hers belonged to some other tree. We later discovered that cousin Maria and her family had moved to Catania twelve years earlier. Even if we had found the "right" house, our real relatives would have been long gone.

Thirty years later, when my mother was in her seventies, we returned to Sicily to connect with our genuine blood relations in Catania. This time, we were *veramente la famiglia*. True family. Once again we were plied with copious amounts of food and drink, and once again we were given the master bedroom. The experience varied little from our first trip.

Maybe I hadn't been so far off, learning about Sicily by reading the *Godfather*. If only I'd paid more attention to the plot, I would have realized it was actually a story about the enduring bonds of family—regardless of whether you were related by blood. If you presented yourself as loyal to the family, you were accepted as family. Our first trip to Sicily was evidence of that. This time we were connected by blood, but I would always be connected to Ma and Pa by love.

Marcy Gordon's narrative travel writing has appeared online for World Hum *and in many Travelers' Tales anthologies including* More Sand in My Bra, 30 Days in Italy *and* The Best Women's Travel Writing 2011 *and* 2010. *She is the editor of* Leave the Lipstick, Take the Iguana: Funny Travel Stories from the Road *(Travelers' Tales, 2012). She also writes* Come for the Wine, *a popular blog that features wine tourism destinations around the world. Visit www .comeforthewine.com for more information.*

MEERA SUBRAMANIAN

❧ ❧ ❧

Of Monarchs and Men in Michoacán

Would you give up sex to live (almost) forever?

They live forever by not having sex. That's one theory. By forever, I mean they live eight times longer than either their parents or their offspring—which would be about 6,400 human years. By they, I mean the generation of monarch butterflies, *Danaus plexippus,* that emerges from chrysalides in the late summer and early fall across eastern North America. Scientists speculate that they discovered the fountain of butterfly youth by somehow delaying their sexual onset. It is called diapause. Although most monarchs live about thirty days, this generation lives eight months, traveling south to slumber chastely though a Mexican winter before heading north again in the spring. It is only in those last few weeks of their life that they sexually mature. Then they mate, and die, while their short-lived young flutter a bit farther north, and so on.

I must have learned about these monarch Methuselahs and their epic migration in third grade but I'd forgotten, and this lesson—half in Spanish, accompanied by drawings on the back of a coaster in a New York City bar, surrounded by handsome men—is much more intriguing. I'm with the adventurers of Papalotzin, most from Mexico, one

from Europe, another an American expat. Papalotzin is the
name of their ultralight painted with the orange and black
markings of the monarch butterfly, and they are in the process
of flying the machine (which is not much more than a hang
glider with a giant propeller in the back, currently stashed in
a hangar in New Jersey) between Montreal and Michoacán,
Mexico. They're raising awareness about threats to the monarch butterfly.

The photographer of the group is named Luis, and he is
like a radiant light and I am like a moth. He speaks little English. My Spanish returns. He is Oaxacan, tall of stature and
broad of shoulder. A great big smile that pulls his dark eyes
down at the corners seems to be his steady state, and I'm hyp-
notized by the easy laugh and the intense interest he shows as
we muddle through conversations. There is a kindness about
him that reaches out to everyone around him. He seems an
innocent flirt with the world. He tells me he is at home on a
skateboard or behind a camera. Or, I imagine, in a woman's
embrace. I show the Papalotzin crew the city as lunch turns
into dinner turns into drinks. They are travelers and need a
place to stay, their group disbanding to various locations. My
place is close. Luis's body is both heavy and light against mine
that night, and I yield.

I will not live forever.

Papalotzin means royal butterfly in Nauhuatl, the language
of the Aztecs who once inhabited what is now Michoacán,
in central-western Mexico. Their scattered descendants still
remain, as does their belief that monarchs are the souls of
the dead. Every year the butterflies come to the tiny patch of
trees that their great-great-great grandparents left the prior
spring. How they get there is a mystery. Maybe light. Maybe
magnetism.

They travel three thousand miles in a matter of weeks.

They weigh less than a gram.

Do I go to see him or the monarchs when I travel to Mexico City three months later? Can I say both? It's early December, and I have missed the monarchs' arrival. Someday, *someday*, I will return to Mexico on November 2nd for Day of the Dead. Someday I will be there when the monarchs descend to Michoacán en masse, souls aloft and arriving, draining from every place where milkweed grows east of the Rockies. Do you think it is a coincidence that Día de los Muertos falls within days of the American Halloween, our holiday of skulls and cemeteries? Do you think it is random that the colors of our Día de Candy are orange and black, the colors of the monarch? I do not.

Ancient dead souls or flying insects, today's butterflies now live in our modern world. We mow down the milkweed the caterpillars feed upon so we can build houses. Genetically modify the plants from which the butterflies draw their nectar. Cut down the last bits of Michoacán's pine forests, a Goldilocks land neither too hot nor too cold that this magical long-lived generation returns to, year after year. In the last quarter century, monarchs have lost half of their overwintering grounds.

The photographer and I head west out of Mexico City to see the monarch reserves, but first we must fly. Valle de Bravo is Mexico's Tahoe, a playground of forested mountains surrounding a huge lake. The weather is ideal, the town quaint and quiet absent the influx of tourists. Families gather at the old stone church, where great white calla lilies overflow from the altar. The church bells ring, a resounding "uh-oh," down the cobblestone streets lined with pink bougainvillea, scaring the roosting pigeons, flowing past the fruit vendors, the firecracker vendors, the church tchotchke vendors selling plastic Jesuses. Rising up into the blue sky where paragliders float down on colorful swaths of fabric. By afternoon, we join them in the skies. He and I leap off a mountaintop, me strapped like a baby in front of him as we sail down softly to the lake's edge, legs swinging in the air. In the evening we fly in Papalotzin, thousands of feet above the lake, our high-flying monarch, the air thin and chilling as the sun descends.

We go to great lengths to fly. The monarchs just spread their wings to let the sun warm them and take off.

Michoacán kindles my longings for man and land. We speak only in Spanish, and he is unlike anyone I've ever met. He has none of the hard edges of my ex. Luis is light, the result of an upbringing in a loving comfortable family but with the freedom given only to an adored youngest child. He wandered and played. Explored and adventured. He skateboarded competitively and photographed intimately. Troubles came to him as they did to all, but their blows seemed glancing. There is an ex-wife somewhere and two children he speaks of swooningly, yet happiness still dominates, even as he describes the pain of not seeing them nearly enough. Always, always, the default is the enchanting smile.

He's different, but the earth is familiar. Michoacán's flora is a living replication of the Pacific Northwest, where I once lived. The monarch's preferred habitat is the oyamel tree, a short-needled evergreen that dominates like the Douglas fir. The ocote Montezuma tree is a long-needled echo of the Ponderosa pine. The understory is thick with replicas of maple, manzanita, and rhododendron. I am at home.

The next morning is cold, with hints of frost on the ground, when Luis and I leave for El Rosario, home of the Special Biosphere Reserve of the Monarch Butterfly. Pablo Angeles, a forester for the World Wildlife Fund, meets our bus in a fire-engine-red Volkswagen bug. He's in his forties, with a thick moustache and eyebrows that are black and long, his hair neatly combed back.

Butterflies, yes, but first, tacos. A man named Salvador serves us meat from a lamb he killed the day before. Each day, another animal, two on the weekends he tells us, is buried in a pit with hot rocks and the leaves of the maguey cactus to slow cook as he sleeps. Now, he asks our preference—legs, back, balls—and lifts up steaming wet cactus leaves to find the right body part, which is thrown on the thick section of wood that is his cutting board. He chops it fine with a large cleaver, but it's so tender it falls apart under the blade, and a woman behind him wordlessly hands him a hot tortilla off a grill. Salvador pressures Luis into having the specialty of balls, tossing a glance at me. Luis reluctantly accepts the mushy meat. We bathe the tacos in salsa—red and green—cilantro, onions, and fresh-squeezed lime. He shows us the skull of the animal.

Satiated, we climb back into the bug and head to El Rosario.

Pablo's hands hold a steady ten and two o'clock on the wheel as the bug putters up the mountain, sliding around switchbacks that open up to expansive views of the cultivated fields and *pueblocitos* cradled amidst forested hills. A man tosses a white chicken into the air as he stands atop a stack of hay. Girls with jet-black hair plaited in long braids walk to school, past roadside altars covered with flowers and candles. We pass stands of poinsettias, piñatas, pottery. We pass police with large guns and blue uniforms. More images of monarchs start appearing, stenciled on walls, accompanying business signs, on the sides of taxis. Pablo has spent his entire life here and laughs about the 1976 "discovery" by Americans of the monarch's winter home.

At 10,200 feet above sea level, we arrive, emerging from the car and entering the reserve. We leave behind the people, the tourists, the women cooking tortillas on smoky wood-burning stoves. We leave behind the children, watchful and covered with dust. One by one, monarchs fill the air.

Within minutes, there's an opening in the forest where a path cuts through, a mini flyway with thousands of monarchs drifting down the passageway, from ground level to the tree-tops fifty feet above. We have entered a church, a holy place, and we fall silent. Pablo encourages us to keep moving; there's more, higher up, he gestures. But every turn in the path reveals more, and we keep stopping, each vantage a new shot for our cameras. Butterflies are covering the benches set up for visitors, lining the handrails, filling the tree branches and trunks. Their flight sounds like the falling of the gentlest of rains.

The path divides, the right fork clearly cordoned off, directing traffic to the left. Pablo hesitates for a moment before lifting the rope and with his WWF credentials, we walk up the path that leads to the right, into the heart of the butterfly grounds. Wings and monarch bodies litter the ground. Pablo picks one up and cups it in his hands, blowing hot breath onto it. He watches it closely, but there is no sign of life, and he tosses it gently off the path. Another hundred feet on, we cross another rope and gasp as we gaze up into the trees.

How to describe what I see? To my eyes they are burls, that thick protuberance in a growth of wood, swirling and knobby. But they are masses of butterflies. Where the monarchs have clustered, the tree branches swell like a dark cloud, the limbs hanging down instead of springing up as usual. It's as though burnt-orange snow has covered the trees, a foot thick, weighing down the branches, clinging to the bark after a gusty, rusty storm had blown through. We walk up a rocky dirt trail, carved by erosion and covered with monarchs, alive and dead. I tread cautiously.

One falls with a soft splat onto the ground from the trees above, and I kneel down on the forest floor to observe. The sun shines off the glossy wings, distinct black veins against orange-gold. It has a furry black thorax, all speckled with white dots, and the wings are ringed with a border of black pixelated with white. It's still early in the day, and it lies motionless for a moment before it begins to vibrate its wings in a shivering motion, making its own heat. When it warms up, it takes flight and joins the thousands of others that are already in the air, seeking the sunny spots, filling the space between earth and heaven. They're bumping into us, us into them. We stand still, watching and breathless as they land on Pablo's hat brim, on Luis's black curly hair, on the back of my neck, where they tickle me.

Scientists like numbers, so the WWF is gathering information, but Pablo shakes his head when I ask him for a figure. Twenty-two million one year. Two hundred fifty million the next. He looks up at the trees, covered with an unfathomable amount of tiny, paper-thin creatures. "Ten thousand or one hundred thousand on each tree? We just don't know. It's all a hypothesis." I imagine trying to count the leaves in a chunk of deciduous forest. Look up at the foliage and guess how many pieces. Stand in leaf litter after fall has come and gone and count the brittle remains. I was always bad at those how-many-beans-in-the-jar contests, but to stand amidst the clusters and think anyone could ever even begin to approximate seems ludicrous.

I see a broken branch on the ground, and it's moving. It takes a moment for the eyes to focus, the brain to catch up. I realize that the weight of the monarchs caused the limb to sever from the tree. The branch is six inches thick at its base and fifteen feet long. I imagine the moment when one butterfly, a fraction of the weight of a penny, becomes too much for the tree to bear and something irreversibly changes in the world. One butterfly is the tipping point, causing the snap, the tumble, the smash, the disturbance, the deaths of the tiny creatures caught below, the trimming of the tree, the shift. The hundredth butterfly.

On the ground the dead are missing wings, thoraxes, heads. Some are intact, fresh-looking but devoid of that elusive energy that means life. Others are long dead, the oils from their body seeped out into the wings, making them dark and greasy. Birds and mice predate on them. Somehow, they often live through the attacks. I see one moving with no wings, another with only half a thorax.

As the day warms up, more and more monarchs lift from their slumbering spots. By one o'clock, it's a blizzard of butterflies. They appear to be blowing in all directions simultaneously, a torrent. The sound of light falling rain has changed into the rush of a distant waterfall, something that at its source is powerful but that has been muted into delicateness.

As we pause on the path, I ask Pablo whether, after more than twenty years of work in this field, he has more hope for the future, or less.

"Less," he says without hesitation. "There isn't enough respect for the environment. There isn't the consciousness."

He is serious, realistic, sad in a resigned way, but he still works, still beams as he watches Luis and me beam at the butterflies. "No one can ever believe it the first time they see it," he says, and smiles.

We descend from the forest and climb back into the bug to head down the mountain, past political proclamations and party announcements, past logging trucks, past monarchs painted on Coke billboards, and under a sign straddling the street that says, "Thanks for coming. Monarch Country."

Within days of my return to Mexico City, I will leave Luis. The butterflies will carry on in their suspended state for three more months, until something finally, belatedly, irresistibly, stirs in them and they awaken to the world of sex. Within just one or two days in the beginning of March, they will make a mass exodus, heading north toward Texas. There, under the cover of dark, the male and female will link bodies for hours at a time, and she will later lay her eggs on the shady side of milkweed leaves, and then die.

"Butterflies that weigh a fraction of an ounce travel 5,500 kilometers in order to make love," one of the Papalotzin men told me back in the New York bar, in delighted exclamation. "Compare this with us. It's the same as going to the moon and back, running!"

For love.

I never see Luis again.

Meera Subramanian is a freelance journalist with a penchant for flying creatures. She covers culture, faith and the environment and is an editor of Killing the Buddha, *an online literary magazine. She not so secretly wishes she had wings.*

ঞ ঞ ঞ

A Thousand Simple Steps

The journey of a single family begins with a thousand steps.

The Great Wall at Badaling curls up the mountains and out of sight like a gray velvet ribbon through a smoke chiffon veil. After three days of delays, sleeping in airports, and checking, claiming, and rechecking luggage, my first sight of one of the world's remaining wonders brings a heaviness to my chest that does not come from the weight of my nine-month-old daughter Liliana strapped to me marsupial style. I step off the embarrassingly lush tour bus, and my hand automatically reaches back, searching, for the large palm and fingers that have clasped mine since infancy: the calming grip of my grandfather, Clyde. The only father I've ever known, he's still a ringer for Walter Matthau at ninety-one.

My grandfather has taken countless steps in his lifetime—on glaciers and ships, in Italian POW camps, into the Australian outback, up Kilimanjaro, down the Grand Canyon, on all the world's continents. He has been a son, brother, soldier, teacher, father, grandfather, and great-grandfather. Five years ago he became a widower, following fifty-five years as a husband. And now he's embarking on what he calls his last great adventure: the steps that will take him to the Great Wall of China. Too old to travel on his own, he has brought my mother, my daughter, and me across the world for this journey, the culmination of his lifetime of steps.

Around us, tourists from various nations pour out of cabs and buses, their heads turned sharply to the left, where the Wall climbs. At the base, a litter of stalls sells every imaginable trinket, shirt, fan, and antique replica. The vendors call relentlessly, their voices creating a dull roar, like squawking seagulls. David, our tour guide, asks our group of sixteen Americans to pose with the Wall in the background and then leaves us ninety minutes to do as we please. The group scatters, fallen leaves in a gust of wind—some begin to climb the first set of stone steps leading up the mountain; others rush to the stalls to start collecting treasures; a few sit on benches, content to look into the distance rather than attempt the stairs in the densely humid air. There are two paths to take: one smooth and flat, another steep and twisting. Grandpa leads us to the steep and twisting path and, with my mother at my side, we take the oldest and youngest visitors to the Wall this thick July day.

From a distance, the Wall zigzags, coiling back on itself so that actually following the line of it by sight is impossible. Standing at the base of this great stone dragon, I'm filled with wonder at its vastness, at the sheer strength of will its construction must have required.

Up close, climbing with a stream of visitors, the Wall is a series of stone steps uniform only in their unevenness and sharp incline. Some are low, like the drop of a curb. Others are higher than our knees. My grandfather's legs are the shortest part of his small frame, so he must lift his knees to his chest, placing one foot on the next step and then using the worn metal rail to pull himself up. Mom lingers on his other side as I trail behind, snapping pictures with one hand, stabilizing my daughter with the other, my weight shifting drastically up and down like a camel climbing dunes. We creep up the stairs, and I watch the

peaked roofs with their ceramic tiles and ornamented gables
fall farther toward Earth as we climb toward Heaven.

We come finally to a flat surface, the First Guard Tower.
It's a wide space, but relatively short and brimming with people of all nationalities. Grandpa leans against an empty corner
and rests. People swarm around me, pointing, smiling, reaching, gripping, wiggling fingers—all captivated by the blond-
haired, blue-eyed baby, cheery through the pouring sweat as
she clings to the olive-green front pack. An Indian couple gestures to their camera and then to Liliana. Their companion
takes a picture of them posing on each side of me, as if we are
dear friends on the trip of a lifetime together. Others don't
ask, just snap pictures of my baby like she's a white tiger cub
found wandering the streets.

"Do you want to go on, Pops?" Mom asks after a few
minutes.

"Are we to the original Wall yet?"

She shakes her head. This is still the rebuilt section. The
original Wall begins at the Second Guard Tower.

"Let's go on."

We climb again. There are fewer rails now and the path
becomes narrow. Mom abandons her post at Grandpa's side,
placing herself in front, helping him ever upward. I am behind,
guiding him forward. In places where the rail disappears, my
mother grips his hand for balance and I place my hands on the
small of his back, arms locked to cradle his weight. The passage becomes so tight that I find myself shifting my shoulder
to allow those descending to pass without bumping me.

Grandpa begins to tire, leaning wherever there's a rail to
rest. Worried that he might slip backward and hurt the baby,
Mom suggests we switch places. I am the leader now, using
one hand to steady my daughter, one to reach back, my fingers
outstretched in coaxing inspiration to bring us up the next step
and the next. The mist turns to rain, a smattering of fat drops

that mingle with our sweat, the film of water dissolving any semblance of traction, making the stones harder to mount.

Even though we are climbing a wall, a simple set of steps made by man, I feel that we are climbing the mountains themselves and the stairs are merely crags of rocks for our feet to find hold. As the rest periods increase, I look out across the valleys and mountains. It's the setting of legends, where time and space cease as the peaks pierce through the mist and increasing rain. The Wall snakes beyond perception, without beginning or end. The deep-hued evergreens blend together, the forest without trees, the dark at the base of the gray mountains, the sky white in the place where fog meets cloud and heavenly bodies conjoin with earthly manifestations.

People stream up one side of the steps and down the other in a fluid and ceaseless motion. We cannot turn back. Liliana begins to cry as the rain increases its attack, and I'm torn between the need to extend a hand for my grandfather and use a hand for my own balance, and my desire to shield my sweet girl from the cold onslaught falling ever faster from the sky. I no longer look out over the side; instead my eyes are trained on the pathway before me, my shoulder cramping as my left arm stretches backwards, more frequently gripping the shaking veined hand reaching out to me from its unseen owner.

The shock of my feet falling on flat stone, first one and then the other, is such that my head jolts. The Second Guard Tower, stately in its simple functionality—it could be a guard tower in Europe—is within finger's reach. My shoulder jerks, and my grandfather comes to stand beside me. I keep his hand in mine and lead him to the flattened gray stones, where the color and texture shifts slightly, where the original Wall, created more than 2000 years ago, begins.

My grandfather moves next to me, his hand absently reaching up to stroke his crying great-granddaughter's cheek, and I notice his other hand is still clasped in my mother's. I take my baby from her pack and turn her into me, snuggling her close. She stops crying and peers over my shoulder. Grandpa pats her back, his hand on mine, as four generations look out over China. The moment fills me with the sense of standing at the edge of eternity, as if I could reach into the air, pinching it like silk between my fingers, tearing through it into the past and future. Even the rain seems to pause.

But the respite is brief. The sky rumbles and the rain pelts us. Some Japanese girls, no more than twenty years old, gesture that they'd like to take a picture with the baby. They lean in to her, and by necessity me, causing me to flash back to the final days of high school when I posed for photos with people I also knew I'd never see again. My grandfather looks out over the mountains for a moment, oblivious to the chatter of the girls as they press an electric blue umbrella with bright white Japanese characters into my hand: "For baby." Instead he removes his thick glasses and, using his handkerchief, wipes his eyes. From the rain or something more, I cannot tell.

The descent is arduous. We are in essence sliding down a great stone chute peppered with broken teeth made of limestone and brick. The rain doesn't help our cause, for the way is slick and our eyes can't see through the sheet of water. My grandfather's legs begin to quiver as he fights to keep his balance, both hands gripping the railing and the Wall alternately, as if he is pulling himself along a rope to a boat after having fallen in the ocean. He rests every few steps for fear that he'll fall blindly down and into the crowd.

We're almost to the First Guard Tower when John, a physically imposing yet affable middle-aged man from our tour, offers to carry my grandfather the rest of the way. Grandpa does not hear the offer. My mother repeats it.

"No," he says, waving John away and lurching from his resting place. The line of people following us grows impatient. I can feel them shifting behind me, looking around me to see the obstruction. They want down, out of the rain. Some try to push around us. Still my grandfather will not be carried, even when he lowers himself to his butt, sliding down from step to step the way Liliana descends our stairs at home on her unsteady legs. He'll do it himself, he tells us over and over again.

When we reach the First Guard Tower, my grandfather refuses to rest, toddling toward the final descent on his bowed legs. John keeps vigil next to us. We pass a boy half my age throwing up, sobbing that the climb is too much. Grandpa begins the final set of stairs.

He is a warrior, sliding, crawling, dragging himself to the end. My mother and I are the squires, holding the umbrella over him, flanking him, but afraid to touch him. John heralds our arrival by repeatedly trumpeting to the rhythmic drumming of the rain:

"He's ninety years old, and he just climbed the Wall! Ninety years old!"

We're fifty feet from the bottom when my grandfather's legs give out. He stumbles, but does not fall, finding a perch on my mother's knee. The Japanese girls locate us once more and throw a rain poncho over Grandpa, a cloak for the warrior. The ninety minutes have ticked away, and the bus will soon be gone. John disappears into the rain, returning with the fraternal twin teenage boys from our tour. Without asking, they slide their arms under my grandfather, preparing to lift him into the air.

"Please," he says to them. "Please give me just a few more steps. Just a few more."

They look to John, to me, to my mother. Her eyes brimming with tears, she nods. The twins remove their hands.

My grandfather rises to his feet and takes an unsteady step. Then another. And another. The twins remain at his sides, ready to catch him. John resumes his cry of victory.

"Ninety years old and just climbed the Wall!"

The stalls of trinkets draw nearer. At the sound of John's call, the hawkers fall silent. Everyone watches as Grandpa lifts his foot, his leg shaking so badly it looks as if it will break to pieces. He comes down off the final step and the air is shattered with applause.

My grandpa crumbles and the twins catch him easily, carrying him away from the clapping vendors and tourists and driving rain, marching to John's excited babbling praise. I fall in slightly behind them with Mom at my side. Somewhere along the way Liliana has fallen asleep. The three of us—my mother, grandfather, and I—say nothing.

On the bus, I settle into my seat while Mom tucks her red rain jacket around Grandpa. He soon joins his great-granddaughter in dreamland. David approaches me just as the engine turns over and hands me a large photograph. It's our tour group of strangers, taken less than two hours before, a fact that baffles me. I feel as if we have been to the edge of the world and back since then. Four generations of our family smile among the faces, and printed across the bottom in English and Chinese it says:

不 到 长 城 非 好 汉
He who has not been to the Great Wall is not a True Man.

Amber Kelly-Anderson took her maiden voyage at the age of nine months to Santorini, Greece. Subsequently she also took her first steps there. She holds a Masters degree in English and the firm belief that traveling companions have no age requirements. When not seeing the world with her family, she teaches literature, composition, and creative writing.

JENNIFER ROSE SMITH

ʃʒ ʃʒ ʃʒ

The Kiwi Hunt

She came for the birds and stayed for breakfast.

The ferns loomed in the damp forest air, and their prehistoric stalks interlaced above my head, filtering the light of the Southern stars. I walked away from the tramper's hut, glancing back at its comforting familiarity. A few steps later it was indistinct, a shadow in a dark, jumbled landscape.

I'd wrapped my headlamp in cloth to dim its blinding beam, but covered with a bandana it gave off an eerie red glow that didn't reach my feet but only intensified the darkness. I turned it off. The night was filled with the sounds of insects and birds. Pushing past the flower-laden branch of a *kamahi* tree, I stopped short, startled by the brassy trill of ringing church bells. It took me a minute before I recognized the song of a jade-feathered Bellbird. I'd heard it for the first time earlier in the day, but in the warm afternoon sunshine it had seemed muted. Now it resonated through the woods, and I stood still in the dark and listened.

For the past seven days I'd been walking the steeply pitched trails of Stewart Island, a jagged scrap of land off the southern tip of New Zealand, where the birds of Rakiura National Park thrived in isolation from the invasive predators of the main islands. It was a rugged spot, and the winter storms that raged across the Southern Ocean reminded its few residents that Antarctica was not so very far away.

It was February, though, and the sun lingered into long afternoons. When the track emerged from the trees, I stood alone on pale beaches, shedding sweaty clothes on my way to the water's edge. I swam in the evenings, too, shivering and whooping from the cold, peeling mussels from the rocks to cook for my dinner, seasoning them with saltwater.

I had three more days of walking before I reached the island's only settlement, where I would board a northbound ferry toward a series of buses, then a boat and train that would take me to Auckland, and finally, a flight to Spain to meet my boyfriend. Just three days left to spot a Kiwi bird, shy, flightless, nocturnal—and a beloved and endangered national icon.

I had made other nighttime forays like this one, creeping through trees, feeling foolish as I looked for . . . what? A roly-poly bird with a slender beak that would undoubtedly prefer I stay in my sleeping bag. A park naturalist had told me (without pausing as he sent the stiff, fuzzy body of an opossum sailing into the bush) that this remote spot would be my best chance to find the birds. I was determined to see one before my three-month trip ended.

It was my first big solo voyage. Although I had pored over travel books obsessively, discovering pre-war Dijon with M.F.K. Fisher and charting the South Pacific with James Cook, it seemed as if the maps were drawn and all the big adventures were collecting dust on library shelves. The frontiers had been conquered, and the casualties included the unassuming Kiwi bird, struggling to survive in a habitat transformed by introduced predators and development.

I felt that spotting a Kiwi would somehow prove that beyond the bungee jumps and backpacker hostels, undiscovered worlds were still shuffling through the earth's dark forests, minding their own business.

Thinking of this, I ignored my timid urge to dash back to the safe, warm hut and continued through the trees, my ears twitching at every snapping twig and falling leaf. For what seemed like an hour I didn't see a thing, and my walk down the trail began to feel like its own endeavor, as if I had come to this island for nighttime orienteering, not a quick glimpse of the local bird life. Then I heard a quiet shuffling in the trees, and I froze, staring hard.

The noises came closer, got louder. My heart was thumping against my ribs, and my surging adrenaline sharpened every sound. With sweating palms, I slipped the headlamp from my pocket and pointed it into the bushes, fumbling with the switch. When I turned it on, the round beam of light illuminated a patch of green pant leg that led to a muddy hiking boot.

I couldn't have been more surprised if I'd seen a Kiwi bird. Standing in front of me was a young man a few years older than I, carrying a notebook and returning my look with a level gaze. He was slight, with dark blond hair that grew toward the wire rims of his glasses.

"Looking for Kiwis, then?" he asked.

"Yes," I replied, aiming for nonchalance. "You?"

"That's what I do most nights," he said, with a smile. In fact, he was spending the summer in a small hut that belonged to the park, tracking the bird population. "I've just seen a whole family of Kiwi. Would you like me to show you where to find them?"

I couldn't believe my ears—or my luck. Of *course* I wanted to see them. Of course.

Without much else to say, he turned in the direction that he'd come, and I followed his slim silhouette through the trees, away from the track and the little hut. Newspaper headlines flickered through my mind, but I stifled them. *There are better places to look for kidnapping victims than empty forests in the Southern Ocean,* I reasoned with myself. We walked on, ducking under fallen trees and brushing aside ferns.

After a few minutes he paused and put a hand out. Then he motioned me to his side and pointed to the ground in front of us. I squinted into the blackness, straining to make out shapes. Slowly, he took out his light and turned it on. In the sudden glow I saw three birds standing about six feet in front of us. Two adult Kiwi were the size of soccer balls, covered in long, slender feathers that swept back to rounded tails. An adolescent huddled between them, covered in fuzzy down. With beaks intent on unearthing bugs to eat, they scarcely seemed to notice us, and as we knelt down for a closer look, the notoriously timid birds didn't budge.

We stayed for several minutes without speaking or moving, until at last the three birds ducked out of the light and into a low shrub, disappearing from view. After our silent observation of the Kiwis, his voice startled me.

"I've been out here for hours," he said, yawning, "and I'm famished. Would you like to come back to the hut for a cuppa and a bite to eat?"

I stood up, thinking of my mother and of newspaper headlines, then shrugged. "I'd love to."

This time we walked with our lights on, and soon after rejoining the track, came across a tiny rustic shack built with unfinished timbers. It was as cold inside as out, and while I sat on the only chair, he knelt by the wood stove, adding kindling to the faintly glowing coals. When flames caught the dry wood, he turned to the table that dominated the room, swept off a pile of maps and papers, and unfolded an ancient two-burner propane cooker.

He filled a teakettle, set it on a burner, and pulled a box of pancake mix from a mouse-proof bin on a shelf. Clearly accustomed to living in a cramped space, he moved with the efficiency of a sailor. He had one teacup, a fork and spoon, one plate. He handed me a steeping cup of tea, made his in a small bowl, then set out powdered milk and a bottle of honey.

It was two in the morning, and my dinner of mussels and pasta had been hours ago. My mouth watered when the batter hit the oiled skillet. Expertly, he flipped a golden fried pancake onto my plate and poured another perfect circle on the hot pan. Reaching the highest plank shelf, he pushed aside tins of beans and dried pasta, then brought out a treasure as rare on that isolated coast as a Kiwi bird in Auckland: a fresh lemon.

We spoke a bit while we ate, I suppose. He asked me my name, and about the paths that had taken me to that remote spot. I must have asked the same, but the details, such as his name, have slipped my mind in the ensuing years. I was eighteen years old, in love with the man who waited for me in Spain, but also with the keenness of being alone, the long days and self-reliance. As I recall the months I spent in New Zealand and my walk around the tiny, rugged island, I often think of that night.

What I remember, along with the dark and the quiet and the dusty comfort of that little hut, is the taste of fried pancakes, soaked with honey and lemon juice. Never before had I seen someone eat pancakes that way, and never since. But I still do, and never without a thought of my great Kiwi hunt, the rustle of feathers in the night forest, and the young man with blond hair and a way with a skillet.

Jennifer Rose Smith lives in Vermont, where she lives a sweet double life. For half the year she writes, travels, taps maple trees for syrup, and plots adventures. During the summer she is up to her elbows in flour and butter, whipping up globally inspired pastries to sell at her farmers' market stand, The Nomadic Oven. She chronicles her adventures on her website, www. thenomadicoven.com.

CAROL REICHERT

༄ ༄ ༄

The Threadbare Rope

A woman discovers the truth about miracles.

I sat alone in my room at a hotel in Santo Domingo and observed what I wasn't thinking about. I wasn't thinking about which sun-soaked beach, what fruity rum drink, or whether to learn the *merengue* at the dance club we'd passed on the drive from the airport. Instead I stared out my window at thick, green blades of Caribbean grass and asked myself if I believed in miracles.

I'd come to Santo Domingo with my brother, Michael, to seek help from a doctor who used fetal stem cells to treat degenerative diseases. Michael had suffered from Parkinson's disease for eighteen years. He shook uncontrollably and walked in short, shuffling movements. He no longer blinked or smiled. His face had become a mask of blankness. My brother believed in the doctor's miracle—and I wanted to believe. Dr. White claimed he could harness the power of creation itself with cells that were biologic chameleons, capable of differentiating into any type of cell the body needed. But I held no more stock in the case studies I read than I did in the eerie voodoo enchantments still practiced in the island's rural villages.

I'd flown from my home near Boston to Milwaukee where Michael lived, and in the airport terminal, my childhood life assaulted me. First the smells: bratwurst, knockwurst, and sauerkraut. Then the sounds: *"Paging Craig Wyznewski, paging Craig Wyznewski."* A name I never heard in Boston. Then a friendliness that startled me: the woman at the rental car counter who gave me explicit directions to the counter of a competitor, the rental car van driver who treated me like a drinking buddy: "I really thought the Patriots were going to win last weekend. Boy, the Celtics are doing great." I remembered that you were a loser in Wisconsin if you didn't follow your teams, and I knew enough to play along.

Outside it was 18 degrees. I picked Michael up at his apartment.

"I'm sorry I'm late," I told him. "I took a wrong turn."

"I don't understand. Who are you?" he asked, staring at me.

"I'm Carol, your sister."

He was embarrassed and I was embarrassed for him. I told him I had changed my hairstyle and that it made me look different.

"That must be it," he said.

I helped Michael pack, and we returned to the airport, where the security guard checked our boarding passes and IDs and told us to have a peaceful day. As we waited for the boarding call, Michael studied my face.

"The circles under your eyes are darker than they used to be," he said.

I pretended to be merely surprised, then excused myself and ran to the bathroom to cover them with makeup. We'd never been close, my brother and I. He was six years older, single, no friends. He suffered from certain social deficits – the worst of which was an inability to empathize. But when he said, "I can't do this trip alone. Will you come with me?" it didn't even occur to me to say no. I left my family in Boston to pick him up in Milwaukee.

"Take lots of pictures," my little girl said.

On the airplane, I walked down the aisle to the bathroom. When I returned, Michael told me that my hips had widened since I'd had children. He said this with no affect—no derision or concern. It was simply his clinical observation about how his younger sister had changed. I wondered how I'd survive the next two days under his scrutiny.

Traveling with Michael, I observed the world through the eyes of someone who seemed to have thawed after a lengthy freeze—emerging severely out of touch. He asked me why the passengers burst into applause when we landed smoothly. "Perfect landing," I told him. He asked me to tell the waiter that he wanted Spaghetti Bolognese because he didn't know how to pronounce it. He was surprised when I tipped the man who pushed his wheelchair from the ticket counter to our gate in Newark. "I never would have thought of doing that," he said.

We landed in Santo Domingo at midnight, and the flight attendant hurried to get Michael a wheelchair. "Good luck," she said from the jetway. It was January, but the night air was tropical and fragrant, and the clinic van was waiting for us.

At the hotel, I fell asleep quickly, exhausted from the journey and the effort of pushing my 200-pound brother through airports and up wheelchair ramps. In the morning, I found a flyer slipped under my door advertising a snorkeling excursion and a sunset amble to the marble burial site of Christopher Columbus. The usual sensations I felt when I traveled—excitement, curiosity, a craving for the exotic—were replaced by anxiety. I worried whether the injection was safe, if my brother was wasting the little money he had on an untested procedure. I feared his disappointment. When I knocked on Michael's door, I heard him shuffle, then he appeared wearing nothing but white briefs.

"Don't worry. I won't look," I said as I entered, shading my eyes.

"Why? I'm not naked. If I were, I wouldn't have opened the door," he said, as if astounded that I might have such a thought.

Why did my brother have to be so strange? I was annoyed by his oddness. It was hard to help someone who made me squirm.

At breakfast, I filled Michael's glass with orange juice and cut his pancakes. I couldn't escape the traveler inside me—always itching to leave home, shed my skin for a while and slip on someone else's. So I ate a Dominican breakfast—fried eggs served on top of boiled and mashed plantains, soft cheese fried in peanut oil, slices of papaya and pineapple, and *café colado*, water poured over a cloth bag stuffed with ground coffee and served with steamed milk.

I looked around the hotel and saw tourists in flip-flops and wide-brimmed hats examining maps and planning itineraries—and also people in wheelchairs, a little boy with muscular dystrophy, a woman with Lou Gehrig's disease who stared into space with her mouth frozen open. Dr. White's patients.

I wondered how the tourists felt—the ones who came here to escape and ended up vacationing among people who were broken.

When I'd told my friends what we were doing, everyone discouraged me. Have you researched this? What are the doctor's credentials? Have any clinical studies been published? I had nothing scientific to offer them. There were no clinical studies, and the doctor was a psychiatrist, not a neurologist. He specialized in treating eating disorders, not Parkinson's disease. I lived in Boston, home of Harvard Medical School, Mass General. So an unknown clinic in Santo Domingo did not give me a sense of institutional worth. I tried to talk Michael out of it. It sounded too good to be true, too mysterious and too expensive. A friend told me she had just watched an exposé on 60 Minutes about offshore clinics that preyed on people desperate for cures. I pictured Dr. White as a flim-flam man operating out of the back of his caravan at *Carnaval*. "Step right up and get your fetal cells!" And behind him, a row of gray fetuses floated in watery jelly jars.

"It's easy to be rational when you don't have Parkinson's disease," Michael said when I told him my concerns, and I was staggered by the truth of it.

That was it, wasn't it? I didn't have Parkinson's disease. It was easy for me to stand in judgment, to question the validity of a doctor who could be a savior or a quack, bamboozling an easy $30,000 from people who still had hope, the threadbare rope they clutched before letting go. As Shakespeare said, "The miserable have no other medicine." Only hope.

The van arrived early to pick us up. Michael sat silently in the back seat while I asked the driver questions in Spanish as he maneuvered through Santo Domingo's busy streets. He said many people were coming to the clinic this weekend—babies, old people. We drove through a poor neighborhood, past women washing clothes on the street in red plastic tubs. In heavy traffic we slowed down, and I saw the open-air market. Normally I would have hopped off here to inspect what the locals ate, to put a frame around the life of the people. Instead we drove on, shuttling past bins of sweet potatoes, yucca, yams, and spices.

I imagined the clinic as a shabby building with cracks in the walls, bad smells, bare light bulbs, used syringes stashed in the trash. But the driver stopped in front of a thick mahogany gate that swung open to reveal a Spanish Colonial villa with a swimming pool and a fountain surrounded by palm trees. The walls were painted a creamy gold.

"It looks like the home of a *conquistador*," said Michael. I saw the driver's eyes in the mirror and wondered if he appreciated this comparison to the explorers who pillaged his country for God, gold, and glory. I wheeled Michael inside, and the interior looked like a movie set: heavy Spanish-style furniture on terracotta floors, gleaming chandeliers, ornate masks, and Mayan musical instruments hanging on thick white walls.

In the living room, a man with a heavy German accent cuddled his two young daughters. Each had cerebral palsy, their legs as thin and shapeless as pipes. A boy with severe autism turned away from his parents and rocked with his eyes closed, occasionally yelling.

"I sure hope it works," my brother said.

I squeezed his shoulder. "Me, too."

An assistant wheeled Michael to a bedroom where we met the anesthesiologist, a Dominican woman in her thirties. She took Michael's blood pressure and inserted an IV needle into the top of his hand. He lay on his back, and his hand shook up and down, involuntarily slapping his abdomen. As the IV dripped into his vein, I felt the rush of hope.

Dr. White entered the room, dressed in a white jacket. He was slender, of medium height with thick, silvery hair swept back over his head. He managed to be both elegant and slightly nerdy. He hugged me and held Michael's hand.

"We'll put a local in your back, Michael, and then you won't feel anything."

Dr. White answered all my questions. He didn't hide anything. I asked him about the fetuses, where they came from.

"In eastern Europe today the number one choice for birth control is abortion," he said, "which doesn't make sense to us, emotionally or financially. Healthy young women come in for abortions. They know nothing about this—they're just asked if they want the material to be thrown away as medical waste or used to help someone. If they say they want to help someone, then we test the cells at one of the best laboratories in the world. They put them into liquid nitrogen at 196 degrees below zero centigrade. I select them, and they're reconstituted. They're alive when Michael gets them."

He smiled at me, and I asked him if I could buy a copy of his book.

"I'll give you a copy," he said.

Dr. White left the room and returned with a copy of his book, autographed.

"Who's the guy on the back?" he teased me.

I turned the book over. Dr. White stared from the back cover with a caring smile. His hand was over his heart.

"Just some handsome guy," I said.

What was I doing? Was I flirting with him? I was buying it, the cure, the miracle, and the supreme confidence of the miracle worker.

I took a break and walked through the house. In the garden were potted palms, scarlet and orange tropical flowers, a thatched hut, and a bench carved from a tree trunk. Wind chimes played a sonorous tune. I opened a thick wooden gate and beyond it was the Caribbean Sea, cerulean blue and sparkling. I wanted to stretch out on the sand, maybe strike up a conversation with the family sitting around a wooden table, eating grilled chicken. Instead I let the sand slip between my toes for a few minutes and then returned to the clinic. A little boy sitting in a wheelchair on the terrace smiled at me.

"My name is Carol," I told him.

"I'm Max. I'm ten."

"What do you have?"

"I'm special needs," Max said, looking away from me.

I saw a gold stud shining on his earlobe.

"I like your earring," I told him.

"My dad just took me out to get it and didn't tell my mom."

"Oh, was she mad?"

"I don't want to talk about that."

He yelled for his mom, a young woman with a sweet, round face.

"Is this your first time here?" she asked me.

"Yes. My brother has Parkinson's disease."

"Max has muscular dystrophy. He had four shots in his abdomen. We're going to come back depending on whether we get results."

The daughter of a man being treated for Alzheimer's joined us and began to crochet.

"Good for the nerves," she said. Her fingernails were so long they curled in arcs.

The families left and I sat alone on the terrace. A worker offered me a *cafecito*, a little cup of coffee. It was thick, like Turkish coffee and very sweet. When I was finished, she told me to turn the cup over and let the dregs drip down the sides.

"It's an old Dominican practice," she said. "I can read the coffee stains on the inside of the cup and make a prophecy."

I thanked her but told her I didn't want to know.

I walked back to Michael's room. His legs were elevated to help the cells travel to his brain.

"I already feel better," he told me.

I wheeled him to the foyer. In the living room, one of the girls with cerebral palsy sat on Dr. White's lap, her head resting on his chest. When he saw us, he gently laid the girl in her father's arms.

"Your eyes are clearer," Dr. White said as he patted Michael's shoulder. "Your posture is better."

"Well, I'm still shaking," Michael said.

"Oh God, give me a break. I'm not Jesus, the healer."

Dr. White handed me his business card. "You might not see any results for six months. But keep me posted at all times."

"You look good, Michael. Doesn't he look good?" Dr. White said, turning to his staff.

I felt uneasy. Was he Jesus or wasn't he? Was it all a hoax?

The driver took us back to the hotel. Michael was starving. In the hotel restaurant, he ate lasagna and I ate *la bandera*, a dish that symbolized the Dominican flag, with red pinto beans alongside white rice, stewed meat, and plantains.

In the morning, we flew out before dawn. I didn't practice my usual travel tricks to prolong the experience—standing outside to soak up the last rays of tropical sunshine, buying the local hot sauce or a CD of some unknown steel drum band in the airport terminal. Anything to hold on a little longer. No. This time I let the country slip right through my fingers. A souvenir would only remind me of life's inequities.

We landed in Milwaukee as the sun set. On the way to his apartment, I was thinking about what was happening inside Michael's body, whether the new cells were multiplying like they were supposed to or just floating around without purpose. Michael, on the other hand, was thinking about bridges. He told me that the ramparts built to support bridges were supposed to last thirty years, but salting icy roads made them start to crumble after only ten. I wanted to know this man, but I wondered if I could, if I could ever get to the heart of who he was.

In his apartment, I noticed for the first time a drawing framed and hanging on the living room wall. I asked him about it, and he told me he'd seen a man at a hamburger joint sketching him.

"I thought that was really interesting," Michael said. "I offered him $20 for it and he said no, just take it. So I gave him $10 and he took it. The only thing is he drew me without any eyes."

He was shaking, and now I was shaking, too.

I made Michael a sandwich and thought *but he does have eyes*, clear and blue, and capable of seeing a life beyond the one he has. Perhaps this was the miracle—that a chronically underachieving, socially isolated misfit who could barely walk or feed himself still had hope, still believed a miracle might be possible.

I told my brother I loved him, and I left to go back home.

ॐ ॐ ॐ

Carol Reichert writes in the sensory deprivation chamber that is the Newton, Massachusetts, public library. She has been a midwife to a cow giving birth in New Zealand, danced flamenco in the mountain caves outside Granada, and learned lomi lomi massage in Hawaii. In addition to writing, she dances flamenco in Boston and Spain whenever the rhythm moves her. She is currently working on a memoir about her family's life in a village in southern Spain.

CATHERINE WATSON

♨ ♨ ♨

Climbing Vaea

A traveler on a trail to remember.

"Pilgrimages," I reminded myself, as I struggled over yet another fallen tree, "aren't supposed to be easy."

But I had thought this one would be. I had gone to the South Seas to meet Robert Louis Stevenson on his own turf—to see the spacious house that was the author's last home and walk the path up to his gravesite, on the top of his favorite mountain.

The flaw in that fantasy was "walk." You do not *walk* to the top of Mt. Vaea, especially not in the rainy season.

The trail was buried in a maze of fallen trees, so big and so close together that the hillside looked like a log jam. Their own weight had brought them crashing down, their roots pulling loose as frequent rains turned Samoa's volcanic soil to slippery muck.

And here they lay—a jumble of branches; leaves in various stages of withering; tangles of jagged roots, and huge, huge trunks caught at angles like oversized Pick Up Sticks.

With a few, there was space to wriggle under; another few let me squirm through their wilting crowns, but with most, my only choice was to crawl over them.

Make that "throw myself on them as if they were horses"—
pull myself up, flop belly-first over the trunk, then roll, skid,
slide, or jump off the other side. Or fall. I did that too, a couple
of times.

Stevenson had been one of my life-long heroes—not
because of *Treasure Island* or *Kidnapped*—but because he
was a great traveler and a prolific travel writer. I'd particularly liked his accounts of sailing around the South Pacific—
voyages that had led both of us to Vailima.

"I travel not to go anywhere," he'd once written, "but to
go. I travel for travel's sake. The great affair is to move." That
became my mantra too.

So did another of his classics: "To travel hopefully is a better thing than to arrive." Stuck on the side of his mountain, I
was no longer so sure about that.

I could have turned around, but that would have meant the
same struggle going back, with nothing to show for it except
torn skin, sore muscles, and muddy clothes. Besides, I couldn't
believe the trail could stay this bad all the way up to the grave.

I was wrong about that, too.

During Stevenson's life, there was no path at all, though he
managed to climb to the top of Vaea and see its magnificent
view over the green slopes that run down to Apia, Samoa's
small capital, and the blue sea beyond.

Samoa was Stevenson's last stop in the Pacific, the place
that the Scottish-born writer finally called home after years
of wandering. In 1890, helped by an American entrepre-
neur, Stevenson bought more than 300 acres of forested land
south of Apia, and he and his American-born wife, Fanny
Osbourne, set about building what is still a grand house at the
foot of Mt. Vaea.

Or rather, she did. Ten years older than her husband, strong
where he was fragile, Fanny served as general contractor,

overseeing construction of the big, veranda-wrapped bungalow they called Villa Vailima.

Working side by side with Samoans she hired, Fanny put
in vegetable and flower gardens, planted fruit trees, and cultivated cocoa, making her a pioneer in modern Samoa's chocolate industry.

She was also her husband's protector, "a violent friend," as
one of her biographers called her. She cleared the way for him
to write, relax, and rebound from the illnesses that had plagued
him since childhood.

He was barely forty when they arrived but already world
famous, thanks to novels that included *Treasure Island* and *Dr.
Jekyll and Mr. Hyde*, as well as travel books, essays, and myriad
poems.

Stevenson wrote a dozen more books in the four short
years he lived here, took sides in local politics, and was much
revered—still is—by the Samoan people. They called him
Tusitala, the Teller of Tales. He died at forty-four, probably
of a brain hemorrhage, while helping Fanny make dinner one
December evening at Vailima.

People told me the name of the place came from two
Samoan words—*vai* for water and *lima* for hand—and that it
referred to a stream, a pool, and a local legend.

The details of the legend varied with the speaker, but
it concerned a traveler (or aged father or tired wife) who
became thirsty, and a traveling companion (or dutiful son
or loving husband) who fetched life-giving water in cupped
hands.

Legend aside, everyone agreed that Stevenson himself had
swum in the shaded, stream-fed pool at the foot of the mountain. Both trails to the top started just beyond it—the short,
steep, "hard" one, which I'd shunned, and the longer, gradual,
"easy" one, which I couldn't imagine being worse.

Now, an hour into this mistake, I was out of drinking water, there were no friendly hands in sight, and I kept losing the trail. I was also starting to panic.

No one in Samoa knew where I'd gone, and if I got stuck or fell or broke an ankle, it would be a long time before anybody came looking. I tried yelling for help then; the only answer was a dog barking, far in the distance. I went back to climbing logs.

Hope eventually appeared in the form of tourist trash—the discarded sole of a sandal, lying in the weeds. The spoor of my kind, I thought, grateful for garbage. Farther on, I found a plastic bottle. Then the wrapper from a packet of Kleenex. Finally, the sole of the other sandal.

And then I was—not on top—but at least out of the woods. A Samoan family was already up there, beside the plain white concrete tomb—three little boys and their mother and grandfather. They were just starting down in my direction. Obviously they thought my trail would be easier.

I burst out of the foliage, waving my arms and screaming, "No, No! Don't go down this way! No!" I must have looked like a crazy woman; I certainly felt like one. We took pictures of each other beside the tomb before they heeded my advice and went back down the "hard" trail, the way they'd come.

The gravesite felt private then. I sat down on the edge of the tomb, read and re-read the famous words on its bronze plaque, and started to cry—as if I'd known the man, as if the loss were fresh. It was Stevenson's own epitaph that made me weep:

Here he lies where he longed to be;
Home is the sailor, home from sea,
And the hunter home from the hill.

Fanny Stevenson died in California twenty years later, but her ashes were brought back to Samoa and interred with her husband's, as she'd wished, under a tribute he'd once written for her:

Teacher, tender comrade, wife,
A fellow-farer true through life,
Heart-whole and soul free,
The august father gave to me.

I took the "hard" trail down, the steep one that grieving Samoans had cut right after Stevenson died so they could carry his body to the mountaintop. It wasn't littered with tree trunks, but in places it was nearly vertical.

It felt like the last run of the day on a ski slope, when you're so tired you lose control, and sure enough, I did fall—hard—trying to hug a tree as my feet slid away. At least that tree was upright.

The heavy air coalesced into rain. By the time I got back to the trailhead, it was pelting down, but I was too sweat-soaked to care. It cooled me, actually—made me feel cleansed, as if I'd swum in Stevenson's pool myself, in the lovely glen where Vailima's waters gathered.

It's true that pilgrimages aren't supposed to be easy, but neither is the way they end. Even hardship doesn't prepare you for that. I mean, what do you do after you reach your Everest?

I just walked back to the main road, bought a two-liter bottle of cold water at a tiny grocery shack and drank half of it without stopping to breathe. Then I flagged down one of the island's gaily-painted ex-school buses, rode it into central Apia and trudged back to my hotel room for dry clothes.

Only later did I celebrate—at Aggie Grey's, a legendary and expensive hostelry that looks like a set from "South Pacific." I went into Aggie's air-conditioned bar, pulled up a stool, ordered a bottle of the local beer—fittingly, the brand name is Vailima—and drank a toast to the Teller of Tales.

Home is the hunter, I thought.

ఎం ఎం ఎం

Catherine Watson is a travel writer, editor, photographer, and writing coach who teaches university-level workshops in the U.S. and Europe. She intended to become an archeologist until she spent a college summer on a dig in the Middle East. Since then, her career has taken her to more than one hundred countries and her writing has appeared in a dozen anthologies. Her books include Roads Less Traveled—Dispatches from the Ends of the Earth, *and* Home on the Road—Further Dispatches from the Ends of the Earth. *Her website is www.catherinewatsontravel.com.*

ॐ ॐ ॐ

The International Expiration Date

Arabian nights just got hotter.

The room was clean and spacious, the floor wasn't sticky, and there was ample seating. The patrons, a sea of mild-mannered men dressed in freshly pressed *dishdashas*—long white robes—quietly sipped Heinekens, carefully using their napkins as coasters. It was the kind of behavior you'd expect to see in the waiting room of a dentist's office, but nobody was here for a teeth cleaning. We were in the largest nightclub in Oman, and we were here to watch the ladies. The three trotting ladies on a stage. It was *that* kind of club. Sort of.

Besides the entertainment, my friend and I were the only girls in the joint. And we wouldn't have been let in at all, except, we were foreign and with male friends somehow rendering us immune to local nightclub law.

The floorshow that night consisted of the same three ladies prancing around like prized show ponies in tight, floor-length 80s-style prom gowns. Arabian women tend to be on the pleasingly plump side, so every curve and jiggle was accentuated as they held hands and sashayed down the runway, seemingly unbothered by underwear lines. Indeed, if these ladies were any example, thick beige bra straps and granny-style skivvies were all the rage in Oman—especially if they cut into the flesh, creating bountiful rolls and folds of sex appeal. They wore their hair in suggestive ponytails, and when feeling particularly saucy, swung them with abandon to the sweet synthesized sounds being played on the keyboard by the Yanni of Oman. This was all considered wild, and the men showed their approval by sitting silently.

At one point, though, someone got a little frisky. He stood up, and with arms wide open and a huge grin, swayed blissfully to the music. I took this as some long-overdue appreciation for these hard-working "dancers," but the bouncer immediately ordered him to leave. The tipsy gentleman didn't even put up a fight. He simply bowed his head and obeyed, while his friend quickly gathered their belongings as if they were late for another dental appointment across town. It was the most G-rated version of a strip club imaginable.

"Let's get another round," Aaron said. He was fidgety. He'd been so all night. He wanted to smoke, but couldn't—not until twelve o'clock. We had a bet: if he smoked before midnight, I'd win, and he'd have to buy a pair of cheap plastic flip-flops and wear them for the remainder of our two-week trip. He deemed this kind of footwear very American, and he said it with a sneer. Even in the middle of the scorching desert, Aaron preferred sensible, sturdy shoes of the kind commonly worn by Home Depot employees. If he won, I didn't know. I had his request scrawled on a piece of paper folded up in my pocket. At midnight, if he hadn't lit up, I could look.

It all started with an advertisement I saw for a position teaching English in Abu Dhabi. The details of the job were sketchy, but I felt confident I had the right qualifications.

"A successful candidate will have the ability to tolerate a high degree of ambiguity."

So when family and friends questioned me about the position, I just shrugged—it seemed like the kind of response my future employers would appreciate.

*   *   *

On a scorching-hot day in June, I was picked up at the airport and promptly driven to the middle of a suburban desert—nothing but swank housing compounds sprouting up everywhere between great patches of beige emptiness. We drove around lost for a while, through a tan, blistering, and seemingly endless landscape.

When we finally reached my compound, a sleepy, shirtless man emerged from a security booth, looking confused and annoyed. It didn't appear that anyone was expecting me—which I found hopeful. Maybe my driver was just asking for directions to the city. A city like Dubai, full of flash and plastic, glitz and glory. After a few minutes, however, my driver seemed to reach some sort of consensus with the guard—hopefully one that didn't include me being sold to a sheik.

I didn't want to be left here, but I had little choice in the matter: the driver unloaded my bags on the sidewalk and told me to get out.

I was the first teacher to arrive. With no contact information, no idea where I was supposed to be, and no clue what I should be doing, I decided to explore the villa while I tolerated the ambiguousness of my plight. It was sensational. Everything came unnecessarily super-sized, which made me feel unnecessarily small. It was like being under posh house arrest or privileged political exile, complete with a pool and a maid.

When the sun finally sank into the sand, I decided to venture beyond the villa, maybe to find the market that the guard had pointed to in an extremely vague imprecise way. Off I went, fully clothed from head to toe, trudging through the vast Arabian Desert, the sand burning my toes. I needed a camel, and I couldn't stop sweating. Sweating from places I didn't know had pores. Perspiration was dripping from my elbows.

Eventually, I spotted some British girls loitering outside their own compound, clad in swaths of fabric no larger than tea towels—risqué even by Vegas standards. Meanwhile, I was dressed straight out of the convent.

"You can wear that?" I couldn't stop myself from blurting out. *Isn't this a Muslim country? Shouldn't we be modest? Respectful?*

"It's fine. It's very open here. We're going clubbing," one replied dismissively and then continued a lively conversation with her two trampy friends.

I had my doubts, but it was really hot. I peeled off my schoolmarm cardigan, hiked up my skirt, and ploughed onward like a true Bedouin.

I met Aaron two days later at orientation. I loathe orientations: a rush of vaguely necessary information that everyone else seems to absorb effortlessly, while I drink paper cups of instant coffee and struggle to make sense of the attendance sheet. Each country has a different system; some like to use checkmarks, others, dots. In Yokohama, meticulous records were required; in Madrid, nobody cared.

Aaron understood my pain. He'd just arrived in the country that morning and was having enough difficulty just keeping his eyes open. We bonded over caffeine—coffee for me, tea for him. I didn't think much of him romantically at first. He had a funny, formal way of speaking, as if he'd just stepped from the pages of a Jane Austin novel, and he seemed a little sweaty. But then, who was I to judge? My elbows sweat.

Classes started the following day, and keeping attendance didn't get any easier. Teenage Emirati girls don't like to stay in class or even come to class. Most of the time I found them at Starbucks or roaming the halls in their designer shoes and custom tailored *abayas*—flowing black robes that made me feel like I was teaching at Hogwarts.

Aaron became a confidant in my quest to win over my thoroughly apathetic students. Every day I had a plan, and every day Aaron listened to how it failed. In the end I let them paint intricate henna patterns on my hands and play Arabic music videos on YouTube. We shut off the lights, the headscarves came off, and we had our own dance party. This they liked. They even taught me the ponytail-whipping move. They didn't learn much from the lesson plan, but they liked me—for that day anyway—and I couldn't wait to tell Aaron.

Compound life had its own set of rules, but a tenacious older teacher—the self-appointed purity police—kept a vigilant watch on us. He seemed to think if the genders started fraternizing it wouldn't be long before the villas were overrun with panty-dropping whores and bathtubs of moonshine. He was probably just lonely, or envious that his panty-dropping days were behind him, but because of him, our budding romance remained innocent.

Aaron and I sat outside his villa day after day in the suffocating heat, drinking piping hot pots of tea. It was like being in eighth grade again: he wasn't allowed inside my villa, I wasn't allowed in his, and any kind of public affection was gravely frowned upon. So we sat, and sipped, and barely touched.

The fourth week into our four-week contract, we finally kissed, late at night with our feet dangling playfully in the pool. He'd spent the past several hours regaling me with tales of the economic collapse of the European Union and the myth of Achilles. For a closet nerd like myself, this qualified as foreplay.

It didn't take much convincing for Aaron to join my colleagues and me on a two-week road trip once school ended. From the creamy, caramel-colored sand dunes of the Emirates to the rocky, sun-cracked land of Oman, we gorged on feasts of hummus and lamb kebabs and ended our evenings with shot-glass sized cups of thick cardamom-spiced coffee and apple mint *shisha*.

One especially balmy evening in a Muscat souk, a shopkeeper lured me in with black sticks of *kohl*, guaranteed to transform me into a harem harlot. Ahmed, the shopkeeper, called me his sister. It was clearly a keen sales ploy, but one I appreciated nonetheless. He seemed to keep his shop tiny and cramped so that whatever he thrust into your hands you couldn't put down again. I had already bought the *kohl*, three jars of frankincense, a few tubes of henna, and a green pashmina shawl when he pulled out a small magical looking bottle from a velvet satchel.

"The Sultan," he said, referring to the bottle, "is an aroma intoxicating to men."

The perfume, Ahmed explained, sneaks up on a man until he's unwittingly engulfed in the woman's seductive scent. He nodded toward "his brother" Aaron, then winked at me. That night while I was sleeping, Aaron returned to the souk and bought me a bottle.

But realistically, where was this going? I was from California but lived in Korea. He lived in Spain but came from London. Geographically speaking, we were a mess. I'd seen it work for other couples—they walked around flaunting their bilingual relationships and work visas for multiple countries. Their babies came out clutching passports in their tiny dual-citizenship hands. For me, international relationships were more like a carton of milk: they came with an expiration date, which you ignored at your own peril.

The no-smoking bet began the night of the green sea turtles. In July, hundreds of these half-shelled creatures crawl ashore to lay their eggs deep in the sand. You venture out at night and wait beneath the stars. Our guide informed us that these mama *"turrrtles"* don't have babies until their mid-thirties. After they lay their eggs, they return to the ocean and embark on a two-year odyssey around the world. Then they return to their birthplace, to this exact same beach in Oman. Meanwhile, the male turtles never go anywhere. I felt an instant affinity with these dynamic reptilian ladies.

The guide said we mustn't help the babies; it was their own destiny to find their way to the sea, or not. We stood in awe for quite a while watching one little fellow waddle in circles—obviously not destined for seafaring life. After repeatedly stating the importance of not interfering with the natural passage of life, the guide eventually grew bored of watching and chucked him in the water, where I'm sure he was promptly eaten by a fish.

I can't remember how it started. Maybe it was because we'd just spent a moonlit evening holding hands and breathing fresh salty sea air, or perhaps being thirty-something myself, I was feeling maternal and didn't want secondhand smoke harming the babies. But by the time we left that beach, Aaron wasn't going to smoke for the next twenty-four hours.

It was a quarter to twelve and we'd moved into the Indian section of the nightclub, where things were a bit more rowdy. More of a PG-13 crowd here. The men were boisterous, and the dancing ladies on stage were actually dancing. They wore bright jewel-toned saris and spun around to a two-man Indian band, whipping their long dark tresses teasingly—a move proving universally provocative.

The place was thick with cigarette smoke, and Aaron was salivating like one of Pavlov's dogs. I encouraged him to break the bet, but he was adamant that he wouldn't give in and had another beer instead. Was he afraid of sandals? Did he have freakish hobbit feet? Or was he just determined to win?

I became fascinated with one of the dancers, the one we'd dubbed "The Fairy." She wore a gorgeous white sari and flitted about like a flirtatious butterfly. She had the attention of every man in the club, and me. Her eyes, her smile, her hair, her body: this woman got what she wanted. Aaron didn't see the appeal. He was mistrustful of fairies; he found them fickle.

He preferred "Midnight." She sat to the side of the stage in a deep blue sari looking bored.

"She doesn't need the attention," he explained. "She doesn't fill you with a bunch of meaningless promises."

I started to see what he meant. The Fairy might be fun for a romp or a heady summer romance, but maybe I was beginning to crave something real. I reached into my pocket and felt for the scrap of paper. It was midnight. I looked across the bar at Aaron. He shot me a cheeky grin before bumming a cigarette off a local, like some nicotine-fueled Cinderella. He immediately relaxed into a billowing cloud of cathartic smoke. As he happily puffed away, I turned my attention back to the stage and the folded note now in my hand. I took a deep breath and quietly opened it.

Buy me dinner . . .

Was that all? He'd stuck doggedly to his non-smoking guns so I could buy him a two-dollar *shawarma*? I felt deflated.

. . . in Korea.

I stared at the words for a minute, a slow smile forming on my lips. Then again, maybe this one had an extended shelf life.

Sarah Katin has been a television host in Korea, professor in Japan, treehouse dweller in Laos, house painter in New Orleans, sangria swiller in Spain, dragon hunter in Indonesia, and fishmonger in Australia. A two-time contributor to the The Best Women's Travel Writing series, she recently retired (pending her success as an unemployed screenwriter) from her teaching position in South Korea. These days you can find her hard at work on her second screenplay at her L.A. office (the cushy chair by the window at Starbucks) or in Costa Rica bathing baby sloths.

🐚 🐚 🐚

Our Own Apocalypse Now

"We are all tourists in history, and irony is what
we win in wars." — *Anatole Broyard*

The Dalai Lama's face looked distorted on the Jumbo-Tron. His eyes peered from behind a pair of twelve-foot-tall glasses into a crowd of 60,000 people in a football stadium. I sat among the masses, my thighs pinned to a blue plastic seat, waiting for him to speak, straining to see the real thing: a tiny orange figure like a blown leaf on the gridded green field below.

I was working as a reporter in Seattle, covering a five-day conference about compassion. The Dalai Lama was the keynote speaker. At the opening ceremony the day before, local scientists had shown a video about an experiment on toddlers, in which a researcher pretended to smash his own finger with a hammer and then cried out in pain. A two-year-old test subject rushed over and, his eyes rimmed with tears, offered the researcher his teddy bear. At the football stadium, the Dalai Lama was talking about how experiments like this prove that compassion is innate. That it's something we feel before we learn its name, and that as we get older, we must be careful not to let it seep out. The crowd stood and applauded wildly.

I snuck out of the stadium before the presentation was over to catch people on their way out and ask what they thought of the conference, but I was too early. The parking lot was almost empty, except for a handful of security guys and a man passing out pamphlets entitled, "Are you going to Hell?" Toward the exit, two Vietnam vets sat on a patch of grass beside a black portable sound system. They were taking turns reading aloud from a binder, thick as a city phonebook, the names of troops who'd died so far in Iraq and Afghanistan: Cpl. Luke S. Runyan, twenty-one, Spring Grove, Pennsylvania. Lance Cpl. Curtis A. Christensen Jr., twenty-nine, Collingswood, New Jersey. The dull cadence of a macabre graduation.

A few feet away, another vet stood in the shade, swaying to the rhythm of the names. He wore a bandana, dog tags, a white undershirt, and wraparound sunglasses too small for his head. He introduced himself as David and, since it was 2008, we started talking about the election, Obama, and the success of the surge in Iraq. After a while, both of us leaning against a cool cement wall, we started talking about his war. Ron Kovic's war. 'Nam. That thick stretch of jungle between his generation and mine.

"Over there, everything's clearer in a way, you know?" he said. "You're killing or you'll be killed. It's you or me. It's live or die. It's simplicity. I'm not saying everything that happens in a war is O.K., I'm just saying it is what it is."

I asked him if there are things people do in a war, during times of simplicity, that don't seem so simple once they're back home. I didn't have the guts to say "you." Didn't have the guts to ask, "Are there things *you* did that don't seem so simple now? Are there things *you* did that haunt you?" But he understood. He looked me straight in the eyes and then laughed a frayed, humorless laugh.

"Listen, in a war, you do what you have to do to live. You kill people," he said, shrugging. "Do you kill women? Sure.

Do you kill children? If a kid is shooting at you with an AK, do you think you're going to care if his balls haven't dropped? You light him up or he lights you up."

David licked his lips and barked that frayed laugh again. "That sound fucked up to you, girl?"

He looked into my face, like he was waiting for me to say something. To agree with him, or judge him, or exonerate him, or start crying—something. But I just stood there, watching him. Feeling stupid or naïve or angry or, worse, as if I both hated him and understood him completely.

"It's fucked up, but it's magical, too," he said finally, quietly. "Remember that, girlie: fucked-up magical. That's war."

I said goodbye and walked back into the stadium, back into the dark, echoing hallways where I could hear the inflection of earnest speeches still going on inside. I hadn't told David I'd gone to Vietnam a few months earlier. I just couldn't do it. *Hey! I took a little holiday to that nightmare place where not long enough ago, you no doubt watched your friends die. Where maybe you killed children.*

To make it worse, when I'd gone to Vietnam, I'd gone with one of those discount student tour groups that give you photocopies of your itinerary with animated, smiling globes on each page. All twelve of us on the tour had fashionable sunglasses and iPods and the same Lonely Planet guidebook, and we all knew the same things every twenty-something American knows about Vietnam: Rambo, peace signs, "Platoon." The drunk vet on the corner by the pharmacy. "Me love you long time." Our collective memory of the place had been rolled over and over in Hollywood's great, gummy maw so many times, its once-sharp edges had been spit out soft as beach glass. We were hipsters on vacation.

That's not to say that most of us weren't old enough to know someone—an uncle, a friend, a sixth grade teacher—who'd been in the war. The girl sitting next to me on the bus, Jenny, said her dad had been a G.I. there in the late '60s. He hadn't wanted her to visit. Jenny thought it was silly, but I understood. The last time he'd been, it was to kill or be killed.

A few days into the trip, a bunch of us rented motorcycles and drove into the hills near Hue to see the cement-topped bunkers where American soldiers used to sleep. We put our palms against the dirt worn smooth by their bodies, worn smoother by the hands of hordes of visitors like us. Then we took a break to drink Diet Cokes in the shade. "Intermission for wartime nostalgia," I'd written in my notebook. "Vacationing in someone else's hell. Or, worse: wallowing in a stale grief, when kids my age were dying every day—today—in my own generation's wars." Nearby, a little old lady in a conical hat hawked buttons and t-shirts decorated in camouflage and the North Vietnamese star.

That afternoon, I left the group and wandered into a gallery showing photographs of booby traps dug by Viet Cong: deep holes full of sharpened bamboo sticks, covered over with brush. A gallery employee explained that when the Americans ran over the top of them they'd fall in and get skewered. I looked at him. He shifted his weight and smiled the way people smile at a casket. Most of the Vietnamese who sided with the Americans were made social pariahs and forced into poverty after 1975, so this wealthy-looking fifty-something guy in this air-conditioned gallery had probably fought my country. Had he been there? Had he tried to skewer Jenny's dad? Had he killed Americans? Had we killed his family? Who do I apologize to? Did it matter anymore?

A few days later, a friend on the tour and I went walking, and within a few minutes a dozen children had gathered around us, begging for money, hanging on our hands and pulling at our pants, until eventually I yelled, "Enough! Enough!" Most of them scattered, and we could see that behind where they'd been, a grown man, deformed by what was probably

Agent Orange, was resting on his forearms in the street, his spine turned backwards like a scorpion tail, his baby-sized feet dangling above the nape of his neck. I closed my eyes. Enough, I thought. *Enough.*

In the football stadium in Seattle, I'd made my way back to my seat. A new face was on the JumboTron, and swarms of children were parading across the field. I let my mind wander, trying to remember my last night in Saigon when five of us from the tour group found a war-themed nightclub called Apocalypse Now, which our Lonely Planets recommended without irony. Sandbags and barbed wire lined the bar and windows, and the elbow-height cocktail tables were painted to look like chemical weapons barrels. A sign reading "Charlie don't serve" hung over the dance floor, where 300 kids slid against each other in the near-dark, the smell of sweat and alcohol and perfume so thick and the music so loud that we couldn't hear or feel anything but the bass thumping in our stomachs, in our thighs, on the napes of our necks.

The five of us stood to the side of the dance floor, yelling over the music, over a sea of black-haired twenty-somethings, until a Vietnamese kid came over and held out a drink. I took it, and we yelled Tarzan introductions in broken English, pointing at each other's chests. You, Bo. Me, Haley. Three more drinks and I felt his arm slip around my back and pull me into him, onto the dance floor, our stomachs touching, and the room began to spin with music and vodka and the red lights from the bar. The DJ, who looked about fifteen, played a techno remix of Bryan Adams' "Summer of '69," and the surge of kids ebbed and slipped against us, thick and warm with sweat, everyone screaming the lyrics. *Back in the summer of '69. Sixty-nine. Those were the best days of my life.*

In Seattle, when the presentation ended, the crowd stood and applauded. Ushers in aprons walked the aisles, handing out braided string bracelets that we were supposed to tie onto our neighbors' wrists, to remind each other to have compassion for one another. The Dalai Lama waved on the JumboTron, his smile as big as a wall, his palms white, unwrinkled.

I thought about David outside, maybe taking his turn now to read the names of the dead, and about Bo in Saigon. I wondered if David had tried to kill Bo's parents, or if Bo's parents had taken a shot at Jenny's dad, and I wondered which of the hot surge of bodies dancing next to me that night had lost siblings, aunts, uncles, cousins to American bombs? Whose big brother was dead because of us? And how long will it be before my daughter goes dancing in Baghdad? How long before she feels an enemy's son wrap his arms around her, stronger than she thought, pulling her into him, the skin of his forearms slipping down her back with sweat? How long before she experiences the howl and surge of music in some red-lit Baghdad basement? How long before she learns about the fucked up magic of war?

The woman in the row behind me in the stadium touched my arm and I startled, pulled back to the present. She smiled and apologized, embarrassed by the look on my face, and asked if she could tie her string bracelet on me. I offered her my hand.

Haley Sweetland Edwards is a freelance writer based in the Caucasus, where she is learning to drive a Soviet-era jeep and detect the subtle differences between regional homemade vodkas, but not at the same time.

BLAIR BRAVERMAN

🜂 🜂 🜂

I Think I Must Be Beautiful

Making scents of the Namibian Desert.

We were in the desert, and Komungandjera was disgusted with me. She shrugged away from the toddlers pulling at her leather skirt and came over to the bush where I was picking resin. I held out my palm—a few chunks of sap, sticks, and leaves, dried blood from where I'd scraped against thorns—and she plucked the sap with two fingers, like a bird pecking, then knocked the rest away with a slap to my wrist. She turned back to the toddlers, muttering.

Karen began to laugh. "She says you pick sap like a man," she translated. "She says you should stick to counting plants."

I had come to the site of the "Perfume Project" in the Kunene region of northwestern Namibia, where a tribe of Himba women gathered commiphora sap to sell to the European perfume market. Karen, a Namibian biologist of English descent, had founded the project a few years earlier. I was staying with her at a place called Marble Campground, which was nearly empty. A low mountain marked the edge of the nearby Himba village, from which the women came every morning, walking barefoot or riding stocky, thick-furred donkeys.

The entrance to the campground was framed by two white granite monoliths, moon-bright and alien in this dusty landscape. They were remainders from when this place housed a marble quarry, a Chinese-funded project abandoned when the village's single access road proved too rutty for the granite to be transported over. This made sense to me: it had taken me eight hours to make the one-hundred-twenty-mile drive from Opuwo, the nearest city, including two stops for popped tires and multiple breaks to allow elephants, giraffes, and oryx to cross the road at their leisure. The land was channeled with dry streambeds, like the markings left after a tide has rushed out.

When I'd arrived at the campground in early evening, a young woman met me at the entrance, introducing herself as Anna, the manager. Anna was from the Herero tribe, an ethnic group that split off from the Himba generations ago, "modernizing" with the first colonialists. She wore jeans and a short, slick-straight wig, and carried a ragged *Glamour* magazine in one hand, her thumb tucked in to mark a page. She led me down a path to a clearing busy with people.

In the center of the clearing, five Himba women sat quietly on a blanket, pressed together, their bodies coated in traditional ochre-red paint. Three of them clutched infants to their breasts. Their color bled indistinguishably from body to body, skin to leather to fabric, as if the group were a single sculpture carved from red stone. Only the whites of their eyes stood out. The women spoke their names one by one, then introduced their leader and spokesperson, Komungandjera. While the other women smiled, Komungandjera glared, at times sighing dramatically. She wore a blanket wrapped around her pregnant belly and frequently used the edge of it to swat the other women.

The Himba were preparing dinner—cornmeal porridge and spicy bean stew served from a cast-iron cauldron big enough to hold a goat—and invited me to join them. As I ate, I watched the others in the clearing. I noticed a conspicuous lack of men; what few there were wore Western clothing, track shorts and worn tanks. They seemed to come from a different world than their painted wives and mothers. Later I would learn that of all the Namibian tribes—except perhaps the Bushmen—it was the Himba who most retained their traditional way of life. Karen thought this was because of the culture's respect for women, and the rights it afforded them.

"Think about it," she said. "Why would the women stop painting themselves, put on Western clothes? The moment they enter so-called modern society, they go from being first to second-class citizens."

When I'd finished my bowl of stew, Anna came to sit beside me. We smiled shyly at each other. I felt like a child at a dinner party, seeking out others my same age, grateful and relieved to find one. "You live here?" I asked. It was a stupid question, and I blushed.

Anna didn't seem to notice. She turned and pointed to a small stone building behind a cluster of mopane trees. "This is my home," she said. "Just me. And your home?"

I pointed to my tent. It was small in the distance, barely visible. After several months of traveling, it did feel like home.

"It is not often," Anna swallowed, as if trying out the phrase, "that an American's home is smaller than my home." She laughed suddenly and patted my shoulder. "I think this means we are meant to be friends."

The local chief wandered over to us. He was tall and wore a long blue skirt, and he frowned and gestured to Anna's *Glamour*—which I noticed was over two years old. She handed it to him quickly. The chief flipped through the magazine, pausing at an article on Angelina Jolie, then again at "The Best Coats for Fall!" He rubbed his chin, handed back the magazine with a slightly pained expression on his face, and flashed me a quick smile before meandering off.

Later, as I set up my tent, Anna watched from a distance. When I waved at her she lifted a hand in return, then turned and entered the stone shed that served as the campground's headquarters. "How long will you stay here?" she had asked me over dinner, in rough English, and when I told her, she grinned. "Two weeks?" she said. "But you should stay forever!"

The Himba women got their color from a fragrant mixture of powdered ochre, butter, and commiphora sap. They blended the mixture in a hollow cow's horn, melting the butter with hot coals. With this they painted their skin, hair, babies, belongings—their whole world a sepia photograph. I'd heard theories about it protecting from the sun, or perhaps masking body odor, but it seemed to me that the paint's primary function—as with much of the Himba women's traditional costume—was to be beautiful. Their hair was woven into cords, coated with the ochre mixture so that each cord seem wrapped in leather, and the paint was so thick on their scalps that it cracked into pieces like an eggshell. Some of the women wore headdresses, and stacked layers of metal beads around their necks, wrists, and ankles.

The perfume project was Karen's idea. She was working for the Namibian organization Integrated Rural Development and Nature Conservation (IRDNC), studying traditional plant uses, when she noticed the women collecting commiphora sap for their own perfumes and thought there might be a market for it. Before starting the project, she taught herself rudimentary Otjihimba—the Himba's language—and organized community groups, spoke to the women, tried to determine their needs. She said it was easy to form a friendship with them. "It doesn't matter the culture," she told me. "Women can always make friends if they talk about jewelry or babies."

Or commiphora, apparently, about which the Himba are passionate. Commiphora plants are stocky, low-lying bushes that bleed fragrant resin from cuts in their bark. In northern Africa, related plants include the biblical myrrh, frankincense, and the "balm of Gilead." Although there are dozens of commiphora in Namibia, the Himba's preferred species is Commiphora Wildii, what they call *omumbiri*.

The sap is produced during the dry season, a time when there is little else to be done—or to eat—in Kunene. In 2007, the first commercial year of the project, 319 Himba, mostly women, gathered five tons of omumbiri sap, with each ton valued at ten thousand dollars. At Karen's insistence, the gatherers were paid immediately for their work; IRDNC offices were not allowed to accept resin unless they had cash on hand. All end profits, too, went to communities, or toward supplies for the project itself.

"Since the omumbiri started," an elder remarked, "we don't need to borrow food from our neighbors. If we are hungry today, we can go and harvest and get money, and tonight we can buy food."

Karen was short and wore oversized black t-shirts and hiking sandals; her curly blond hair looked fastened to her head as an afterthought. She was, quite possibly, the last person you might expect to work in the perfume industry. But she'd managed to sell the omumbiri to major European cosmetics companies, including Estee Lauder, marketing it as "Namibian Myrrh."

Unlike myrrh, though, the scent wasn't sharp. She described it as a mixture of citrus and pepper, with a hint of pine. The first time I rubbed a ball of sap between my fingers, I was struck by its stickiness; it seemed like once on the skin, it could never be fully removed. It smelled like lemons and saltwater and soil.

On my second day in Orupembe, I took a walk in the afternoon, a time when most of the others had retreated into shaded tents and awnings to wait out the sun's worst. After twenty minutes or so, I came to the Himba village. Huts were scattered loosely in a sandy plain, domes made of mud and sticks with occasional pieces of cardboard, PVC pipe, or plastic bags. A few sparse grasses grew, but mostly there was just dirt, packed with the layered prints of bare feet and donkey hooves. The plain was empty but for a little boy of around two, playing in the dirt by the roadside. When he saw me, I waved. The boy froze for a moment, staring, then ran into the nearest hut.

I stopped walking, startled. The boy was right: this wasn't my place. I remembered something Karen had mentioned—rules the Himba have about passing between a fire pit and a house, and the proper way to approach a chief's home—and decided it was wise to turn around.

As I did I heard a voice calling, "Hey, hello!" I paused. Anna ducked out of one of the huts, waving. She was carrying a large box of powdered soup mix. I took one side of it, and we started back toward Marble Campground together.

Anna wanted to talk about boys. Was I married? I was not; no, definitely not. I was twenty, I said. I didn't even have a boyfriend.

"I had a boyfriend," said Anna. "Four years. When I was eighteen he came to my mother and said he would like to marry. He was Herero and older than me. He was handsome."

"What happened?"

"He died in Khorixas. He was hit by a truck." She said this apologetically, as if informing me of a minor inconvenience.

"Now," she continued, "I think I will wait some years, until I am twenty-three or twenty-four. I want to be like an American girl. I don't want a husband yet." She laughed suddenly. "The Himba women, they feel so sorry for you! They think you are—that you cannot have babies. They think no man wants you, and your life is, what, a sorrow. And you are so far from home."

This stopped me for a moment. Out of all the emotions the Himba might have felt toward me—indifference, curiosity, even resentment—I had never considered pity.

"They do not understand how you are so alone," Anna continued. "I agree with them. I could never be so far from my mother."

"Where does your mother live?"

"In Opuwo. I had to leave her to work here, but it is worth it. Because maybe here I can become permanent staff."

By now we'd reached the campground. We dropped the box at the office, and then Anna invited me to her home. It was a single room, maybe six by ten feet, and the walls were covered with pages from fashion magazines—women in dresses, men with thumbs tucked into their jeans, clothing and perfume advertisements. A cot with a mosquito net was pressed against one wall, and an open Bible rested on the pillow. Anna pulled a few photos from a pile of papers in the corner, handling them delicately. Here was a little girl beside an older woman; here a young man in a Tupac shirt; here Anna standing in a heavy Victorian dress, beaming under a cow-horn headdress. "That is my Herero costume," she explained, "what I am to be married in." The dress was orange with black markings, like a cat's stripes, and I asked her if that meant something.

Anna frowned. "I don't know," she said. "I think it means that I love Jesus."

Just then there was a commotion, voices. We stepped outside to find that Karen had bought a goat, and the Himba were gathered around it for slaughter. It was dead by the time we reached it, hanging by its back ankles from a tree. One of the men skinned it quickly, spread the skin beneath the body, then slashed the stomach with a knife and released the organs, which puddled like jelly on the bloody side of the skin.

Anna clasped my hand in excitement. "Meat is my favorite food," she said, "except for macaroni." Then she hurried into the crowd of Himba and was gone.

The Himba had their own system of classification for the commiphora plants. What I learned by Latin name—C. Anacardifolia, C. Crenato-Serrata, C. Multijuga—they called omutuya, omuhanga, omuzumba. That is, they had names for species that were of use to them; anything else they called omunbungu, the "Tree of the Hyena."

This wasn't the only case where Himba and Western names differed. Those Himba who worked closely with foreigners tended to adopt their own English names; Karen said that when she first came to Kunene, her three guides were named Capacity, Ability, and Never Lose. "And of course, with them on my team, the projects turned out splendidly," she recalled. "How could they not have?"

Karen had hopes for one of the omunbungus. Last year a professional "nose" had come to Orupembe, a man sent by the perfume industry to evaluate the region's scents. He walked past one of the hyena trees, a type known for its awful stench, and paused; he leaned down, sniffed, and scooped a gob of sap onto his fingertip. He smelled it, his face expressionless. Then he reached into his pocket and pulled out an orange peel from earlier that day, upon which he wiped the sap. This time, when he sniffed it, he smiled.

"It was remarkable," Karen remembered. "It smelled . . . amazing. Somehow he just knew, knew that the orange peel would bring it out."

The Himba were perplexed when Karen expressed interest in the hyena tree. But they humored her, as an adult humors a child's illogical requests, by collecting a sample. The perfume industry liked it. Now, to the Himba's bemusement, Karen wanted to know whether an omunbungu harvest, like the omumbiri's, would be sustainable.

While Karen and I counted omunbungus, the Himba women collected resin. Komungandjera was in charge; she would gather the women and speak to them, pointing to assign their routes. She still never smiled, but she seemed less angry now; maybe it was just her manner. Karen handed out bags—a few younger women protested when handed burlap, sulking until Karen gave them a woven plastic bag instead, a type they could later unravel and braid into jewelry—and they scattered, silent and barefoot on the hot sand. Every now and then I'd come across one, crouched by an omumbiri, plucking hardened drops of sap from the tangled branches. One woman, carrying a tiny baby on her back, pulled an umbrella from somewhere in her skirt and opened it for shade. The umbrella, too, was coated in ochre; there was a hint of plaid pattern underneath it, but unless you saw it at the right angle, you'd never even notice.

We went camping in the desert, the Namib desert, with the Himba women. Anna wasn't pleased; she had to stay behind to work, and made me promise we wouldn't be gone more than a few days. We drove in two trucks, and Karen brought her car, a Toyota. She didn't offer seats to the Himba. "They know how I feel about paint on my seats," she said. The Himba didn't seem to mind: they climbed cheerfully into the back of the trucks, clutching one or two babies each, and as the engines started several more women came running and clambered aboard.

Three hours later we pulled into a dry riverbed and pitched tents, started a fire. As dusk fell the Himba joined us around it, speaking animatedly to each other. One of the women stood up and began shouting, beating the air with her hands, and two others rose to calm her; they took her shoulders, whispering and stroking her arms until she sat down again. Karen translated quietly. A child had died that morning in the village, a small boy bitten by a snake. In the past few weeks, a law had been passed that all deaths must be reported to the government. To do this would mean a long journey by donkey cart to Opuwo, to reach the government offices there. Some of the women were inclined to oblige. What point is there? the others argued. By what authority does the government make these rules? We owe them nothing. Let us bury him here. Let us do it our way.

When the stars came out, the sky seemed made of static, a million shimmering pieces, as much light as there was dark. It curved overhead, and the smoke rose up and spread to fill it. The Himba took off their jewelry and hung it on a tree, and the babies wandered around in the dark. I slept outside in my sleeping bag and woke up soaked with fog.

In the morning, the women sat around the fire and played with each other's hair, smoothing ochre around each thick cord while the babies picked their noses and stared at the flames. Last night's argument seemed forgotten. The women giggled often; sometimes a single word would set them off. They touched each other constantly.

Back at Marble Campground, Anna was excited. She'd been approved to attend a two-week training course in Sesfontein for wilderness guides. Out of twenty participants, she was the only woman accepted, possibly the first woman ever to do this. If she graduated, the certification would allow her to apply for a promotion—a chance to become, as she said, "permanent." And on the way there, she'd be able to stop in Opuwo and visit her mother.

"I want to take you somewhere," she told me.

We set off in the late afternoon. She led me up a trail, around the skirt of a low hill, past the edge of the campground. Along the way we walked through the Himba's clearing, the place where they rested between commiphora expeditions. There was a small hut and a fire pit and the same large cauldron we'd eaten from the first night. The Himba were gathered around the cauldron, eating porridge with their fingers. They hooted as we approached, calling to Anna, offering porridge and juice. One little girl came up and took hold of my wrists, pulling me toward the others. When she let go, there were perfect red handprints on my skin. Anna linked her arm through mine and pulled me closer.

One of the women stood up and spoke vehemently, waving her arms. There was a moment of silence, and then everyone began to howl. Anna translated, laughing. "She says I will lose you in the quarry, because your skin will not show against the white rocks."

We continued on, the sun low in the sky behind us. As we rounded a hill, the quarry appeared, brilliant white against the yellow-brown of the hillside. It looked as if an enormous mouth had taken a bite from the base of the mountain, leaving gnawed-off blocks of white rocks, sharp edges, tiered ledges leading down and around the cavern. The marble faces were cool even in the sun, cut perfectly flat and surprisingly rough, like fine sandpaper. Little chips were scattered about, glistening. Anna pressed her cheek against the rock wall, closing her eyes. I walked along the bottom ledge, then climbed to a higher one. I had never seen anything so bright.

Anna climbed up beside me, and we sat in the shade of one of the walls. We were silent for a while. "Someday," she said suddenly, "I would like a cat." She pushed a chip of marble around with the tip of one finger, flicking it away and pulling it back again. Then she said, "I think I must be beautiful."

"You are beautiful," I said.

"That's what *they* say," she said, after a moment. "The men who come here. Men from—England, Germany, I don't know where. They come with their wives."

She was sitting very still. We both were.

"Sometimes," she said, "they want to—" she stopped.

"What do you do?" I said, careful to keep my voice neutral.

"I tell them—" she cleared her throat and tried again. "I tell them I have a boyfriend."

The pebble had rolled too far for her to reach. I stood up and brought it back for her, then sat down again. She took it and flicked it some more. Shelf by shelf, the quarry was falling into shadow.

"Anna," I said quietly. "Then what happens?"

She didn't answer. I thought about the pictures on her walls, the women in ball gowns, bikinis, designer jeans. The jewelry advertisements, the perfume. I thought what it might mean, to be admired by a man from the same world as the magazines come from. *My* world.

Before we left the quarry, I pulled a notebook from my bag and we exchanged addresses. Anna's was care of the Marble Campground's post office box in Opuwo. "Tell me when you become permanent," I said. Anna squeezed my hand.

"My real name is Wakakomba," she said.

On our way back to the campground, we passed a group of women talking excitedly on the path. One of them said something to Anna, who shrieked.

"Did you hear?" she said to me. "Komungandjera has had a baby! A boy. Her sixth!"

She turned back to the women and opened her arms, a question. Where was it? The nearest woman pointed down the trail, toward the village. She called out to the group, and as one they turned in that direction, half-skipping in their haste. Several of the women waved goodbye, but they did not slow down.

"He is home in the village," said Anna. "With his mother. A boy!"

We came to the place where the path split, and after a hug we separated, Anna toward the stone shed and me toward the tents. It was dark now. A light wind rustled the mopane trees by the office and carried with it the sound of a donkey braying. When I passed the barrels where the omumbiri was kept, the air seemed to grow warmer. It took me a moment, but eventually I found it: the slightest, drifting scent of lemons and salt.

Blair Braverman is an MFA candidate at the University of Iowa's Nonfiction Writing Program. Her writing has appeared in Orion, Agni, High Country News*, and other publications. She has worked as a dogsled guide in Norway and Alaska, a naturalist in Colorado, and a mapmaker in Maine.*

ॐ ॐ ॐ

Passion and Pizza

A slice of seduction in Buenos Aires.

"I can't take you anywhere, because my favorite restaurant is there." The pot-bellied *taxista* with the silver hair pointed across the intersection, where three plastic pigs danced on top of a sign that read "*Los Chanchitos*." The Little Porkers.

"Get in," he said. "I'll drive you."

It was silly for him to wrestle his cab across the street when I could easily walk, but I got in anyway. I looked at the pair of sky-blue baby shoes hanging from the rearview mirror. The *taxista* wasn't flirting with me. He was just being kind.

"I don't want to cheat you," he said, making a U-turn and braking in front of the restaurant. "Go in and have a great lunch."

I wished Liliana were with me when the *taxista* refused the pesos I offered him. A few days earlier, over coffee at Café La Paz, when I told my Argentine tango mentor that I was getting into random cabs and asking drivers to take me to their favorite restaurants, she tore off the end of a *medialuna*-croissant and shook it in my face. "*Taxistas* are the biggest cheats in Buenos Aires!" she said, "They'll drive you in circles, or rob you, or rape you, maybe even take you someplace dangerous."

Perhaps she was right. So far I'd only taken a few taxi adventures, and maybe I was just lucky nothing horrible had happened. But when the silver-haired *taxista* shooed me out of his cab and into "The Little Porkers," where the pancetta-wrapped pepper steak was so tender I could cut it with a butter knife, I felt it was more than luck. We were dealing in trust.

Months later, I was looking for a cab at the corner of Diagonal Norte, near the mad midday traffic around the *Obelisco* in downtown Buenos Aires, wondering where I was going to eat lunch. Buses wheezed by, mopeds wove between the Fiats and Renaults on Avenida 9 de Julio, and I could hear the drums of a workers' protest getting closer when a taxi stopped in front of me. I climbed in.

The last thing I wanted was an *aventura* with another Argentine. After the fling with Joaquín ended, I carried my disappointment all over the city: I didn't know where he ended and Buenos Aires began. As predictable as the end was, as stupid as I'd been to believe Joaquín would keep calling me—who ever heard of a sustainable relationship with a tango teacher?—I still felt sliced in half.

I glanced at the cab driver. His eyelashes were so long they brushed against the lenses of his sunglasses. Even if this *taxista* was the most beautiful man I'd seen in a city full of beautiful men, I told myself the only thing I was interested in was his food. If he had to leave Buenos Aires tomorrow, I asked him, where would he eat today?

"Aren't you going to invite me to eat with you?" he said.

I rolled up the window. There are few things more dangerous than a man who's well aware of how good-looking he is, except maybe an Argentine man who's well aware of how good-looking he is.

"Only if it's lunch and nothing else," I said.

"No kisses?" He turned down the techno on the radio.

"No kisses," I shook my head.

"Not even a kiss on the cheek?"

"*Mirá*," I said. I wanted my heart to slow down, and I wanted to stop blushing, but that only made me start to sweat. "This is how it's going to be. You take me to your favorite restaurant. We have lunch. I take the bus home. You drive away in your taxi. And that's it."

"So it has to be on your terms?" he asked.

"Yep," I said.

"Then I don't accept."

I laughed. I was tempted. I was flattered that the *taxista* with the Johnny Depp cheekbones wanted me, even though I tried to remind myself that flirtation was a fact of life in Buenos Aires. The cab driver was no different from the bureaucrats at the immigration office or the dentist who'd given me a root canal. If I wanted to keep from repeating my mistake with Joaquín, I had to learn to handle seduction the way Liliana embraced sweet talk from her tango partners at the *milonga*: "Lie to me," she said. "I like it."

"Once I picked up this redhead near the casino," the *taxista* began, ignoring a red light on Avenida Córdoba. "She was about forty. *Belleza*. We got to talking, I invited her for coffee. We ended up at my house, in the shower, didn't come out until dinner the next day. I took her to La Taberna de Roberto—"

"Oh, yeah! I know that place," I said. "It's great!"

The *taxista* went on uninterrupted. So I listened to his stories of his conquests—he'd met most of his girlfriends, and other men's girlfriends, in his cab. I was hungry—my stomach had begun growling when we'd started our journey, and now I was in that dangerous, hypoglycemic zone that's the reason I always try to pack a snack in my purse. I was also confused about why such a beautiful man felt he needed to go over his sexual resume, wishing he would try to seduce me some other way. *Lie to me*, I thought, *I need it*.

We crossed Avenida Rivadavia. The asphalt ended and the cab bounced over the cobblestones. I felt the same vertigo

I experienced every time I started to tango: I didn't know where I was going or how I was going to get there, and I was leaving it all up to a stranger.

"Have you ever had a one-night stand?" the *taxista* asked.

"That's something you'll never know."

"Oh, come on! That's not fair. This is an even exchange, isn't it?"

"I'm guessing you've had a few?" I said.

"Of course."

"So your taxi is literally your vehicle to love," I said.

"Love? No, no, no. Passion, maybe. But not love."

We were in Boedo now, on the south side of Buenos Aires, where abandoned factories faced soot-covered houses. I still didn't know where we were going. I didn't like the uncertainty, but I had to contend with it. Now I was in a neighborhood I didn't know, and I was starving.

"Do you like pizza?" he asked.

"Yes, I love pizza. Yes."

He stopped the taxi on the corner of Avenida Boedo and Juan de Garay, in front of a pizzeria called "San Antonio." There was a life-sized painting of a halo-topped, brown-robed, pizza-bearing saint on the window. Behind the saint, the restaurant was full.

"Are you sure you don't want me to come with you?"

"Well . . ." I wasn't sure.

"At least let me kiss you," he took off his sunglasses. His eyes were hazel, a lighter shade than Joaquín's.

"By the way, I'm Hernán."

If I started to kiss Hernán, I reasoned, I wouldn't be able to stop, and I'd become the brown-haired gringa he told his next conquest about. Also, if I started to kiss him, I'd have to wait who knows how long before I could eat his pizza.

"I'm Layne," I said, quickly shaking his hand, "You know, like Luisa Lane. Superman's girlfriend?"

He grinned.

"You don't want to kiss me," I said. "I'm too much trouble for you."

"What? You have a boyfriend?"

"Yes."

"I don't believe you."

"You're right," I said, "but believe me when I say I'm too much trouble for you."

I handed him ten pesos and climbed out of the taxi.

"Wait!" he called, "Luisa! What about your phone number?"

I shook my head, staring at him as he leaned out of the passenger-side window, trying to memorize the sculpture of his face—the Roman nose, the dimpled chin, the double curve in his upper lip. I blew him a kiss, then turned around and walked into the pizzeria.

I was still thinking about Hernán's eyelashes when I squeezed into the only free seat and studied the menu on the wall. Like most *pizzerias de barrio*, San Antonio's pies fused Italian pizza-making techniques with the Argentine preference for puffy dough and excessive cheese. *Fugazzetta*—a Buenos Aires staple that was invented in the late 1800s when local pizza makers added heaps of mozzarella to the focaccia that their Genovese ancestors brought across the Atlantic— was what I noticed on most people's plates. There were two men at the bar, bald spots gleaming under fluorescent lights, eating their *fugazzetta* with slices of *fainá* – chickpea flat bread—stacked on top.

A server in a thin white dress shirt shared a joke with the beer-drinking retirees at the table next door before he took my order. He returned minutes later with a piece of *fugazzetta* and a slice of *fainá*. Individually, neither was anything special. But together, the *fugazzetta*—a mound of melted mozzarella and a pile of sliced onions on an inch-thick crust—and *fainá*—garbanzo bean flour and olive oil baked into a dense slice—made a delicious combination. Chickpeas checked the richness of the cheese. Onions, oven-roasted and paper-thin, added a strong, sweet accent.

I watched the neighborhood come and go as I ate my lunch. The retirees nursed their beers, studied the soccer scores in the *Clarín*, and pretended not to notice me. Young couples fed toddlers who couldn't sit still. Teenagers in school uniforms schlepped stacks of twine-bound boxes of pizza to go. I spotted a sign between a pair of thirsty philodendrons: the pizzeria had been there for more than sixty years.

I was almost finished with my *fugazzetta* and still wondering whether I'd been an idiot to turn down Hernán's proposition—I couldn't deny that the attraction was mutual. It was only for a ride, but he'd distracted me from the pain of Joaquín. And after all my doubts about where he might take me, the *taxista* had led me to this spot. I felt like I was on the inside in this slow old neighborhood. A wooden statue of San Antonio watched over the dining room from a shelf above a plastic Pepsi sign. I stared at the pile of mozzarella and the tangle of onions on my plate, glad I had a few bites left.

Layne Mosler is a writer who did restaurant reconnaissance and danced tango in Buenos Aires for nearly four years before moving to New York City to drive a taxi. This story is an excerpt from Driving Hungry, *forthcoming in 2014, a book based on her taxigourmet.com blog.*

LAUREN QUINN

⁊⁊⁊ ⁊⁊⁊ ⁊⁊⁊

Bones Surfacing in the Dirt

The cost of ammunition is not included.

I watched the boy move. Thin, dark, in tattered pants and flip-flops, he walked slowly along the river's steep embankment. He carried a wooden spear, his eyes hunting the small black birds that flitted from crevices in the cement.

It was dusk on my first day in Phnom Penh, exercise hour along the gleaming new riverside. Men in running shoes swung their arms in circles; couples played badminton; elderly women in sun visors lifted their arms in unison, mimicking the aerobic instructor's movements. Behind them the orange sky struck the Royal Palace into silhouette. Its decorative roofing rose from the spires like snakes, twisting like incense smoke. Around me, people smiled.

It didn't feel like a city that had been deserted.

That's all I'd been able to think that first day, walking through streets exploded with the yellows and purples of flowering trees. I tried to imagine it the way the parents of my childhood best friend had left it, as the Khmer Rouge marched into the city and evacuated its two million residents: burned-out carcasses of cars, buildings crumbled, rubbish strewn across empty streets. I couldn't.

I sat drinking a papaya shake when I spied the boy along the embankment. I watched as he approached a bird. A swift stab, a flurry of wings. He brought the stick toward his face, plucked the creature from its spear. He pressed his thumb against its throat and pushed in slow, hard strokes.

Then he placed the small black body in his pocket—a ragged strip of cloth—and continued walking, repeating, repeating.

It wasn't so much the action of it that unsettled me; it was the slowness with which he did it—the calm.

He continued along the steep slope beneath the riverside's bustle, stabbing and gathering.

"It took four people to die for me to be born."

My best friend Lynn and I were sitting on her bedroom floor, in a little yellow house that flinched every time a bus passed. We were nine years old, coloring and eating crushed ice, sun-sleepy from another day spent at the public swimming pool down the block.

Lynn's comment came out of nowhere. She counted them out. First, on her index finger, her mother Lu's first husband had to die. Then, bending back two fingers at once, Lu's children, the two that came before Lynn and her brother Sam— they had to die too. On her pinkie, her father Seng's daughter.

Another daughter had already died, before the war. Sometimes that other daughter had died because of suicide, because Seng hadn't allowed her to marry the man she'd loved. Other times, that daughter had died because the man Seng had been tricked into allowing her to marry had killed her. I don't remember which it was that day, just that neither that daughter nor Seng's first wife got a finger.

Those were the conditions that created Lynn. If those half-brothers and -sisters and a former husband hadn't died, her parents wouldn't have been arranged to be married. They wouldn't have walked across Cambodia to escape; Seng wouldn't have dragged Lu, pregnant, through a waist-deep river in the middle of a monsoon; Lynn's brother Sam

wouldn't have been born in a Thai refugee camp and Lynn
later in a farmhouse without heat in northern New York,
where the people who'd sponsored their family forced them
to live and work until they escaped to Oakland, California.

It was a simple statement, as concrete and non-debatable
as the date of one's birth. We'd done a family tree project that
year in school; I remember looking over at Lynn's. After two
sturdy branches of "Lu" and "Seng," the tree turned to thin,
wispy branches, then nothing. She'd finished the assignment
early and stared off, looking bored.

I counted them with Lynn, looked down at my fingers.
"Four people," I repeated. There wasn't anything else to say,
so we went back to coloring.

Lynn's room had two doors, one to the living room and one
to the hallway. We always shut them both. We locked them
sometimes, too—it felt safer that way.

"So everyone you see here," Cindy looked out from the *tuk-
tuk* onto the bustle of the dusty road, "who's over the age of
thirty-five lived through the war?"

I nodded.

"God. It's hard to imagine. Every single person . . ."

Cindy and I were traveling out of the city center. The pavement gave way to dirt, sidewalks to mud puddles, as we made
our way closer to the Killing Fields.

I'd just met Cindy. She was a fellow travel writer, passing through Phnom Penh on her way to Siem Reap. We'd
arranged to meet up and spend an afternoon together.

I could relate to her observation: my first few days in the
city, all I'd been able to think about was the war. I'd come to
Cambodia looking for answers. I wanted to understand the
war, the Khmer Rouge, and everything else that had never
been openly discussed in Lynn's family. I sensed it was a kind
of key, the beginning of a story I'd walked in on halfway, a

story Lynn and her brother Sam—and perhaps an entire generation—had also walked in on halfway.

Our *tuk-tuk* rattled along the unsteady pavement, taking us closer to the mass-grave and execution site, one of Phnom Penh's two main tourist attractions. The other was the Tuol Sleng Genocide Museum, the former S-21 torture prison under the Khmer Rouge. All the travel agencies along the riverside advertised for tours of the two, sometimes combined with a trip to a shooting range where travelers could fire AK-47s left over from the war (cost of ammunition not included).

Most travelers stayed in Phnom Penh only long enough to see S-21 and the Killing Fields, then they scattered from the city. It was what Cindy was doing, and what I would have too, had I not come searching for answers. I'd been putting off visiting the Killing Fields, not wanting, I'd rationalized, to spend the $12 *tuk-tuk* fare venturing out solo. Cindy offered an opportunity to split the cost—but more than that, she offered companionship, and a buffer.

Without buildings to block it, the wind grew stronger, and I blinked bits of dust and debris from my contact lenses. By the time we pulled into the dirt lot in front of the Killing Fields, stinging tears blurred my vision.

"This happens every day here," I laughed, and dabbed my eyes.

The Killing Fields were set in a peaceful country landscape, with birds chirping and the echo of children singing from a nearby grammar school. Incense burned in front of the bone pagoda, where skulls were separated into tiers by age. We walked past ditches that had been mass graves, trees against which guards had bludgeoned children. None of it seemed real.

A sign told us that when it rained, bits of victims' bones and scraps of their clothing still surfaced through the dirt, more than thirty years later. As we walked, we kept seeing faded pieces of cloth, half exposed in the earth.

Groups of Westerners in cargo shorts and sun hats wandered through the lot with clasped hands and concerned expressions. I saw only two Cambodians—young monks with round faces, their orange robes blazing against the brown earth.

After about an hour, we exited the front gates. Dark-skinned men leaned against their bikes, chatted in the shade, napped quietly in the backs of their *tuk-tuks* as they waited for their fares to return. Many of them, I thought, looked over thirty-five.

I remember laughing.

Not a funny laugh but a *you-have-got-to-be-fucking-kidding-me* laugh. Beside me on the foldout bed, my duffel bag was still packed.

It was the end of my first semester at university, and I'd just returned from my grandmother's funeral on the East Coast. I'd sat down on my bed, turned my cell phone on for the first time in five days, and listened to a string of messages, vague and urgent, from Lynn, Sam, other childhood friends: "Something happened." "Can you call us?"

"What is it?" my roommate asked.

"The parents of my childhood best friend died while I was gone," I told her, staring at my phone. I closed my eyes as I said, "Her dad shot her mom, then himself."

"Oh my God," was all Rose said.

I walked out of our dorm room and roamed up and down the hall's thin carpeting, a muffle of hip-hop and the smell of Nag Champa leaking from behind the doors, shaking my head and half-laughing. Friends poked their heads out of their rooms and asked me what was wrong; I told them. I didn't yet have the distance I'd develop in the following days.

"They died in a domestic violence dispute," I'd say, which was softer, more detached. In the hall that night, I kept saying, "He shot her, he shot her," and people backed away—unsure, I guess, of how to respond.

At some point, I finally stopped walking and stood still at the end of the hall. I slid open the window and breathed the sharp December air. I looked out at the quiet bustle—students carrying books, standing around smoking in the dim light and fog. I realized I wasn't surprised.

I remembered strange things about Lynn's house: footsteps at night, insomniac murmurings from down the hallway. In the weeks to come, more specific memories would return. Bruises across Sam's shins; how Seng would hit him there because it wouldn't show; an image of Seng—pointing at something, screaming, a flash in his eyes and a glint off his silver tooth.

"My dad might be moving back to Cambodia," I remembered Lynn leaning in, an excited whisper. "He could start his business again, and live over there, and we'd stay here. Like, maybe in six months." I remembered us sitting cross-legged on the bedroom floor; us lying on our bellies on the swimming pool deck; us standing amid the morning glories waiting for our turn on the monkey bars.

And I remembered the hallway—the muffled sound of heavy things moving, coming from behind a locked door, when I'd gotten up in the middle of the night to use the bathroom. It had scared me, made me afraid to get up to pee—afraid of that narrow hallway with its mirror at the end.

"I just didn't think it was that bad," we'd all say, in the days and weeks to come. But even then, no one would say what it was that had made us think it was bad to begin with. Had we all observed little things—bruises and passing comments—that we'd dismissed, ignored, convinced ourselves we'd made up and eventually forgotten?

I didn't remember any of it that night, the night I got the news—when I pressed my head against the mesh screen on the third floor of the dorms, stared out of the window, and tried to breathe. All there was that night was a vague sense, like the uneasy feeling you sometimes have waking up from a dream, and the words I kept repeating: "He shot her, he shot her."

"What do you think of how the Khmer Rouge is taught to the next generation?"

The question came in a French accent. A standing-room-only crowd had come out to the German-run Meta House cultural center for the screening of *Enemies of the People*—"the best documentary to be made about the Khmer Rouge," Meta House's director had assured us, "because it is the only one to be made by a Cambodian."

I counted five Khmer faces in the crowd, none of whom had stayed for the Q&A session with Cambodian director Thet Sambath.

Sambath paused after the question, smiled that bashful Cambodian smile. "This I don't know so much about," he carefully evaded. "I know for many years, Khmer Rouge history was not taught in the schools."

The audience was nodding. With nearly three-quarters of the population born post-war—the so-called "new generation"—formal curricula about war history had been conspicuously missing from the schools for thirty years.

"In the beginning, it was still very sensitive," a young Cambodian had explained to me. "How do you talk about it—especially with Khmer Rouge still in the country, in the government?"

Over the years, that initial avoidance of the subject had deepened into a de facto silence. Young people were left to piece together what they learned from their parents, which often wasn't much.

A massive disconnect formed. Many of the new generation began to doubt the Khmer Rouge even happened. They suspected that their parents were exaggerating.

"How could Khmer people kill other Khmer people like that?" challenged a teenager interviewed in a documentary I'd watched. His mother sat behind him, looking away.

I was shocked. These were young people living in Cambodia, amid the physical and psychological evidence: mass graves and landmines, astronomical rates of post-traumatic stress disorder, and their own absent family members.

"It's time for Cambodia to dig a hole and bury the past," Cambodian Prime Minister Hun Sen, himself a former low-ranking Khmer Rouge, famously stated. Westerners often used this quote to exemplify the culture of silence around the war in Cambodia. Hillary Clinton cited it after a 2010 visit, when she urged the country to continue with the Khmer Rouge trials, because "a country that is able to confront its past is a country that can overcome it."

I'd read Clinton's statement and nodded, thinking of my own attempts to understand the things I had been through, what I'd witnessed in Lynn's family.

"But, since 2009," Sambath continued carefully, "there is now a textbook for high schools just on the Khmer Rouge. This is very good." He paused again. "But I think this is not enough."

I thought of the entire section at Monument Books, the high-end, air-conditioned expat bookstore, dedicated to Khmer Rouge histories and memoirs. I thought: no, it's not enough.

I was walking out of the market, poised to dodge motorbikes with arms full of bananas and plastic bags of fish, when the smell struck me.

A particular kind of incense, thick and ancient smelling, wafted from the wats and streetside altars in Phnom Penh.

Obscured behind the jumble of market umbrellas, I'd forgotten that I was right beside the enormous Wat Ounalom. I stopped, blinking my eyes as the memory billowed back.

Lynn's parents' funeral was held in East Oakland, a faded funeral home with two stray bullet holes in the street-facing window. I went through the ceremony in a daze, coming away with only a handful of images: Lynn smiling, greeting us casually in the entryway as though we'd come over for dinner; Sam crying at the podium as he read lyrics of an R. Kelly song.

Old Cambodian women, hunched in their thin Chinatown blouses, rocked slightly and muttered to each other in the pews. Young Cambodian-Americans in baseball caps and baggy jeans talked on cellphones in the back and kept reaching into deep pockets as if to dig for items they never pulled out. A mix of Americans, parents from other families we'd grown up with, filled the rest of the seats.

"Well, I just loved Lu so much," Mrs. Reed had said. "She was a real nice lady."

No one mentioned Seng.

The ceremony was both Buddhist and Christian. For the Christian component, an open casket had been elected. We filed past to pay our respects, and I winced at the sight of Lu; beneath the framed photograph, her reconstructed face looked like Silly Putty, a wax figure, a melted doll head.

I walked past Seng without looking.

After that came what I supposed was the Buddhist component. The caskets were closed and wheeled out of the room. We followed in a crowd, confused, behind the cluster of older Cambodians murmuring, raising incense sticks to their foreheads. Down a narrow hallway, a narrower doorway, to the crematory. The first casket, I didn't know whose, was eased into the machine. Lynn and Sam were made to push the button.

The smell began to filter out: embalming chemicals and burning body mixing with the musky incense. I blinked against the sting, lowered my head. I felt the smoke envelop me. When they began to cremate the second casket, I looked at my mom and whispered, "I have to go."

The smell stayed on our clothes and skin; we carried it in the car, back into our house where people gathered to mourn and eat casserole. We balled up our funeral clothes and put them in plastic bags to be taken to the cleaners. But the smell stayed with me, in my nose and hair for days.

Silvio clutched a can of Angkor beer with dust-stained hands. He'd arrived in Phnom Penh that morning, on a motorbike with another Italian friend. Their backpacks and film equipment sat in a dirty pile in my friend Tim's flat, where people had gathered for dinner.

Silvio and his friend were making a documentary, they told me, on Indochina. They were in Phnom Penh for three days and wanted to interview people about the Khmer Rouge. Did I have any contacts?

"Well," I began slowly. "Not really."

"But you were researching this topic, no?"

"Yeah, but as an outsider," I glanced around our table of Westerners, Styrofoam boxes of take-out and cigarette smoke. "It's hard to have access, you know?"

I'd been in Phnom Penh six weeks. I'd learned a lot about Khmer Rouge history—read histories and memoirs, researched the state of mental health and trauma services in Cambodia, attended documentary screenings, become a regular fixture at Bophana, an audiovisual historical archive center. But, I had to admit to Silvio, that was as far as I'd gotten. I'd only sat down face-to-face with a handful of people, and even then we only discussed subjects tangentially connected to the war history.

"It's a lot to ask," I told Silvio, "for people to talk about it, open up." I was vaguely aware that I was talking mostly to myself.

"Yes, but it wasn't so long ago," Silvio said. "There are still many people who lived through it. I think it shouldn't be so hard to find a person who wants to talk."

I nodded slowly. I tried to explain how people didn't really talk about the war. Sure—it was referenced a lot, was always kind of there, but there wasn't any open discourse, any real or meaningful discussion.

I paused. I realized I could have been describing Lynn's family or her parents' death, Pol Pot or her father Seng. I could have been describing myself.

"Yes, but they should." Conviction flashed through Silvio's dark brown eyes. "This is how you move forward. It's not good to keep quiet."

I know that, I felt like telling him. We know that.

"Yeah, but it takes time," I told him instead.

He gave a nod, the kind that could mean anything at all, and lifted the can to his arched Roman lips. I watched the smoke twist from his cigarette. It looked, I thought, like incense.

ॐ ॐ ॐ

Lauren Quinn is a writer from Oakland, California. Her work has appeared in 7x7 and The San Francisco Chronicle *and on websites such as* World Hum, Matador, *and the* Huffington Post. *She writes the blog Lonely Girl Travels and is currently living in Phnom Penh, Cambodia.*

❦ ❦ ❦

Mare's Milk, Mountain Bikes, Meteors & Mammaries

A nipply night in nomad's land.

"Oh, no, Kirsten!"

My Kyrgyzstani guide's warning came too late, and stepping in poo had never felt so good. My cycling shoe sank into the dreadful yet luxurious warmth of fresh animal dung. I was chilled to the point where I was actually lingering ankle-deep in feces, by choice.

Yena shone the light of her cell phone, its only feature that was still working, onto the molten mound enveloping the bare skin of my lower leg. The droppings looked like something a brontosaurus might have deposited. A meteorite seared across the night sky, so close that you could actually hear it crackle as it hissed down the vertical gorge to the Chong-Kemin valley.

The point of light from Yena's phone caught me in the eyes. When I'd first met her, yesterday, after traveling thirty-six hours from Canada, I'd told her that I had two irrational phobias. The first one—fear of the dark—I fabricated as an excuse for not wanting to climb the unlit, steep, winding stairs of an eleventh-century minaret. I wasn't worried about the lack of lighting; I was being lazy. The second phobia—which I'd added to brighten the mood after she looked disappointed that I didn't want to go up the tower—was real: I was terrified of meteorites. I was seriously scared of being struck by a shooting star. I'd lie in bed at night imagining them out there in space.

Now here we were on a mountain, in the dark, unable to make it across the pass with our bikes because a fresh rockslide had strewn unstable boulders and scree for several kilometers in every direction, including on the slope directly above us. We'd had to turn back and were descending on foot from an altitude of 4,000 oxygen-deficient meters above sea level, as night smothered Chok-Tal Mountain. The blinding dark was being shredded by the Perseid meteor shower—shooting stars so close it seemed I could even smell their trails of smelting iron and sulfur. I snuggled into the poop.

"Yena, why did the old Kyrgyz nomad ask me if I was afraid of wolves?"

"I no know why. Is very strange."

It *was* weird. It was the only thing he'd communicated, as we'd left his family's yurt in the afternoon to head up over the mountain chain. He had a wind-whipped and sun-lashed face, a riding crop, a long white moustache, and a traditional white felt hat that made him look like he was wearing a small yurt on his head.

"I'm not scared of wolves," I said to Yena as she skidded away down the rocky trail beside her bike.

"I know, you say dis already." Just a few feet ahead of me, and she was invisible.

Suddenly, she shrieked. A clatter of falling rocks started above us and immediately bounced and slid past on all sides. Stone and shale tumbled over the sheer precipice.

I screamed. I didn't know what was going on, but screaming felt right.

"A horse!" Yena cried.

"Oh, God. Did it go over the edge?"

"It go off." My guide was somewhere near the edge of the gorge. I couldn't see her.

"It went off the edge?" All I could hear were the glacial rapids roaring thousands of meters below.

The light from my twenty-two-year-old guide's phone darted around the nearby mountainside. There was nothing to see in its beam but rocks balancing on good will.

I was too old for this.

Wait, did I seriously just think that? I was furious with myself for even entertaining such a thought. I was *not* too old for this. I was forty . . . something. Mid-forties. I'd been lying about my age, saying I was older than I was, for so long that I'd actually need to do the math to figure out my real age. I had never understood why movie stars claimed to be younger than they were. If you lie up in age, then people are amazed by how good you look. But today's mistakes were those of a twenty-two-year-old. I'd made such errors in judgment decades ago and there was no excuse for repeating them at forty-five-ish.

We had no water, food, supplies, flashlights, or gear of any kind. Everything we needed was in our support vehicle with our driver, Alexey, and my Kyrgyz cultural guide, Cholpon. Everything that could save our lives was on the other side of this snowy mountain range, a six-hour car ride away—if we had a car. When the sun vanished, the temperature had plunged below freezing, and I was wearing shorts and a t-shirt. I'd suggested turning back hours ago, when I'd begun to suspect that I'd misunderstood the plans for the day; I didn't want to get caught high in the mountains at night.

"Hello, Alexey, hello. . . ." Yena tried her useless walkie-talkie and her useless cell phone for the hundredth time. I knew she was just putting on a front for me. She was fully aware that there was no cell service here, and the transceiver radios were only good if you had a line of sight with the other person. "Hello . . ." Static.

There had been a tense fight last night at camp between my guides. Alexey had said—in English, for my benefit— "The lady is tired and she has come from living at sea level. We are too high in elevation. Change tomorrow's ride. Do a small ride, Yena. Don't cross the mountains." I agreed with Alexey. Then the arguing continued in Russian, the common language of the three guides supporting my bike trip across Kyrgyzstan.

I didn't normally travel with a team of babysitters. I'd hired them all before arriving in Bishkek, back when I assumed I'd have a group of cyclists accompanying me. But it turned out nobody else in the world wanted to come to Kyrgyzstan, mostly because of a recent revolution and government over-throw and killings. I'd even received death wishes from an Arizona prison guard on an online mountain biking forum for daring to invite Westerners to a Muslim country. He'd lusted for guns pointed at my head.

Maybe Yena hadn't understood Alexey's English when he said we shouldn't cross the Celestial Mountains. She spoke Russian and French. I could barely understand a word of her English and none of her French, and I was beginning to think she didn't understand my English, either. Or perhaps she'd won the argument, and nobody thought to tell me. But when we'd left so late in the day, and when I'd watched her hand two bottles of water back to Alexey, complaining they were too heavy—these two clues had indicated we were doing a shorter, easier ride, and not crossing the mountains. She'd even thrown out our food, at which point I was completely certain we'd just be doing a quick jaunt.

Four hours later, when I was vomiting horse milk, clam-bering over rockslides, carrying, pushing and dragging my bike continually upward, I realized we were doing the full mountain crossing.

Now, one foot in front of the other, defeated, we were feeling our way back down the mountainside, trembling with cold and muscle fatigue. The incline was so vertical that I was using my bicycle brakes to help slow my pace. I winced as a rock tore the skin off my shin, and again as a shooting star whizzed in front of me. I didn't make a wish. I wasn't superstitious. I was just fully freaked out.

The nomads, though—they were superstitious. The Kyrgyz woman who'd served us fermented mare's milk and bread with jam and clotted cream in her yurt this afternoon had stared at my upside-down bread on the table and shot me a look of horror. I'd also pointed with my foot at her adult son. I was showing him the hardware that attached my shoe to my bike pedal. He'd jumped back and protected his face with his hands. You'd have thought I was going to kick him in the head.

Before traveling to Kyrgyzstan, I'd been sent a warning list on how not to offend or upset the nomads. One of the items on the list said, "Do NOT put your bread upside down on the table," and the other said, "Do NOT point at anyone with your foot." I'd cursed the Kyrgyz family with bad luck and brought the devil into their yurt and now I'd startled one of their horses to its death. Maybe they wouldn't notice. They had lots of horses.

"We leave the trail, now. Here. Here. See light. Is yurt. We go there." Yena pulled my handlebars to direct me off the trail toward a wavering speck of light in the far distance.

"What? No." Leaving the trail was insane. Bad things happened when you left the trail. Besides, if we stayed on the trail it would lead us right back to the yurt we were at today. Unless the light was coming from the first yurt we'd stopped at earlier in the day, not the second one.

At the first yurt, a nomad woman had made cheese balls with her bare hands, and I could see her dirty handprints in the sour cheese. My stomach turned at the thought of putting it in my mouth. I pretended to enjoy my golf balls of cheese but palmed them into my pocket, intending to drop them in the outdoor toilet. But when I went to the squat latrine, I realized my cheese balls would be visible to anyone who looked in the shallow hole, so instead I feigned washing my hands in the stream and ditched the cheese there. They instantly sank to the bottom and stayed. The nomads had probably found my cheese after I'd left. They'd know it was my cheese. I didn't want to go to the first yurt, but then I'd insulted the nomads at the second yurt as well. Plus, there was the issue of the horse.

Following Yena, I stepped off the trail onto an impossible incline of slick wet grass. I turned my bike wheel sideways, as not even the brakes helped stop the downward slide. My front tire suddenly plunged straight down and stopped.

"What's that?"

Yena shone her cell phone light. It was a marmot hole. She cast her light over the slope. Between where we stood and the far-off flicker from the yurt was a minefield of marmot holes, all just several feet apart. Before leaving for Kyrgyzstan I'd learned that the marmot was the second deadliest creature known to man, but that was because the marmot carried the flea responsible for the Black Death, or Bubonic Plague—not because their holes were waiting to trap and snap your leg bones like twigs.

Using my bike like a senior citizen's walker, I inched my way down the hill as slowly as possible. It was still too fast. A compound fracture out here would mean certain death. I wasn't going to die at the hands of Muslims, as the Arizona prison guard had been desperate to prove—I was going to die by marmot.

Just then I became aware of motion, black moving against black, and far too large to be a marmot.

"Yena, what's that? There's something out there. No, not something, lots of things."

We were being surrounded. Large shapes were closing in on us.

"I no know," Yena whispered.

"Oh, it's just cows," I said, relieved.

Except that right then, we heard a deep, guttural, angry growl above us on the mountain. A T-Rex-sized beast was roaring and approaching fast.

"Bull," Yena cried out in dismay.

The bull circled. I couldn't see it, but I could hear its hefty hooves impact the soil. It started to paw. It was going to charge. Yena and I made a barricade with our bikes. I heard myself panting—tight, short, breaths that sounded exactly like *The Blair Witch Project* whimper puffing. People really did make that silly noise. I couldn't stop doing it. The Minotaur was bearing down on us. We'd be gored.

In a split second, the bull rounded our makeshift bicycle-fence. We were now on the same side of the bikes as him. Yena fumbled with her phone and the weak ray hit the bull's eye. He charged. We scrambled around our bikes and held them in front of us, sidestepping with them, our bikes locked together in a panicked tangle of handlebars and spokes. I closed my eyes, bracing for impact. He thundered past and around us again. We were an awkward, gasping, four-legged matador.

"Call the nomads to help us," I begged Yena.

She cried out in Russian, shouting her pleas toward the swinging lantern that marked the safety of the nearby yurt. Then all of a sudden, Yena let go of her bike and ran at the animal—all eighty pounds of her, shrieking threats as she waved her arms over her head and hurtled toward the horned mass of muscle.

I heard men's voices to my right, speaking in Kyrgyz.

"Help us," I whinnied.

Where were they? I was still making that pathetic whimpering-huffing noise.

A shepherd whistled a command. A lantern was lit. Dogs. Dogs and nomad men. Muslims. Muslims with guns. I was so happy to see Muslims with guns.

We were ushered into the family yurt. It was the second yurt.

"*Kumis?*" The mother offered me mare's milk that had been fermented in a smoked goat's stomach, again. I'd been up-chucking her *kumis* all day. Even in my dehydrated state, there would be no swallowing horse milk; the alcohol content was too low to be worth the risk.

I declined politely as Yena spun our adventure to the nomad woman who poured me the traditional half-full cup of tea, which I drank in one gulp. This happened ten times in a row. I wished she'd just pour me a full cup of tea. I wasn't superstitious.

Her eldest son, whom I'd pointed my foot at earlier, eyed me from under his pile of colorful quilts. It was midnight, and the family lay on the floor, shoulder to shoulder. Where would we sleep? I wasn't entirely comfortable wedging myself between the nomads on the ground; maybe I could spend the night huddled with the manure-burning stove and the teapot.

"I tell her about rock slide," Yena said. "I tell her we cannot cross the pass and she say she know this. The same thing happened with Germans on bikes. They come down the mountain last night and sleep here."

The nomad woman smiled at me with her gold teeth.

"Why didn't she tell us that this afternoon?" I asked.

"I know. I no know. Is strange," Yena replied. "We go now. They make bed for us in barn yurt."

I was so thirsty. I hadn't had nearly enough half-cups of tea, and as I followed several nomads back out into the freezing night, to the "barn yurt," I was shaking with what surely the beginning stages of hypothermia. My teeth rattled in my skull. Yena wrapped her icy, spindly arms around me. I don't like being touched, but I could feel the warmth from her heart on my back, so I didn't pull away. We shook together as nomads kicked the dogs out of the barn yurt and moved saddles, boots, and riding tack.

"I d-d-don't mind d-dogs," I chattered. The dogs ran off into the darkness in a barking frenzy, chasing something unseen.

Yena was handed a lantern, and we stepped into the yurt. I took off my poopy shoes—not that it mattered in the barn, but the nomads were superstitious about shoes—and one tipped over on its side. That was bad luck, too. Now I'd brought bad luck to the barn, as well. I quickly righted my offensive cycling shoe, but not before it was noted by the old man.

On the ground was a mat for us to share. Yena snuffed the lantern, and we crawled under the mountain of handmade blankets on the felt mat and spooned for warmth, feet of course pointed to the flap of the door, for luck. I heard the flap move, and then something else.

"Something is in the tent with us," I whispered.

"No," Yena answered.

Something sat down. "Maybe a dog came back," I suggested.

The dogs responded by barking maniacally in the distance.

"Yes, something is in here," Yena agreed.

We heard scratching. "Dog," she sighed.

I suddenly had the feeling that it wasn't a dog. It was the wolf. But I wasn't afraid of wolves, I told myself.

Then I coughed. It was a horrible racking cough. Yena rubbed my chest.

No, she was rubbing my boobs. Yena was rubbing my breasts.

O.K., this was worse than wedging in with the family. Did she think I was paying for this service along with her guiding skills? It was beyond awkward.

"Yena," I coughed, "I'm not scared of shooting stars anymore." I barked painfully.

"Dis is good."

"Yeah, now I'm scared of pulmonary edema." I could feel my lungs filling with fluid. I choked on mucus. Yena rubbed my boobs again.

Day one was over—I hoped. But there were three more weeks to go.

Kirsten Koza is an adventure travel writer, speaker, and the author of Lost in Moscow. *Her articles and photographs have been featured around the world in newspapers and magazines. Kirsten has mountain biked (badly) across twenty countries, was rewarded with a ham for the first mountain bike ascent up Romania's Mt. Cocora, has driven the intercept vehicle tornado chasing for 19,900 kilometers, kayaked inches from alligators, was held at gunpoint in Honduras for twelve hours, was tattooed by a Rapa Nui tafunga, and has put testicles and penis and many other unusual food items in her mouth. To see pictures and read more about Kirsten's misadventures visit www.kirstenkoza.com.*

ॐ ॐ ॐ

Letting Go on the Ganges

India held her ticket to transformation.

Our boat dropped anchor in the middle of the Ganges, and a slight breeze brought relief from the October heat. Two men interrupted the live, languid sitar music by scurrying like beetles around our wide-hulled rowboat, setting out forty leaf plates big enough to hold a scoop of ice cream. Inside, rose petals cradled votive candles, which the men quickly lit. The light made feet and faces glow. Our tour guide Ganesh, a tall, gangly Indian from Bangalore, stood up, momentarily taking center stage away from the sitar player.

"Please take a bowl with a candle and place it in the Ganges," Ganesh instructed. "When you do, make a wish. It is said that when you do this, your wish will come true."

We were offering our wishes, he explained, to Ganga—the goddess of the river that bears her name. A bath in her waters was the ultimate symbol of redemption and purification, and a wish was perhaps amplified here more than anywhere else.

I looked at the water. It was black. No place for a wish.

"If you can't think of anything to wish for, wish for world peace." Ganesh smirked, as if reading my mind, and then hustled to the front of the boat.

I heard his instructions but rebelled. I already knew I wasn't going to make a wish.

Eight months ago, I was married with a comfortable urban apartment and a dual-income life. On a rare cloudy day in Los Angeles from my perch on the living room futon, I told my husband of seven years that it was over.

"Why?" he'd asked. Shocked. Baffled.

"Being married is not conducive to the life I want to live," sounding like I was running a meeting.

"What life is that?" He tilted his head.

"I want to travel the world."

There it was. I'd never said it out loud before. Freed from a dark recess of my heart, the words seemed almost to vibrate in the daylight.

"But where do you want to go?" What was this paradise that could be so much better than the life we'd created?

At the time, I had no idea. I just knew I had *always* wanted to travel. In our first year of marriage I wrote three pages a day in my journal, more often than not trying to reconcile wedlock with the desire to pack up and hit the road. On our third anniversary, I'd given him one of those narcissistic we're-really-a-couple books called *The Book of Us*. I'd answered the question, "What are your dreams for your life together?" in ballpoint ink: "to travel around the world." Then I added "together" to bind words and hope.

There was nothing wrong with him, nothing wrong with me. But I wore despair and denial like a heavy winter coat—my dream, to voyage out like Freya Stark and discover myself amidst the sands of Arabia. I denied myself study abroad in college and backpacking through Europe, shuffling from school to a "good job" and finally a big Catholic wedding to a really nice guy who I loved and couldn't see beyond.

My ring even held the promise of travel. A simple gold band with twelve small diamonds, it was both wedding and engagement ring. As the date of our wedding had approached, my then-fiancé was in his second year of law school, and his money was going to tuition and car payments. He couldn't see peeling out a few grand for a matching band, so instead of a wedding ring, he promised we'd put the money toward a future trip. "Wouldn't that be better?" he offered.

The travel never happened as promised. Instead, we used our sparse vacation days and bonuses to travel for ten days to China, two weeks to Europe, sixteen days to Thailand. But these trips were more a retreat from home life in a grand setting—not enough for me. I wanted deeper, more. After seven years, I had spoken the truth at last and breathed for the first time.

For three months we separated, each day removing a layer of our life together—the mattress we'd just purchased, the Noritake Colorwave Green china, and the joint DVD collection. Over time, he agreed that our separation was for the best. He dreamed of a house, a family, and a silver anniversary party. I dreamed of a camel ride to visit the Great Pyramids of Giza. When he eventually admitted that it was better to be fulfilled than be together, the cement block of guilt weighing down my newfound freedom began to lighten.

I spent most newly single nights on the bare floor of my apartment reading travel magazines and drinking red wine. The photos of far away comforted me more than any sympathetic therapist or cathartic girls' night out could. I wanted to take these pictures of sunrise at Machu Picchu, the Acropolis's stately grace, and the desperately blue French Polynesian waters and rub them over my body in a baptism of travel and desire—I wanted them in my veins.

My nights settled into this familiar routine of turn page, sip, and sigh; turn page, sip, and sigh—until one page turn resulted in a destination. An image of the golden Taj Mahal appeared at sunrise beneath bold text: INCREDIBLE INDIA.

I took another sip of wine, swallowed, and breathed. I have to go to India, I inhaled. I'm going to India, I exhaled.

Five months later, my tour group arrived in the holy city of Varanasi. The day was jungle-hot and sticky, with dive-bombing insects. We found our way to the river's side through the walled city, where sacred cows shared paths with lost tourists. Cafés and temples provided views of the expansive mud-brown river, but we traversed the famous ghats, the long, uneven stairways pilgrims took to enter the holy Ganges.

Revelers celebrated the Durga Puja holiday by dancing in the shallow waters. Men splashed and clapped their own music at the base of the stairs and between boats. A lone woman took part from a distance, covered completely in a wet sari. Large stacks of logs and sticks signaled the crematory ghats. Out of respect, we avoided them, casting our curious eyes away from the smoldering piles where Hindus made their transition from this life to the next. A haze had settled over the river, the tired humidity catching the smoke and smell of recent fires.

As I passed funerals and dancing bathers, I decided that this river, this place of transformation, would be the final resting place for my marriage. I would release my engagement-cum-wedding ring into this sacred river with a ceremony of my own.

That evening as the sun faded into a haze, we filled a blue wooden boat big enough for a tour group, crew and sitar player. The river slurped the ghat stairs, sucking Durga Puja remains into her current. A campfire smell pervaded the sludgy damp of the riverside. The brown of the Ganges blended into a muddy pink sunset. The bathers had gone home.

The sitar's high-pitched plucks were the only sound as our boat glided toward an outer bank that looked like a ribbon resting along India's girth. Night turned the Ganges from brown to black, and Varanasi's lights became fireflies in the dark.

In the pocket of my jeans were two things: the ring that had been feeling smaller with each passing day and each advancing adventure, and a slip of paper—a eulogy. It was a departure from the vows promised to husband and God seven and a half years earlier. Divorce vows to be read aloud to ring and river. This little leaf plate with the small dancing flame would be the funeral pyre for my marriage. With her flowing current, I hoped the Ganges would somehow redeem and purify me.

I hunched over, my curved back shielding the ceremony from the surrounding cackles and laughter of my tour group. Too much had been splayed open over the past eight months; I needed to sew it back up amidst the frivolity. Possessions spread over two apartments, bank accounts scrutinized by a judge, a mother-in-law who wrote to me on my anniversary, "If you want to travel, take a vacation. Don't end your marriage."

With some semblance of privacy, I faced the river, the burning cup in my lap, ring and vows in hand. I settled into where I was, resigning myself to the lack of seclusion. I had done something similar once on a bright March day in Wisconsin. This time, there were no nervous mothers, no stoic fathers, no 267 guests—just the Ganges and me.

I could do this—with more honesty—in the middle of this holy river, in the middle of India.

By the light of the small candle, I read the vows in a whisper, hoping the sounds of the sitar would cover my words so that only the river would hear them. I placed my ring on my finger and read aloud.

Thank you for the seven years together.

Thank you for your kindness, your love, and your forgiveness.

Whatever anger you have, please release. Whatever blame I have, I release.

Thank you.

I love you and I let you go.

I love you and I let you go.

I love you.

I let you go.

My tears started at the first "you." I ripped the paper into tiny shreds, placed them next to the rose petals, and removed my ring. After a moment of hesitation, I set it beside the flame. The gold caught the firelight and lit the bowl even more. I bent over, placed the package on the water, and let go. The Ganges took the cup from my hand and carried it along in her current. Soon, my candlelight joined all the others.

When not doing things abroad that make her mother and aunts cringe, Kristin Zibell writes to inspire women to live their travel dreams on her blog TakeYourBigTrip.com. Kristin lives in San Francisco, traveling locally and always planning her next big trip.

EMILY MATCHAR

✿ ✿ ✿

Birthright

Was this the land of her people,
or just another foreign country?

A few hours after landing in Tel Aviv, we were sitting
in the fluorescent-lit conference room of a 1970s-era
hotel in the Judean Hills, listening to a man named Momo
talk about love.

"This trip is a gift," said Momo to the three hundred of us.
"All we ask in return is that you fall in love with Israel, fall
in love with a Jew, marry Jewish, make Jewish babies, make
aliyah and move to Israel. Is that so much to ask?"

I snorted involuntarily.

Momo was Shlomo "Momo" Lifshitz, a retired IDF officer
and president of Birthright Israel, an organization designed
to introduce young American Jews to the homeland. With
an unrepentantly bald head, linebacker's build, and a gruff,
Israeli-accented baritone, Momo had what you might call
"stage presence." Much of the audience seemed rapt by his
words. Or maybe it was the jetlag.

I was twenty-four years old and visiting Israel for the first
time on a free Birthright trip. Though as a travel writer I preferred going it alone—and often by the seat of my pants—I
wasn't one to turn down a free trip to a new foreign country,

even if it meant riding on a tour bus with a strict minute-to-minute itinerary. Plus, it made my parents and grandparents happy. My paternal grandmother had fled to Palestine from Poland during the 1930s when things started getting ugly for Jews in Central Europe. And my father, who grew up in Baltimore after my grandmother immigrated to the U.S., spent his childhood summers at Zionist camps, learning the Hatikvah and doing wholesome collective labor like building basketball courts.

Still, I wasn't counting on all the propaganda—though I suppose I should have known. Birthright Israel is often referred to as "Birthrate Israel" because so many former trip participants (there are some 250,000 alums) go on to marry and eventually procreate with each other.

As a non-religious North Carolina-raised Jew who hadn't seen the inside of a synagogue in years, the very idea of "marry within the tribe" or "Israel-as-homeland" seemed the antithesis of all my liberal multicultural values. And I'd recently begun dating a non-Jewish grad student—a blue-eyed, blond-haired son of the American West whose forebears had trekked across the country in covered wagons nearly a century before my ancestors fled the shtetls of Galicia. It had only been a few months, but I thought there might be something special there.

The day after Momo's speech, I filed into a bus with two dozen other twenty-somethings and set out to see the country. And within a few days, I began to wonder if there was something wrong with me; despite our group leader's strenuous efforts, I wasn't falling in love with Israel.

At a kibbutz in the Galilee, I rolled my eyes through a group-bonding exercise that involved crossing a moat with a rope. In Tel Aviv, I yawned through a rousing lecture on Israeli history and foreign policy. In Eilat, the "Vegas of Israel," I sat in the corner of a cheesy bar while Israelis dressed like Gucci models gyrated on the dance floor. In Jerusalem, our tour leader berated me for straying from the pack to buy a disposable camera from a street vendor. Somewhere along a stretch of desert highway, the boy behind me on the bus made out noisily with one of the young Israeli soldiers brought along on the trip (both male and female), presumably for this express purpose. I just wasn't feeling it.

At the Western Wall, the men and women split up to visit their respective sections of the old temple. As we approached, Orthodox women in long-sleeved t-shirts and headscarves passed us walking backwards, leaving the wall but avoiding turning their backs to the holy site.

I reached out and touched the wall. It felt rough and chilly under the cold, white December sun. Next to me, a tiny elderly woman in black prayed silently, her chapped lips moving as she rocked back and forth with her eyes closed.

"Did you feel it?" a woman from my group later asked.

"Feel what?" I asked.

"The power," she said. Some kind of thrilling, voltaic energy lit her eyes from behind.

"I could tell that it's a very powerful place for a lot of people," I said, limply.

"No," she said, turning her shiny eyes on me. "There was definitely something there. Something that can't be explained."

"O.K.," I said.

What was my problem? Did I lack a sense of awe? Or was I so disconnected from my roots that I couldn't sense the power that had drawn my ancestors to this place for thousands of years?

Then something started to happen. I began spending the long hours on the bus sitting with Jeff, a Yale medical student, the two of us geeking out over our mutual affinity for bad 1980s kids' movies. And I bonded with a few of the other women after we were forced to share a tiny room on a kibbutz in the Golan Heights. Someone gave me a nickname. I'd never had a nickname.

In the Negev, we rode camels and ate dinner beneath the stars, a nomadic feast of couscous and spiced meat stew. We slept in a Bedouin tent on stacks of Persian carpets, piled up together like a litter of puppies, encircled by the deep, languid smoke of our hosts' slow-burning shisha pipes.

As I dozed off under the cold, cloudless sky, it occurred to me that I was becoming part of a group. It was a novel feeling for me—I'd always been the kid at summer camp hiding in the bunk with a book while everyone else linked arms and swayed to the camp anthem during sing-along time.

A few days later, at a Dead Sea bathhouse, we females changed into bikinis in a communal dressing room where several hefty Eastern European *bubbies* sat in plastic chairs nodding into their ample bosoms. Soon we were cracking each other up with Yiddish-tinged imitations of our grandmothers:

"Oy, what a *shayna maidel* you are! The boys must be beating down your door!"

"You've got such a beautiful *punim*, if only you lost a few pounds!"

"Have you had your bowel movement yet today, sweetheart?" I chimed in, channeling my notoriously nosy Polish immigrant grandmother.

Outside, the sea was swimming-pool clear and flat as glass all the way across to the pink-tinged mountains of Jordan. It was cold outside, and the only other people on the salt beach were a few goose-pimply Russians floating nonchalantly in their white briefs.

We waded in, the hard-packed salt ground pricking our feet. The water was warmer than the air. I walked in a ways, then sat back and let the water bounce me back to the surface like a cork. My sense of gravity was distorted, my limbs no longer under my control. We all laughed as we slipped and bobbed through the slick, salty water. The sun was beginning to set, turning the surface of the water orange. Someone took a picture.

I called my grad student boyfriend on a pre-paid cell phone later that night, and his voice sounded thin and far away. Next door, the boys from the bus were having an impromptu sing-along with a borrowed guitar and several bottles of kosher wine. Their voices rose, rich and jocular, across the thin room divider.

Are these my people? I asked myself.

On our last day in Israel, we went to Yad Vashem, the Holocaust museum, where we filed solemnly past grim piles of shoes and broken eyeglasses.

Again my thoughts turned to my grandmother, who fled Poland after her uncle was attacked in the street by teenage thugs hopped up on Hitler's rhetoric and their own youthful meanness. They'd cut off his long beard. My grandmother's father, my great-grandfather, saw which way the wind was blowing; he abandoned his factories, packed up his family, and headed for Palestine. They got out just in time. A few more months and their shoes might be on the bottom of a dusty heap in the necropolis of Yad Vashem.

Later that evening, we met with Momo. Once again, he spoke deeply and charismatically about Israel's splendors. The beaches! The gorgeous women! The brotherhood! But then his voice turned more serious and his eyes began scanning the audience, falling upon our faces one by one.

"The Jewish culture is three-thousand years old," he said, slowly. "That culture has been passed down to you in an unbroken chain. You do not have the right to break that three-thousand-year-old chain by marrying outside the faith. YOU DO NOT HAVE THAT RIGHT!"

And just like that, the spell was broken. The happy, among-my-people feeling drained from my body as if a cork had been pulled from the sole of my foot.

In college I had dated, very briefly, an orthodox Jewish boy with black hair and green eyes and the cutest little gap between his front teeth. Even though we had nothing in common, I'd fantasized about what it would be like to marry him. I'd have a clear role in life, well-defined loyalties, a distinct place in the community. It might be nice, I thought. Easier.

That's what it would be like, I realized, to accept Israel's embrace, to reach out and take those pamphlets on "Volunteer Opportunities in Israel" and "Making Aliyah." I knew kids who returned from Birthright trips fired up with a sense of purpose and belonging—the success stories. They'd go back to the homeland after college, marry an Israeli, wind up doing their Ph.D. at the Hebrew University of Jerusalem. Their parents would be thrilled.

It would be easier. But it wouldn't be me.

I'd like to visit Israel again, but this time on my own terms. My husband and I are thinking of going next summer. We'll buy slabs of halva and bags of dried sumac at the Mahane Yehuda Market in Jerusalem and scoop up piles of creamy hummus with pita bread in Tel Aviv cafes. We'll hike Masada in the glowing dawn, then float like seals in the Dead Sea beneath a pink sky. We'll see things I wasn't allowed to see on the Birthright trip, like the sunlight streaming through the dome of the Church of the Holy Sepulcher and the lively neighborhood markets of the Muslim Quarter.

Yes, my husband. When my grandmother met my grad-student boyfriend, by then my fiancé, she declared him "a lovely boy." She was dying then, and we'd gone to visit her in Florida knowing—even though she didn't—that she wouldn't be able to make it to our wedding. Later, after we'd flown home, she said to my aunt, "He's not Jewish, you know." But that was O.K., she added—he was a lovely boy, and we were in love. She couldn't wait to dance at our wedding.

Emily Matchar is a freelance culture writer and Lonely Planet *guidebook author. In the line of duty she's hot-wired a pickup truck, ridden up a Mexican volcano on a horse with a wooden saddle, and eaten at thirteen different Memphis barbecue joints in 36 hours (not recommended). A native of Chapel Hill, North Carolina, Emily studied English and Spanish at Harvard University. Now she writes for publications like* Salon, The Washington Post, Men's Journal, Outside, Gourmet, *and many others. See more of her writing at www.emilymatchar.com.*

༄ ༄ ༄

Spiral-Bound

She found what she was seeking
in the last place she looked.

The day I met Teddy, the heat and the grimy streets of
Pune had mixed a muggy haze outside, which leached its
way into the bookstore, slicking our foreheads and necks. As
I examined the travel section, the bell above the door clanged,
and Teddy stood for a moment in the doorway, backlit by the
sun, and then walked to where I stood, so close I could hear
him breathing. I watched from the corner of my eye as he
scanned the horror novels and selected an old hardcover. I
caught a glimpse of the curling binding: *Carrie*, by Stephen
King. The bell above the bookstore door clanged again; hot
wind blew in.

Teddy was a tall black man with close, tight curls and white
teeth, save for a brown one toward the molars, which he'd
learned to hide by keeping the left side of his mouth closed.
Because of this, he talked with only half his mouth, and that,
combined with the rotting tooth behind full lips, gave him a
sly, crafty look. I wouldn't learn why he smiled the way he
did until later, of course, and so on the day he walked into
the bookshop, all I saw was the crooked smile. He was careful about hiding the tooth, practiced at concealing it after so

many years. We were four hours northeast of Mumbai, in a city known mostly for an ashram built by the guru Osho.

Teddy's eyes sidled to mine as we browsed, but I looked away. Aman, my host, had warned me of certain people on my first night in this city. There were those who came to Pune for the money that could be made selling drugs to hippies at the ashram; there were the ones who slipped pills into tourists' coffees at the German bakery, or took them away by motorbike into the night. Aman was a friend of a friend, a second cousin of a farmer I'd met picking apples near Dehradun, and I figured he was exaggerating a little, protective and trying to scare me into being extra-careful. Still, I took the horror novel in Teddy's hands as a sign; I kept my eyes averted and continued to browse.

The books on the shelf before me bore beaten bindings and dated titles, and I set my attention on those. *The USSR Today*, one stated gloomily. *Myanmar: Temples of Splendor*, read the cracked yellow spine of another. When I tugged it down, opening the long cover that drew stickily back, a flattened moth broke off and spiraled to the floor. The pages showed Technicolor tourists admiring a crumbling, sunlit temple.

Those books were like the labyrinthian, rutted streets outside, the old men on rickety gray bicycles, even the street children, their cries at once pitiful and joyful, and the beggars with their practiced wheedling. I would remember each one as an enduring Indian staple: worn by time, accustomed to crowds, doggedly resilient. Teddy, on the other hand, was fresh, with pearl buttons on his Western shirt and pointy shoes on his feet. "Have you read this?" I heard him ask. I looked up; he waved *Carrie*. I couldn't help it: I smiled, shook my head, and pretended to look grim. No, he wasn't at all like India's enduring things; he was tall and upfront, his face unlined, his eyes flickering.

"What's wrong?" Teddy asked, seeing the look on my face. "What's it about?" His question was mockingly innocent. Even if you knew nothing about *Carrie*, the cover, with the heroine's body covered in cow's blood, told you everything. "Just joking," he said at my raised eyebrows and flipped fast through the pages like he was just seeing how long it was, how closely set the type.

"So, you can't stand the gore?" he asked after another moment. When I looked at him, he winked. *Be careful,* a voice inside me said. But Teddy continued talking, and I kept listening. How welcome his English sounded, because everyone who'd told me that English was spoken all over India had been wrong. In the cities, sure—the language was used, marked with that charming and plucky accent, but in other parts of India, it wasn't nearly as common as I'd expected.

"That Stephen King—he's something else," Teddy remarked, lowering his voice a little as an elderly Indian couple brushed past us. "He's American, like you?"

I could tell by the way he said it that he knew the answer, but I nodded anyway. His own accent sounded imprecise, a little off-kilter, rolling and round. He was from South Africa, if I had to guess.

He looked at me like he was waiting to hear me ask where he was from, but I remembered Aman's warning and said nothing. *Don't push it.* When I looked up from the Myanmar book again, he'd bent to examine the rest of the Stephen King section. I slid my book back beside the others on the shelf, and as I walked toward the door to leave, I ran my fingertips along the soft spines once more. I love the way old books feel, the way they leave their scent on my hands, the way their pages can feel leathery or dusty, brittle and crackling or soft as butter. Anywhere you'll go, you'll find books, if you look hard enough. I like knowing that.

Just before I reached the end of the stack, the pad of my first finger caught on the broken coil of a spiral-bound book, and I drew my hand back. I thought I felt a tiny spark as my fingers left the book. I stopped, peered at it, then eased it out from between the others. It was a loose-leafed notebook, the kind you buy in American drugstores. I felt Teddy glance over, but in that moment, nothing could keep me from lifting the cover and looking inside. There was something funny about it, I just knew. There'd been a spark.

Handwriting choked the inside cover and the very first page: all Sanskrit and all in pencil, delicate marks made by a trembling hand. The words spilled onto the next page, and then the next and the next. In places, the writing ran over itself, and as I turned the pages the characters grew smaller and began to march up and down the margins and snake between each coil of the binding. It was as if the book had been the writer's only source of paper for a very long time.

"Someone's journal," I heard Teddy whisper beside me.

"Maybe," I said. *Put it back*, the little voice said, *and leave Teddy. That's what Aman would want you to do.* But I just couldn't take my eyes from those pages. The notebook felt both heavy and flimsy, like the words were weighing down the cheap paper. Teddy didn't try to take the book, didn't say anything else, and together we looked at the pages the way little kids look at picture books without reading the words. The tightness of those lines; their growing frenzy.

Toward the very end of the notebook, we came across a nearly clean page, startling and white like a flat, smooth stone in grass. The lines resembled veins on a wrist, and the only other thing on the page was a signature at the lower right. The signature was both scratchy and looping, if that can describe it: hard at its points, but soft in its curves. How had it happened, this page? I heard Teddy's breath quicken a fragment. Had the writer waited as he filled up every other page for the person who would sign their name on the only blank one? I imagined a prisoner, or someone exiled. Someone banished. Was it a hastily scribbled prayer?

Teddy brushed the signature delicately with one calloused thumb. I reached out myself and felt the way the writing cut into the page. It was impossible to tell whether the signature was a man's or a woman's, in the way it both rolled and cut into the page. I glanced at Teddy; he shrugged. When I returned to the book I felt a little chill, even in the hot store: looking at that page was like seeing a secret.

I felt increasingly guilty as I held it in my hands. What was it doing on these shelves, anyway? I glanced toward the counter at the young shopkeeper, who was typing into her cell phone intently, perched on a stool with her legs crossed. I closed the book, knelt down, and slid it onto the lowest shelf, taking care to tuck it in so that it wasn't easily visible to a browser. Teddy didn't protest. It didn't occur to me to even ask whether the book was for sale, for it seemed a mistake, placed on these shelves by accident when really it belonged in a locked drawer, or behind a pane of glass in a museum. For one selfish second I imagined waiting for Teddy to leave, and then slipping the book into my purse, hurrying back to Aman's and holding it open again, this time alone.

We stood there silently for a while, looking at the place where I'd slid the book back. What could be said, after all, except that those pages held a mystery?

Teddy broke the spell. "Can I buy you a coffee?" he asked, and then, all of a sudden, I was aware once more of the shouts of chai wallas and the shotgun explosions of motorbike engines. No, I didn't have time for coffee; meditations started in an hour, and I still had to meet Aman beforehand. I shook my head.

"Can I at least get your name?" Teddy asked, and I told him. *What the hell; we'd already shared one secret.*

"I'm Teddy," he replied, and plucked *Carrie* back up off the shelf. "I'm taking this one," he added, grinning.

"Good luck with that," I said, and without looking again for the spiral-bound book on the shelf, I left the store and went back out into the sunshine.

The ashram wasn't like the rest of Pune, which was built, as far as I could tell, around the wide, trash-littered, dried-up river that divided the city. Aman lived on the northern side, opposite the ashram, up a little street lined with apartment buildings built in the seventies. Most of Pune's streets were unpaved—except for the wide avenues that circled the city center—and were crowded with vegetable stands and bidi shops, vegetable wallahs and munching cows. The deeper you walked into the old city's heart, the farther you stepped back in time: no cars, just cows and bike rickshaws and a crumbling red temple, centuries old. Strings of marigolds for sale.

But the ashram was perpetually manicured, forever gated to keep the scented flowers protected, the wood floors gleaming, and the servants immaculate in their starched white linens. Beggars gathered at the ashram gates, but guards planted there day and night made sure they'd never get inside. You could feel the shift as soon as you entered; gone were the noisy cars, the shouting hawkers, the trash on the ground. Fake waterfalls obliterated all unpleasant noise, and neatly shorn grass or tall, carefully planned stands of trees replaced the city's broken pavement.

I was late to meet Aman after the bookstore, even though I'd been rushing. It always took longer than I thought it would to race back to the flat and change into my red robe. Everyone at the ashram had to wear the red robe, even the guards and front-desk agents. The robes kept us all looking the same, and the most enthusiastic attendees wore the red robes everywhere. Those devout, red-robed souls stuck out like sore thumbs among the city's chai wallahs and rickshaw drivers, fruit vendors and street children. As for me, I hated

my robe—it chafed my skin and made me sweat profusely—
but when I didn't wear it to the ashram, Aman took offense.
He'd given it to me as a gift and wore his each day, washing
it carefully in the evenings and putting it out on the little
balcony to dry in the night.

I didn't tell Aman about Teddy as we sat sipping our tea
before meditation. Of course I didn't, for he'd only frown and
warn me. Aman was a little man with large, dark eyes and
glasses that magnified them further. I knew he took pride in
showing me his city, his ashram, introducing me to his friends
and neighbors. It was strange to be led around the city by this
little man who'd taken me in with delight; sometimes, I just
wanted to walk by myself. Still, I was grateful for Aman's
kindness, and I tried not to let my occasional grumpiness
show.

I didn't mention the notebook to Aman, either. Instead,
I held it in my mind like some precious stone, a thing to be
guarded and saved. Aman and I just drank our tea, and he
went over our schedule: noon meditation, another at two, and
then the White Robe ceremony in the evening.

Aman had taken great pains to ensure that I attended at
least one White Robe ceremony. In the first few days after
I'd arrived, we'd both been too exhausted; meditation at 5
A.M. followed by afternoons of touring Pune tired us out. But
today, Aman was determined. The morning before, he'd sent
me across the street to his neighbor's, a woman who lived with
her teenaged daughter. They lent me a white robe stamped
with cream-colored flowers. Aman laundered it again for
me after I brought it home—just in case, he'd said. *In case of
what?* I wanted to ask, but bit my tongue; anyway, I figured I
knew why. While Aman kept his flat spotless, right down to
the shoes lined up by the door, the neighbor's house was just
two rooms, smaller than Aman's and stinking of cigarettes,
the windows shut tight to preserve the air conditioning. I

didn't mind the smell much, just the close, freezing air. The television blared.

Aman drank down the last of his tea, and we made our way to the meditation room. It was just like the website pictures: the whole room sparkled with mosaics made of mirrors. A few dozen people already sat cross-legged on the low, wide steps that rose toward the back of the room, their eyes closed. Silently, Aman and I joined them, and he settled into a lotus position, closing his eyes and slowing his breath.

I tried to let my thoughts slip from me, but my legs fell asleep right away, still unaccustomed to the position. I cracked my eyelids open: everyone around me kept their backs straight and their hands folded. Someone had dimmed the lights, and when a gray-haired woman wearing lots of turquoise jewelry lit a candle up front and clicked two little chimes together, the room fell into an even deeper quiet, steady breath the only sound.

But I couldn't keep my mind still. This wasn't like the yoga I'd practiced up in Rishikesh, in an old man's living room that became a studio every afternoon. In this glittering space, thoughts crowded in on me and raced around. Little twinges in my muscles and on my skin grew into itches, cramps. I wanted to stretch but knew that doing so would disturb my neighbors, breaking them from their trances. The candle smelled sickly sweet, and the room grew heavy and warm with all the bodies. *Notice your breath*, I reminded myself, but my thoughts just shot away again. I was hungry, and where was that scarf I bought last week from the woman on the corner? I hadn't seen it lately. Meanwhile, my leg pricked and my foot fell numb. My mind circled over itself, reeling.

Then I remembered the journal. I thought of the words that filled the pages and the startlingly empty sheet. I thought of the scrawled signature, and imagined touching the penciled words. Teddy's breath on my neck. When the gray-haired, turquoise-clad woman touched the chimes together again, I blinked in the light with everyone else, understanding for the first time the way opening your eyes after meditation can feel like waking from a dream. I hadn't emptied my mind, but at least I had thought only of that creamy blank page for the final long minutes of the session.

After meditation, we ambled to the German bakery, still in our robes, and ate soup together at a long table where other soul searchers congregated. Outside the German bakery, vendors displayed long racks of red and white robes for sale. I tried not to meet their eyes on the way out. How foreign I felt in my robe, how conspicuous.

Aman liked to wash before the White Robe ceremony, so after we'd attended the second meditation and eaten dinner, he went into the bathroom. I could hear the water running as I changed into the white robe. At least it was cooler, sewn of thin cotton instead of scratchy polyester. Aman emerged from the bathroom eventually, his hair slicked back with water, his white robe cloaked over him. He'd ironed it that morning; I told him it looked nice. He nodded humbly, and I thought I caught him blushing; this ceremony was where he shone, I realized. We walked back across the river to the ashram, where a hundred other people in white robes waited outside the big auditorium, its silhouette reflected in the meditation pool that lay before it.

It took a while to get to the door, because everyone needed to remove their shoes and place them in cubbies, then grab a handful of tissues for the breathing meditation. We all murmured and mumbled in line, but no one spoke loudly or laughed, unwilling to break the stillness of our reflections in the meditation pond. Slowly we made our way up the stairs and into the cavernous auditorium lobby.

"Miss," I heard a woman call from behind me. I turned; "Miss," she said again, and beckoned with her hand for me to come back.

"I'm sorry, miss," the woman said as I pushed back through the doorway, against the flow of white. "You can't attend the ceremony today." She glanced at my robe. "It's the flowers, these little flowers here. The robe needs to be totally white, just plain." She shrugged her shoulders—*sorry, they're the rules*, her look said.

"Are you serious?" I asked her, and a few heads turned. I was making a commotion, I realized, but *really?* After Aman washed the robe, the one we'd taken pains to borrow?

The woman nodded. "Sorry," she said, out loud this time, then coolly moved her gaze from my face to monitor the others still trickling in. I glanced through the doorway to see if I could find Aman—he'd been ahead of me in line, talking with friends. I didn't see him. So I laced my shoes back up and left, taking the stairs two at a time, my face aflame.

Mostly, I was annoyed—after the initial shock of being banished wore off—that I didn't have a change of clothes. I figured, as I tried to steady my breath and slow my beating heart, that I had two choices. I could go home, or I could wait for the White Robe ceremony to end so I could still walk back with Aman. After pondering the walk home alone, across the bridge beneath the dimming sky, I chose to wait, and so I walked out the ashram gates, white robe and all, toward the German Bakery, where I thought I'd get a coffee and try to find a magazine or someone to talk to. Something to take my mind off the shame and frustration.

Stupid white robes, I muttered as I walked past the beggars and into the bakery. *Damn flowers.* And then I saw Teddy, standing there at the counter, and my cursing stopped short.

He turned and grinned, recognizing me immediately, then took a moment to study my white flowered robe and my flushed face. "Everything okay?" he asked carefully.

"I'm okay," I said, then blurted it out. "I got turned away from the White Robe ceremony just now."

He grimaced. "Was it the flowers?"

I nodded. "How'd you guess?" I asked, half sarcastic.

"I've been to a few of those White Robes in my time," Teddy said. He put on a grim doctor's face: "I've seen this before." I laughed at his tone, which compared the ceremony to a serious condition that lacked a cure. I felt, all of a sudden, less embarrassed. How silly it all was, and how funny I must have looked in the banished robe.

"Let's have coffee and make fun of the ashram," Teddy suggested.

"Or maybe something stronger," I joked, but I was grateful for someone to sit with. Teddy eased the moment, and while we sat and talked, I forgot all about the empty page in the journal and the little voice that had warned me about Teddy. How kind he was being, paying for the coffee and then leading me outside. The air had cooled, the wind smelled sweet, the tables outside were littered with newspapers and crumbs. Our coffee was hot and thin and laced with sugar.

"So what do you do here?" I asked him as we sipped. I could smell chocolate emanating from the bakery.

"I'm a Ph.D. student," he answered. "Anthropology. I'm especially interested"—he paused, put down his books, and stretched his hands out before him—"in the palms."

"*You read palms*?" I asked, then immediately regretted my dubious tone. A true Westerner I was proving to be, doubtful of the softer, spiritual sciences. Sure enough, he looked offended.

"I don't just *read palms*," he insisted, as if he'd dodged the question all his life. "I read them in the traditional, voodoo-ey way." He wiggled his fingers in the air to emphasize *voodoo*. "But my degree has many levels. Astrology, physiology, human biology, psychology . . ." the list petered out. He set his coffee down beside him and leaned back on the heels of his hands. "It's a complicated degree," he finished, drawing a pack of cigarettes from his pocket.

I watched him strike a match and light a cigarette. As an afterthought, he offered the pack to me. I shook my head. "So, what can you see in the palms?" I asked him. I looked at my own; they were sweaty, for one thing, with a few scooping lines.

"Oh, you can read many things," he finally said vaguely, maybe still miffed. He drew on his cigarette and blew the smoke into the street. He took another drag, exhaled. "Many things," he said again, this time as if to himself, drawing the words out like honey scooped with a spoon. I guessed he was going to make me beg. He turned and looked at me for a long moment, his gaze uncomfortably piercing. I looked away.

"You don't have to tell me," I finally said. *Two can play at this game.*

"It's not that I don't want to tell you," he said, and just like that, the tension hovered and eased. He smiled again. "It's that . . ." he paused, "I'm afraid to tell you what the palmist sees."

I waited for him to explain.

"Everyone wants their palm read," Teddy said, "but when they hear what the lines mean, they often see them as . . ." he waved his hands, looking for the right word. "As ugly. People are afraid of the truth in the lines." He looked over, down at my hands, and only then did I notice that I was running my first finger along the lines of my left hand.

He grinned at that. "Do you really want me to read it?" he asked.

"Sure," I said, and though I made my voice casual, I realized I meant it. I wanted to see if he really was who he said he was, but more than that, I wanted to hear the ugly bits.

"You sure?" he asked. "Because I will. I'll tell you what it says." His voice was still lighthearted, and I nodded. He smiled that half-smile, the one I'd seen creep across his face in the bookshop.

"Okay then, hand it over. Ha, get it? *Hand* it?" He laughed, and I caught a glimpse of the molar, the rotten one his lips usually concealed.

I faked a laugh. "I get it," I said, sticking my left palm out.

"I need to see both," he said. He put his cigarette out on the bottom of his shoe and flicked the thick gold filter into the gutter. Then he took both my hands in his; how warm his fingers felt, how they nearly pulsed against my skin. He rubbed my outstretched palms with his thumb, as if to draw out the lines. For a very long time he stared at them, looking back and forth between my two hands.

"It's a very interesting hand," he muttered finally. "A very, *very* interesting hand." Again he went quiet, pressing my palms again with his thumbs. Then he let both hands fall.

"You will have an ordinary life," he said with a shrug. He wouldn't meet my eyes.

"That's it?" I checked my palms myself; what was so wrong with them? "Tell me, Teddy," I urged. "I won't be hurt." Even then I think I knew it was a lie.

"Yes, you will," he affirmed, and inhaled deeply, letting his breath out slowly. "This is why I never read the palm of a friend," he said, going for his cigarettes again. "They never leave me alone after that."

But I wanted to know! I *had* to; now that he'd seen, we couldn't go back. "Please tell me," I said, and now I really was begging. What could be so terrifying in the lines?

"Okay," he finally said, after a few long drags on his new cigarette. "Okay. I can tell you about now, because the hand is always changing to show the present. Here," he reached for my right palm and poked a finger into the longest line, "in India, you're afraid. You're suspicious. And, you're often alone?" he looked at me. I nodded, unimpressed—any female traveler would feel those things. "But, you feel as though you are searching for something here?" he continued. "And," he added, "you worry you'll go home without it." Again he looked at me, confirming. I nodded yes. "You're expecting something. Not *expecting*," he laughed, "as you Americans say, but *expectant*. You're waiting for something."

"That doesn't sound so horrible," I said. It was all I could think to reply. Only later would what he said really sink in: all throughout India, I felt oppressed by the constant eyes upon me, the omnipresent crush of people.

"There's something else," he told me. "Something happened, before you were born. Maybe something happened with your parents, or in your family. I think," he paused, took a drag, let the cigarette fall, "it was something bad."

Teddy stood, his coffee cup empty. He stretched his arms high and glanced down at me. I must have looked bewildered, because he said, as if to comfort me, "Don't worry; luck will be on your side." He mumbled something about how he had to meet his friend inside. "You okay?" he asked. I nodded.

"See you, Teddy," I called softly as he walked away, but I couldn't be sure whether he heard.

Instead of returning to the ashram, I walked toward the city center. This walk was always rich for the senses, and I let my mind wander into everything I passed. I couldn't think too much about what Teddy said—I just couldn't. It was as if he'd seen me, watched the movements behind my eyes, the shifting beat of my heart. His words were like the empty page of the journal we'd found together: meaningless without context, yet somehow important, too. The most frightening thing was his hesitation, the way he'd glanced at me, tight-lipped.

I walked home, letting the sights of the walk replace the nagging curiosity of what he'd withheld. Vendors tended stands from dawn until dusk, and the cigarette and sweet shops stayed open through the night. Boats on the river pulled up to the banks, and bums and sadhus slept on the shores,

shaded by day and protected from the wind by night with
trees and boulders. Taxis pulled up from the train station;
buses came through from Bombay and sometimes from as
far away as New Delhi. The buildings alongside these roads
crumbled with peeling paint and broken blocks, and I thought
that those signs of age, of wear, gave each structure a rugged
beauty. How many years those layers marked: a decade of
cream, another of blue, each shade revealed in patches. Thin
old men pedaled bike rickshaws as I approached the city center, their rubber sandals flapping on their dusty feet.

The wealthier, more modern side of Pune came next, with
paved roads and expensive restaurants, a shopping mall and a
university. The center pulsed with people on bicycles, scores
of buses, cars that slunk through the crowds. The visitors
ambling around the mall were dressed in Western clothes;
almost everyone wore sunglasses, their skin tanned. I forgot
about my white robe and let myself observe: the women could
have stepped onto Fifth Avenue and been admired for their
beauty, their cutting-edge style. I hadn't seen Louis Vuitton
in months, but suddenly I was surrounded. There was Jimmy
Choo and Vera Wang, draped over the wrists and arms and
heads of the women who glanced at me, taking in my robe, the
sweat at my hairline. They didn't interrupt the flow of chatter into their cell phones, just raised curved eyebrows or half-
smiled to themselves and turned their eyes down, amused.

I got lost in the winding streets of Pune, and it was dark
before I took a rickshaw back to Aman's flat across the
river. He'd been worried sick about me, it was clear; when I
knocked on his door, he opened it immediately, relief in his
eyes. His hair was greasy, like he'd run his hands through it
over and over. He'd changed out of his white robe, but still
had his black sneakers on.

"Oh, dear," he gushed, before I was even inside. "I heard
about the robe." He looked me over. "I guess I should have

known. They're very strict about the white robe." He went to the stove to start tea. "Oh, *darling*," he went on as he filled the kettle, "where were you? Oh, I'm so sorry. I apologize. What a long night you must have had."

He turned to look at me, to check whether indeed I'd had a long night, and perhaps to hear where, exactly, I'd been. But I couldn't think of an excuse. How could I tell Aman that a palmist had seen something bad in my hand, and I'd wandered the city as a way to escape? I apologized, explained that I'd gone to the bookstore and lost track of time.

Aman and I resumed our routine. For three more days we rose in the morning, walked across the river for morning meditation, sipped tea at the ashram. Aman and I did not attempt the White Robe ceremony again, nor did we speak of the night I'd been turned away.

I tried to give the place another chance—Aman loved it so—but the sealed-off grounds and surly guards wore on me. The ashram tried to push India out, tried to erase the sounds, the pulse, of this country, and this was not what I'd come to India to find. So far, the closest thing to peace I'd encountered was the blank page in the journal, the one I could settle my mind upon. And so after my seventh day in Pune, while Aman and I stood in his kitchen, preparing tea, I told him I'd be leaving the next day. He was kind, helping me buy a ticket to Goa, my next destination. I could tell he was sorry I hadn't loved the ashram the way he did, and I was grateful he didn't plead with me to stay.

Aman still slept as I crept out the door in the darkness of early morning. I scribbled a note on the pad beside the phone: *Aman: thanks for everything. Will call when I get to Goa.*

Then, as I let myself out, closing the door quietly behind me, I saw the envelope on the ground, tucked halfway under the door.

It could have been mail, an electricity notice, some apartment document, but something compelled me to pick it up and lift the open lip. Perhaps it was the spark I felt on my fingertips, seeing the unmarked envelope lying there. Opening it, I saw that it wasn't meant for Aman at all. I drew the page from the envelope slowly, knowing just what it was and at the same time hoping it was anything but.

It was the empty page, with the signature in the lower right corner.

The edge of the paper was ruffled from where it had been torn from the notebook. Ripped from its context, it had been folded and smudged, and now resembled trash. I held the envelope and the piece of paper with trembling hands. I remembered my train. With the papers still clutched in my hands, I ran down the stairs, through the gate, and onto the main road where I caught a rickshaw that would take me to the station.

I don't have the empty page anymore. When I got to Goa, I looked up the address of the bookstore and mailed it back with a note of explanation. I don't know why Teddy tore the page from the book, or how he knew where to leave it. But the memory stays with me, even as my time in the ashram has fallen away. The ashram was a place where I failed, spiritually and logistically, but Teddy and the empty page remain unanswered questions in my mind—as does the palm reading. I've never asked my parents or my brother, but his words have stayed with me.

Maybe, holding that journal in my hands, with Teddy looking over my shoulder, I did find what I was seeking in India. Maybe his smile was never sly after all; maybe he only used it to conceal something ugly from the world. Meanwhile, places that glimmer aren't always made of gold, and the truest beauty can be found in the clamor of an unpaved road, or in the layers of paint on a building—creamy white beneath robin's-egg blue, or coral cracking over teal. Secrets sometimes live in dusty bookshops, even when they're impossible to locate in the glistening reflection of a mirrored mosaic, or in the rhythm of a hundred people breathing.

I think of the creased paper, the texture of the scrawled words, and I hope that whoever wrote that journal will someday come to claim it again, that they will open the cardboard cover, check for the scrawled name, and find the page where they left it, torn from the spiral rings but intact, blessed in its comparative bareness.

Kate McCahill is a writer, editor, and visual artist from Lake Placid, New York. As the 2010 Mary Elvira Stevens Traveling Fellowship recipient at Wellesley College, Kate spent a year traveling overland from Guatemala to Patagonia, teaching English and writing along the way. She holds a Bachelors degree from Wellesley College and an MFA from Vermont College, and she currently lives in Santa Fe, New Mexico.

ABBIE KOZOLCHYK

✌ ✌ ✌

Meat and Greet

"Vegetarians . . . are the enemy of everything good
and decent in the human spirit." — *Anthony Bourdain*

The Traveler's Code of Conduct—a body of oral law
etched indelibly into the collective nomadic consciousness—is very clear on matters of food: however unfamiliar,
unappetizing and/or squirmy, nothing a host serves may be
turned down. Especially when you're a stranger in a strange
land. To violate this rule is to violate one of the most ancient
and sacred precepts of hospitality—and to reveal simultane-
ous provincialism and schmuckiness of the highest order.

Here, then, one schmuck's tale.

I became a vegetarian twenty-five years ago, during a
tenth-grade biology lab, when my designated dissectee turned
out to be the pigeon that broke the camel's back. Deceased
animals placed before me, whether as meals or science projects, had long since induced guilt and a gag reflex. And for
some reason, with this one squab au jus de formaldehyde, I
was done.

Alas, some twenty years later, my hosts on Yao Yai didn't
get the memo.

No, really. There was a memo. Or at least a *Special Dietary
Requirements* section of the paperwork I'd filled out for my

trip to this southern Thai island. I was heading there to write about a nascent homestay program, and my friend Lon—always up for a dose of the different—was joining me.

Thus did we find ourselves the newest residents of an isolated wooden shack. It was surrounded by rice paddies and water buffaloes, propped up on stilts, and filled—in our honor—with freshly prepared fish.

Yes, our appointed island home—where two men on motorbikes had just deposited us after a dock-to-door off-road derby—harbored the ichthyological mother lode. Name the Andaman Sea subspecies, however obscure, and it was represented in our welcome buffet. Highly identifiably, in fact: whatever had happened to these fish between their last swim and their appearance on the day's menu, nary a scale, fin, tooth or eyeball was out of place.

So I knew Lon wouldn't be the one to get us out of this mess. Normally she'd act as my omnivorous wingman, making at least a respectable dent in any non-veg offerings. But anatomically correct entrées were her deal breakers—grounds for a poker-faced declaration of vegetarianism. And I could feel one coming on.

I panicked. And the heat and humidity—augmented by a thousand steaming fish dishes, all enclosed in the house's tiny central room—didn't help. Within seconds I felt woozy. But apparently, no one was the wiser. Our host parents, each a good decade our junior, beamed expectantly, gesturing toward what had clearly taken them hours (him, on the fishing end; her, on the cooking end) to produce. Just for us. The esteemed guests. Oy gevalt.

As much as I hated being *that* tourist—the philistine who rejects such generously, lovingly, painstakingly prepared food—I saw no alternative. Especially as Lon was giving me the "can't help you, dude" shrug.

"I'm SO sorry," I began, looking back and forth between our new parents, who spoke next-to-no English.

"So, so, so, so sorry," I continued. "I really can't tell you how sorry I am. But there seems to have been a misunderstanding."

Their brows—until now eagerly raised—suddenly descended to the mildly concerned elevations. But still, not a glimmer of comprehension.

So I tried again.

"You've prepared *such* a beautiful meal. So, so, so, so beautiful. Wow. Really, wow. The only problem is, sadly—very, very, very sadly—we can't eat it."

Nada.

Between the fish haze and the fear of offending—both intense to begin with and rising at equal rates—I wasn't sure how much lucidity I had left.

My mind raced several years back to another such episode, when Lon and I were in Frankfurt, and I was struggling to order a meat-free meal. After attempting every possible pronunciation of the word *vegetarisc*—only to be met with the waitress's blank stares—I finally blurted out, *kein fleisch*.

No meat.

Plain and simple. Crude and desperate. The fumbling vegetarian's version of the Hail Mary pass. But it worked.

I thought I'd try it again.

Not knowing the Thai words for *no meat,* however, I resorted to miming them this time. And in a show of solidarity, Lon was soon in on the act. With a succession of moves not seen since my Red Cross Advanced Swimmer certification circa 1980, I did lap after lap around the tiny living room as she did the universal "no-no" wag. But the unfortunate thing about breast, side, and back-strokes is that fish tend not to use them. By the time anyone got what we were saying, we had performed a veritable Macarena of *we-no-eat-seafood* gestures.

Nevertheless, *something* finally clicked, and our hosts nodded accordingly. Then they started laughing hysterically.

Some things—the unbridled joy of watching two grown women make giant asses of themselves, for example—are indeed universal.

With our plunge into idiocy, the group dynamic changed radically. No longer were we a collection of strangers, smiling and nodding at a polite distance. There was something familiar, even familial, about the way we were cracking each other up now.

Still, our Charades skills went only so far. We failed to convey to our hosts that the plain rice they'd already cooked would more than suffice, so an hour later—to our mortification—a replacement feast showed up. The motor-bikers had been sent back to "town" (a relative term on a one-road island), where some mystery chef had devised an all-you-can-eat vegetarian buffet—from the curries whose estimable coconut, coriander, and lemongrass quotient immediately overtook any lingering fish smells, to the garlicky, gingery stir-fries that finished the job. And for dessert, every possible combination of banana leaf, sticky rice, mango, and taro.

Absent a table and chairs, which don't come standard with Yao Yai stilt houses, we sat in a circle around the food on the linoleum floor.

By now, we were famished—and so were, apparently, all the neighborhood ants. They showed up as soon as we were served, and without ever breaking formation, marched militantly over our ankles, calves, and thighs to get to the goods.

Lon and I once again exchanged glances, but to our surprise, no one else did. There was evidently nothing out of the ordinary about 100,000 ants showing up for lunch.

Abstinence was not an option. Was it?

No, we silently confirmed to each other; it wasn't.

So without even speaking, we arrived at a system. Pretending not to notice our ant-covered bodies and plates, we'd wait for breaks in the foot traffic. Then—our chopsticks precocked—we'd go in with laser-like speed and precision, hoping to minimize the insect protein content. Because really, what was a little syncopated stick work, given our already curious eating habits?

Soon enough, we all started chatting again—and rarely stopped during the three days we spent on top of each other in this tiny home. Of course, no one had the faintest idea what anyone else was saying, but that seemed a minor detail.

So taken were we with these impossibly warm, open, and lovely people, that even activities we normally wouldn't sign up for—the admiring of doomed fish, for example—now seemed a perfectly acceptable form of bonding. When our host father and his fishing buddies took us by long-tail boat to behold the waterborne holding pen they'd set up in the middle of Phang Nga Bay, their giddiness was palpable. Forget the surreal limestone formations that protruded from blue-green waters, or the secluded, powdered sugar beaches—or any of the other greatest hits of Phang Nga Bay. Though we were dutifully escorted to all of them, nothing lit these boys up the way a mackerel in a net did. How could we *not* smile and nod appreciatively at every last detainee?

We repeated the exercise (or a variation on it, anyway) later that day, as our host mother expertly handled a succession of carcasses in the kitchen. She was so solicitous—always looking up from her work to smile at us and make sure we were having a good time—that we dared not disappoint. If we were going to commit the cardinal traveler's sin of not eating the day's catch, we could at least ham up our audience participation. And judging from our oohs and ahhs, you'd think fish gutting was our favorite spectator sport.

That night, our last on the island, even the ants endeared themselves to us as we dodged them to get to our farewell feast: ten curries, stir-fries and sticky rice confections for every one that had appeared on our first day.

After dinner, Lon and I gave our host mother a pair of earrings we knew she'd love. (They were the same enameled bohemian jobbies we had loved at her age.) And the following morning, they kept catching the sun as she waved goodbye to us from the dock. But as we waved back—our ferry slowly maneuvering out of its slip—we noticed a much subtler glimmer: tears were running down her cheeks. Down our host father's, too.

Within seconds, Lon and I were crying too—at which point we realized how quickly we'd all formed this funny little family. The process wasn't graceful—but God, was it delicious.

ॐ ॐ ॐ

Abbie Kozolchyk, a New York-based writer and editor, has contributed to National Geographic Traveler, Travel + Leisure, *the* San Francisco Chronicle, Outside, World Hum, Concierge.com, Forbes Traveler, *Traveler's Tales, and a variety of women's magazines. Visit her at www.abbiekozolchyk.com.*

.🙞 🙞 🙞

Death and Love in Kenya

Kenya would teach her to cope—
whether she liked it or not.

The morning James died, I was on my way to visit a
neighbor.

December is Kenya's summertime, hot and dry, dust from
the baked plains rising in lazy clouds and settling onto sweaty
skin. My home, a little concrete bungalow, sits on the edge
of a dingy Nairobi bedroom community stretching its gangly
legs in the African version of urban sprawl—tin slum houses
creeping beyond the town limits, tin slum bars springing up in
small, social clusters. Across the highway, the town gives way
to savannah, the long plain clouded with dust from cement
factories, the scrubby grass green during the bi-annual rainy
seasons, crisply brown the rest of the year.

"Carry your phone," urged my sixteen-year-old foster
daughter.

"I don't want to carry my phone," I said. "I'm relaxing, I
don't want to be disturbed."

"But someone important might call!" she said. Scandalized
that I would consider violating social etiquette by being unavail-
able to speak with someone who wished to speak with me.

I was not a hundred yards down the road when the phone
rang. "I heard a rumor," my colleague said. I stood in the

concrete-brick street, staring at the bougainvillea climbing up the fence, its blossoms too bright, the day too beautiful, for the news that a friend had been killed.

That December was my second in Kenya. The previous year, just as my marriage was freefalling into crisis, I had come alone to Africa for what was meant to be a brief stint of volunteering. Daily I walked a circuitous route through the dusty town to perform my Do-Gooder White Girl duties, visiting low-income women living with HIV/AIDS. There was Violet, huddled in a tin house at the end of an alley running with wastewater, too weak to walk or speak; her seven-year-old daughter Elizabeth, coughing wetly with TB, would climb in my lap to sing. Hellen, wrapped in flimsy khangas, begged me to find an orphanage for her children so they would at least be fed. Adhiambo lay in a hospital bed pointing from her baby to me: "Samuel, you mama, *you*," she declared, but to my relief she rallied, returning to her dirt-floored shack to continue raising her baby herself.

During those first months, Kenya kicked my ass. Its sheer, unstoppable poverty—the withered women extending pleading hands; the copper-haired children weak with malnutrition; the glue kids staggering past with an open bottle to their lips, breathing in the fumes that made the misery go away. I was crushed by the knowledge that nothing I could do would fix it. And I was constantly embarrassed by being so other, my white skin guaranteeing that my Kenyan experience would occur from a distance, viewed through a lens of plenty, of pity, of knowing *this will never happen to me*. I imagined the Kenyans despising me for it.

Nonetheless I felt, for the first time, that I was doing what I was meant to do. And so, when my husband and I decided to split up, I stayed.

One year later, I was living in a small, comfy bungalow in a quiet estate outside Nairobi. I had wanted to live "among the people," but while I was comfortable using a squat toilet, carrying my water home in a jerrican, and sweeping my concrete-floored house with a small bundle of twigs, it's not called "Nai-robbery" for nothing, and security was one thing I was unwilling to go without. So I and my laptop, iPod, camera, and phone had taken up residence in a new housing estate, sheltered by chain-link fences cloaked in purple bougainvillea with guards standing bored but vigilant at the gate. I had, of necessity, traded full-time volunteering for a good job in advertising. Daily I cloaked my otherness beneath my adaptability, slowly learning Swahili, shaking hands with everyone when I entered a room, always carrying my own toilet tissue. I was falling in love with Africa. I was making it.

Then James died. And I saw a deeper layer of life in the developing world, one where the suffering *could* happen to me.

My neighbor, a rotund woman with a Kenyan good nature, found me bawling under her avocado tree. "Sorry, sorry," she soothed. It's what Kenyans say when something bad happens to you—if you so much as stub your toe, a stranger on the sidewalk will cluck an earnest "Sorry!" In a land of so much suffering, sympathy is abundant.

"My friend died," I sobbed, anxious to justify my maudlin American tears. "He was shot."

"The one with dreadlocks?" Mary asked. I shook my head, ashamed to feel relief.

In fact, James had been my first Kenyan friend. The day I'd arrived, petrified, for my supposedly brief African experience, James had singled me out from the other volunteers; as we were shuttled to our homestays, he dared me to drive the van, knowing it was the wrong side of the road for me. I called his bluff and drove a tentative half-kilometer. He cheered, and we were friends. Over the next year I came to know him as a deeply kind-hearted man, devoted to his wife and daughter, passionate about helping his fellow Kenyans. His was one of those "why him?" deaths. There is never a why, of course, death just is, but I was fresh from several crushing losses and didn't know how not to go there. He shouldn't have died, because his death hurts *me*. Grief is a selfish emotion, in the end.

The one with dreadlocks, on the other hand, was my boyfriend Austin. My first boyfriend since the divorce, since promising myself I would never be vulnerable to a man again. Dating had been easy to swear off in Kenya, where the single men (not to mention many non-single ones) were fond of pickup lines like "So where can I find a white wife?" But Austin was special, a courteous, compassionate man, devoted to his work as a soccer coach for children in the slums. The dreadlocks, which he'd grown after ending his career with the Kenya national soccer team, hung halfway down his back, giving him a tough appearance (dreadlocks were often associated with Kenya's ruthless political gang, the Mungiki) that belied his extraordinarily gentle nature.

I've never been able to resist gentleness.

Each phone call I made that morning confirmed James' death, and each Kenyan, much closer to James than I was, comforted me. "Sorry, sorry," they soothed, genuinely distressed at my pain, as if their own was not infinitely greater. Had I been braver, I would have called James's wife to offer my condolences. I knew a bit about grief; in the preceding three years I had lost my mother and my two-year-old niece to cancer. But my bereavements, while crushing, had not affected my survival. Grace's sudden widowhood, on the other hand, rendered her an unemployed woman in an impoverished, jobless land, with no way to support herself or her child— and I, who could lay down the plastic and be sipping a grande macchiato in my hometown Starbucks twenty hours later if Kenya got too tough for me, was ashamed to claim any common ground with her catastrophe.

I'd planned a party at my house that afternoon for the HIV women and their families. The death of a friend entitled me to cancel, but I would have been compelled to join the crowd of mourners filling Grace's home, and I was too chicken. And too socially unacceptable—while Grace's status as new widow gave her carte blanche to weep, I had no such excuse and would have embarrassed myself and everyone else with my inappropriate sniveling. So the party was on.

Violet came, dressed in her best purple dress, strong enough now to walk short distances. Hellen, resting in my small yard, watched her daughters skipping rope and managed a weary smile. An hours-long Monopoly game took place between an HIV-positive white friend who blew Kenyans' minds (you mean you can get it too?) and the children, too poor to go to school, too smart to be daunted by the complex Western game; they acquired fictional property with heartbreaking glee.

As a little girl, I had occasionally visited wealthy friends whose splendid homes amazed me; I was both warmed and astonished to realize my simple concrete bungalow must be the same to these children, its flush toilets, five rooms, and all-you-can-eat snacks a veritable wonderland. Looking through their eyes, I tried to count my blessings, to stop my infernal weeping and remember how fortunate I was. As a Kenyan hostess should, I chatted and entertained my guests, I stuffed them with chapati and lentils and rice—and every so often, as the afternoon passed, I remembered with a sick shock that James was still dead.

Finally I told Austin. He had invested himself for years in the lives of kids who grew up and got shot by police, or were executed by the Mungiki, or drank the mind-altering illegal brew called changa'a and set themselves on fire. He knew what sudden, senseless loss was like.

"Anish, what is wrong?" he asked as I dissolved in tears again.

"James was shot last night," I blubbed. "He died."

"Ah," he sighed. "Sorry, sorry."

Tearfully, I recounted James' death. Austin listened in silence, nodding, then urged me, "Be strong."

Be strong? My ex-husband had never asked me to be strong. He probably *still* had stains on his shirts from how often I'd bawled in his arms. But Kenyans are accustomed to disaster; they can't afford, or won't permit, the luxury of acting tragic over something so common as a young father shot dead by thieves at the gate of his home. "Don't cry, Mama," my foster daughters exhorted, and I heard their disapproval—orphans since girlhood, they knew a thing or two about suffering themselves. Still, I was irritated; as an American, I firmly believed in my God-given right to express my emotions. But as a Kenyan, I was expected to suck it up. I wasn't sure I could. My ache for James, for the pointlessness of his death and the suffering of his wife and child, felt like the first bruise of a beating that would break me if I stayed.

I thought of Grace again that night, after I finally saw my guests off, waving them home on the matatu minibus with relief. The house quiet at last, I rested with Austin, studying his face by lamplight—the long scar above his eyebrow, the dreadlocks framing his jaw, the silky black skin of his cheeks where I stroked my thumb. I had been so determined not to fall in love again. Yet there we lay, on a thin foam mattress on my white-tiled floor, cuddled in a posture only love takes. I had loved my husband, but I left him; Grace loved hers, and she stayed. Yet for her this was the first of a lifetime of nights without her husband, and for me it was another night in my lover's arms. Grief is selfish, and so is love—that I, who had love once and walked away, was taking more.

I thought, after the death of my mother, my niece, even during the self-inflicted severance from my husband, that losing someone I loved so much would destroy me. But an

African will tell you: everything is lost in the end. Love is no guarantee, not for the man to whom I whisper *ni yangu*, "mine," not for the two delightful, trying teenagers who call me Mama, not for the dying children skipping rope in my front yard with deceptive vigor while their weakening mothers watch and smile. You can love someone and lose them in an instant, or across the path of years. But you will lose them in the end.

In Africa, you must grow like the acacia tree, twisted by the wind but continuing to stretch for the sky. Life is harsh, but it is beautiful; so you care for your loved ones when they suffer, you say "sorry, sorry," and together you go on.

Anena Hansen still lives in Kenya, still gets her ass kicked by deep poverty, and still plans to stay because now it's home. With a helplessly American perspective, she blogs about her Kenyan experiences on her website, www.anenahansen.com. *In addition to freelancing for local and international publications, she balances a power-suit day job in advertising with running a soccer program for high-risk teenage girls in the slums. Austin, naturally, is the football team's coach. They're engaged to be married, and she is stoked.*

LAURA FRASER

✿ ✿ ✿

Dance of the Spider Women

A traveler to Italy is bitten by
a mysterious, ancient rhythm.

*T*he road that runs down through Salento, a region in the
heel of Italy's boot, is almost completely deserted at night.
I am driving to a folk concert with two Italian friends, and we
pass only a few sleepy villages, many gnarled olive trees, and
scarcely another car along the way. When we reach the town
of Alessano, situated a few kilometers from the point where
the Adriatic and Ionian seas meet at the tip of the peninsula,
we park on a narrow cobblestone street. No one is out, and the
air is dry and hot. The place seems scrubbed bare of inhabit-
ants. We trudge up a hill, round a corner, and then—a blaze
of light. Before us, the central piazza is packed with thousands of people. The crowd stretches from the town's ornate
neo-Gothic church to the clock tower, everyone staring up at
the brightly lit stage.

Singer Enza Pagliara, the evening's main act, is just warm-
ing up. Fernando Bevilacqua, a local photographer who has
brought my friend Giovanna and me here, elbows his way
to the front of the crowd, sidling past elderly *signoras* in car-
digans and pumps, scruffy kids with dreadlocks, men with
slick black hair and neat red pants, and young women in

diaphanous skirts and eggplant-tinted curls. The crowd is *di tutti i colori*, as they say in Italian, all types and all colors. Giovanna, who is short, climbs the step of a fountain to get a better view.

A few strums of guitar, several staccato taps on a tambourine, some mournful cello sawing, and Pagliara steps up to the microphone, reaching wide with her long arms as if to embrace the entire crowd. The sound that emerges from her mouth isn't like blues or jazz or opera or anything else I've ever heard. It's an Arab-tinged wail of close harmonies and dissonance, full of longing, lust, and lament. Her clear voice carries over the thousands of upturned faces, and the song seems as ancient as the limestone buildings of Alessano.

Maybe it is. When I tell Bevilacqua I can't understand a word, even though I speak Italian, he explains the lyrics are in Salentino and Griko, dialects spoken here that date back to the Greeks who colonized the area long before the Romans arrived. Pagliara sings hymns to endurance, plaintive tunes for gathering wheat under a beating sun; come-hither courtship dialogues with back-and-forth verses between voice and instruments; and pieces with polyphonic overtones that sound like Balkan ballads. Pagliara invites her elderly aunts and uncle on stage to sing a few traditional lullabies and other songs from their childhoods. The crowd is swaying, entranced by the mystical music, which is called *pizzica*.

Then a frenetic song starts up, and Bevilacqua whispers that this is a *pizzica pizzica,* which translates to "bitten bitten." The tambourine, accordion, and cello pick up speed, and Pagliara sings faster and faster. The words are coming so quickly now, they're just sounds. Pagliara is dancing so fast that her long black hair swishes wildly and her feet barely touch the stage. The earth vibrates with thousands of feet pounding the cobblestones in the square. Bevilacqua glances at me and says, "It's impossible not to dance, no?"

and I realize my feet are tapping, too. I give in to the rhythm and start twirling with the music. The crowd in the square breaks into small circles as people stomp, spin, and pair off for impromptu courtship dances. The pace is dizzying; no one can resist the song's contagious energy.

Tonight, the mood is celebratory, the antithesis of pizzica's seemingly tortured beginnings. Legend has it that in the distant past, musicians played these songs when someone, usually a woman, had been bitten by a tarantula spider. Contemporary pizzica, while paying homage to the customs of the past, represents a reawakening and reclaiming of the region's culture, turning something morose into a joyous event.

When the concert is over, many in the crowd continue playing tambourines, their bodies shaking and feet tapping, and we wander amid the stalls that sell CDs, instruments, jugs of local wine, and t-shirts emblazoned with big black spiders. The people around us keep dancing until we straggle back to the car at two in the morning.

I'm here in Salento in the middle of a scorching August for the Notte della Taranta, or Nights of the Tarantula, a weeklong festival that celebrates the tarantella, the famous folk music and dance of southern Italy. Concerts are slated for almost every night in different town squares throughout the region. Pizzica is the Salentine variant of tarantella, and its homeland, the southernmost part of Puglia, is still relatively untouched by tourism. It feels like the Italian countryside foreigners visited forty years ago. During the day, the villages are deserted, motionless, and oppressively hot; during the cooler evenings, the shops open, and people slink out as if from under rocks.

I've come because I'm fascinated with Salento's myth of the tarantula, in which women throughout history have claimed they'd been bitten by a tarantula, possessed, perhaps in order to escape their otherwise dreary lives. I'd seen images of these women in a dramatic film, *Pizzicata*, and heard it mentioned among my Italian friends. I wanted to understand more about this culture—and its music, which has made a decided comeback.

Since antiquity, and until only a couple of decades ago, life in Salento was desperate, particularly for women, who had little say in their destinies. Occasionally someone would sink inward, glassy-eyed, and begin writhing on the floor, delirious. Neighbors would whisper that she'd been bitten by the tarantula, and would circle around her playing instruments. The spider's poison would cause her to convulse and become manic. The afflicted *tarantata* would eventually rise up and dance in circles, stomping on the ground to the music (particularly the tambourine), as if trying to kill a spider, until the episode subsided. The ritual lasted, on and off, for up to three days, and the symptoms allegedly returned every year in June around the feast day of San Paolo (Saint Paul), who protects against venomous animals.

Today, Salento is better known for its craggy coves and Baroque architecture than for its *tarantate*, who—like the poisonous spiders that supposedly caused their frenzied state— have mostly died off. Yet on my first trip to Salento, three years ago, I noticed signs of those spiders everywhere. Faded posters of tarantulas were tacked up on village walls, advertising traditional *pizzica* music concerts. Happy-looking spiders beckoned from highway billboards, encouraging tourism in the area.

How had Salento transformed the tarantula—a grim symbol from its past—into a cheerful icon celebrating the region and its music?

To find out, I had to start with history. In the 1950s, a handful of anthropologists and ethnomusicologists started recording pizzica music. Alan Lomax, for instance—famous for discovering Muddy Waters, Leadbelly, Woody Guthrie, and other American roots musicians—amassed a collection of traditional Salentino folk songs. Another researcher, anthropologist Luigi Chiriatti, recorded music and oral histories in the early 1970s and has written several books on *tarantismo*.

After the concert in Alessano, I call Chiriatti, and he invites me over to his house in a town near Melpignano. His living room walls are covered with relics from his long career in anthropology: masks, ancient musical instruments, and black-and-white photos of Salento's past.

Chiriatti, a modest man in his seventies, is energetic and impassioned when talking about his region's deepest traditions, and we chat for hours about the history of the tarantula rites, how they came to Salento (probably from the Greek Dionysian cult), and the varieties of stories he has collected from tarantate over the years. What puzzles me, I tell him, is how *pizzica*, which he says by the 1980s was mostly forgotten or considered hillbilly music, is packing town squares in 2009.

"We had to revisit what identifies us as Salentini," he says. Previously, most associations with Salento had been negative. "It had been considered a land of remorse, a land from which people emigrated because there was no work, a land with no partisan heroes—a land that had been silenced and forgotten."

But when ethnomusicologists began rediscovering the songs and musicians began playing them, Salentini realized that *pizzica* music and dance are what makes their territory unique. Their view of the music—which is, at its heart, upbeat in sound—began to take on a positive cast, and this affected the way Salentini saw everything about their culture. "Through the music, we started seeing the territory in a truly different way, rediscovering the land, the rocks, the churches, the piazzas, and the sea," Chiriatti says. The music fits the place.

In the 1990s, a small underground pizzica scene started to percolate, partly boosted by *Pizzicata*, a 1995 neorealist film that included interviews and sessions with traditional

Salentine musicians. The film recounts the story of one tarantata, a young *contadina* (peasant woman) who was "bitten" by
a tarantula and fell ill after her lover was killed and she was
promised to his murderer.

Local musicians, including Bevilacqua—the photographer
who was my guide in Alessano—started organizing small
concerts and booking gigs throughout Europe. In 1997, some
young administrators of Salento's small towns recognized the
modern appeal of the spider and decided to use pizzica to pro-
mote regional identity, staging the first Notte della Taranta.
The event has grown exponentially ever since, bringing tens
of thousands of tourists to the area and making Salento syn-
onymous with pizzica, the way Argentina means tango.

"By freeing the music from associations with the spider,
the ritual, and religion, we've turned something negative into
something profoundly positive," Chiriatti tells me.

On the day before the final concert of the week in Melpignano, a town of about 2000 people, I find my way to the ruins
of the sixteenth century Carmine church. A stage has been
built there, and musicians are preparing for a dress rehearsal.
Enza Pagliara sits on the grass, pressing a sweating bottle of
water to her face to stay cool in the hundred-degree heat. I
sit down next to her and ask about pizzica's tarantula-related
origins.

Pagliara, forty-one, who has studied tarantismo and pizzica
for more than twenty years, says that most people think the
tarantulas were a myth. In 1959, the anthropologist Ernesto
De Martino set out with an interdisciplinary team of physi-
cians and psychologists to study thirty-five women afflicted
with *tarantismo*. His work was published in English as *The
Land of Remorse* (and "remorse" in Italian has a double meaning: re-bitten). Today, Pagliara says, most Salentini believe
that the tarantula bite was an excuse, a way for people in the
villages to express rage, repressed eroticism, and frustration.

"It was a territory that was extremely poor," Pagliara says. "People worked like serfs, and until fifty years ago, the *padrone* even had the *diritto della prima notte*," meaning the local landowner had the right to sleep with a bride first on her wedding night. "For women"—she makes a strangling gesture around her throat—"it was untenable, and the tarantula was the way to let loose of everything, a form of therapy before psychotherapy."

Pagliara grew up singing the songs with her aunts. She began recording, she says, because "I knew there was something precious in this music." She went to early pizzica gatherings in the '90s and learned to dance and play the tambourine. When she began to record her relatives, at first they were ashamed and wanted to sing songs from the radio instead. "Their songs have a real sense of this territory from the older days. They're the sound of the land, and I've wanted to keep them alive."

Pagliara performs at large concerts, but also at small pizzerias and at parties, sometimes until five in the morning. "I don't know how to sing pop or anything else," she says. "Our oldest music was therapy for the tarantata, and so maybe I am a little crazy, because I have to sing. I need it for myself more than anything. I can't help it; I feel like I have the living soul of the music inside me, the soul of the land."

I hear similar sentiments from other Salentini I talk to. The tradition is in their blood. Before the last show, I meet Giorgio de Giuseppe, who dances to pizzica almost nightly with small gatherings of musicians. We sit in a café outside a gas station in a small village near Otranto. De Giuseppe is a slight, fit retiree of fifty-six who worked as a jail guard. He tells me that his father, an illiterate *contadino* (peasant), was one of the rare men bitten by the tarantula, before Giorgio was born. His father never felt the bite, but became vague and depressed. Then, every year on June 29, he turned manic. The family took him to the church of Saints Peter and Paul in the village of Galatina to join the other *tarantate* in the region, who likewise became agitated on that day and went there to be calmed. For the rest of his life, even when he walked with a cane, his father had to dance whenever he heard a tambourine. Now de Giuseppe says he's inherited that urge. "A little bit of the spider's venom has been transmitted to my blood," he says. "I don't fall to the ground and have convulsions, but I *need* to dance when I hear the tambourine."

De Giuseppe's belief in the spider venom is unshakeable. "Why," I ask, "did the spiders mainly bite women?"

"They wore skirts—that made it easy to get bitten," he explains.

"Do you think that saying you were bitten by a spider might have been a way for people who were extremely *stressato* to let off some steam?" I ask. "Maybe the spiders weren't even poisonous. I mean, no one else in Italy went *pazzo* (crazy) after being bitten by a spider."

De Giuseppe becomes agitated. "Look, Laura," he says, tapping the table. "There are no more spiders because of pesticides, and so there are no more *tarantate*. If you go looking for a spider, you can't find one. They're extinct."

On the final night of the Notte della Taranta, Melpignano is transformed into a huge fairground with food vendors, camping tents, craft stalls, and remote video screens for dancers who want more space. De Giuseppe the dancer is there, peddling hundreds of little tambourines to tourists. Backstage, I pause to talk to Giuseppe Spedicato, thirty-three, the acoustic bass player in Pagliara's band. Spedicato tells me he became interested in pizzica while studying ethnomusicology in Lecce, the largest city in the region. I ask him why tens of thousands of people are gathering outside right now, from all over Italy, and he says there's a huge interest in traditional music now among his generation; these days it's cool.

"You go to anyone's house, or to a party, and people will make a circle and play pizzica and dance," he says. People love the music because it's so rhythmic and hypnotizing. "There are moments when the tambourine and the voice send people into a trance. It's a way of getting outside yourself." So, too, there's a fascination with the music's history. "Pizzica is popular partly because of the magic associated with it," he says. "The spider, the poison, the music as an antidote—we've got a collective infatuation."

The concert begins at dusk, and soon the crowd swells to more than 100,000 people, as far as I can see, all swaying together in front of the moonlit monastery ruins. Band after band takes the stage, starting with traditional acoustic music, and heading toward rock. Special guest stars—world musicians from other countries—join the Orchestra Notte della Taranta in compulsively danceable collaborations. The audience is transported, moving together as though under a spell. My friend Giovanna is here, along with several of her friends who've traveled all the way from Bologna in the north for the concert, which they say they wouldn't miss. Mesmerized by the music, the audience speeds up as the hour gets later and later.

When a man taps me on the shoulder and tells me I've been "bitten by the tarantula," I check my watch and notice I've been at the concert for seven hours straight, most of it dancing, packed into a crowd. The concert finishes around four in the morning, and it feels as though it just got started.

Afterward, Giovanna and I walk the streets of Melpignano as the wine sellers pack up, the jewelry makers take down their stalls, and the crowds disperse to the far corners of Italy. In the main square, dancers twirl and stomp on imaginary spiders. One by one, they drop off, a few curling up on the stone steps of San Giorgio church. As they finally sleep, exhausted, the sky grows light and the pale limestone glows a faint pink, already beginning to warm.

Laura Fraser is a San Francisco-based journalist and author whose articles have been featured in The New York Times, Mother Jones, Gourmet, *and* O, the Oprah Magazine. *She is the author of* The New York Times *bestselling travel memoir,* An Italian Affair. *Her most recent memoir is* All Over the Map.

೫ ೫ ೫

On the Macal

**A beat-up boat in Belize brought
a traveler back to herself.**

Yellow-headed swallows dipped in and out of thick mist
resting on the river. That fog probably followed the
water's curve for miles, I thought, maybe the whole length of
Belize. I wouldn't see a thing from the boat.

Atop a bank overlooking the Macal, I stood with my arms
crossed, waiting for full dawn, feeling miffed. The fog had
burned off along shore, but the water wouldn't let it go. As
I watched, a chunk of the white stuff seemed to break sideways and soar above the river, a white king vulture erupting
as if born of the mist. It tacked and flew close over my head.
I saw its magnificent wings trimmed smartly in black, each
feather distinct. Shaken from myself, I watched the bird
become ever smaller in blue sky, like a rocket launched into
space.

"Just you?" came a voice from below.

A young man, very young but no longer a boy, stood tall
and tanned, barefoot on the sand. He was talking to me. I
nodded.

"Good," he said. "We be light."

At the water's edge sat a feeble-looking craft about ten feet long, maybe a near antique, a fiberglass canoe scratched and dull with age. This tableau below me, I supposed, was what I had purchased at the hotel desk the night before: "River Trip, Laid Back, No Frills, Local Guide."

The young man's smile wasn't mocking, but he was enjoying something, all right. "Yo best be comin' down then," he said. Had I been staring at him?

On the beach, I extended my hand, and he took it softly. "Do you want to see the receipt?" I asked.

"Henry," he said. His long, dark hair was braided into a thousand tresses, each secured at the bottom with a single cocoa-colored bead. I wondered who did it for him, then wondered why I wondered.

"So Henry," I said, more curtly than necessary. "Do you want the receipt?"

He shook his head no. The smile became even wider, but it was kind. Bright teeth. Full lips. He lifted the bow of the boat and raised his eyes to the aft, a signal I should push. I slipped off my sandals and dropped them into the canoe. When Henry tried to help me board, I waved him away. Lowering myself to the middle plank seat, however, I lost my balance and almost tipped us both into the drink. He didn't meet my eyes then. I felt spared, but mad at myself as we pushed off from shore.

"Yo wantin' a ride on da river, Miss Lady," he said to my back. The engine sputtered. "Yo want to re-lax."

He was right about that, but I didn't like hearing it from someone I had known for five minutes. Younger. Who spoke oddly. I had not dropped biology for years of studying literature without carrying around some proper respect for the language and—admittedly—some misplaced disdain for those who did not.

We floated under San Ignacio's tremulous, one-lane bridge. The rumble of tires on old metal rolled in my ears, beat on my head from inside the skull. I closed my eyes. *Re-lax*. Indeed.

"Like a thunder," Henry said. And I didn't want anyone reading my mind, either.

As we left the town behind, the harsh sounds of the bridge faded too, exactly like thunder receding. The small engine's soft putter became as much a part of the atmosphere as the birdcalls. In the mid-distance, three white egrets swooped low on wide, smooth wings, synchronized like a team of competitive divers.

I turned around and saw Henry perched on an aft plank painted gray-pink, right hand on the tiller. His khaki pants were cut off above the knee, about halfway up thighs that looked strong as the trunks of young mahoganies. I suppose I had turned around to get my bearings, but I am not sure. Henry steadied the tiller with an elbow as he pulled his shirt off over his head. He was slim, tight across the stomach.

"Da sun, yo know," he said.

"Da sun," I said. Then quickly, "Yes, the sun," and turned to face forward again.

Sharp-billed kingfishers perched on boughs that reached low over the water. Sometimes one spread its wings and leapt to another branch, bright red breast like a shooting dart. A blue heron, neck feathers still adolescent brown, posed on a green canoe, the boat tied up empty, its owner unseen. They bobbed gently together, blue heron, green canoe.

I don't know how long we'd been floating when I realized the sun had burned away almost all the mist. We came upon a rock that looked covered with brown lichen, and slowed. I dared to turn around once more, and as I did, Henry cupped his hand, scooped up water, and broadcast it over the rock; the brown mass burst into a cloud of tiny insects, thousands of vibrating wings sounding a high-pitched hum. Answering some signal known only to them, they tightened ranks in mid-air, then settled again as one upon another rock, silent and seamless as a prayer rug.

I could let go a little—why not? I gave Henry a congratulatory nod of the head. He grinned, proud of the lovely trick.

For an hour, Henry rowed from the forward plank. I watched his arm muscles strain now and then, but mostly he pushed in the current without effort. Once, when he pointed to the nearby shore, I focused my eyes and picked out iguanas in the trees. They were about four feet long, the kind called "green iguanas," but which turn brown with age to match the mottled boughs on which they stretch in the sun. I startled myself; I recognized the animals, even though so many years had passed since I'd studied them and their brothers, recognized them even though I had never seen the real thing outside a zoo or a lab. The iguanas might have lain there a million years, I thought, crested backs and long dinosaur tails motionless as high noon.

Below them, spiny-tailed wishwillies scavenged the beach for food. They were the iguanas' low-caste cousins, smaller, nervous-looking, and perpetually scurrying. Tree iguanas were herbivores, I knew, and wishwillies carnivores. I didn't need Henry's description of their repulsive behavior but laughed despite myself when he delivered it.

"When one person is buried an' everbody leave da grave, dem wishwillie go an' haf dem a party sure ever time."

I wondered what else was out there, what lived from the river, what existed in that porous green jungle wall. "Any monkeys or crocodiles?"

Yellow fever "wipe out da monkeys," said Henry, and hunters "ice da crocs" on this stretch of the waterway. But farther along where the Macal joins the Belize River, "they exist," he said.

"I do believe da crocodile come back heah someday again," Henry said dreamily, as if wishing it so.

For no reason I can give, besides the fact that we shared a capsule in time and space, floating hours together now on a river turning warm, I touched Henry's arm to get his attention.

"I do too," I heard myself say. "Wish da crocs come back."
No response.

"I studied all this, you know," I said. "I studied all this once."

My thoughts came fast now, thoughts long frozen defrosting faster than I could catch them. I wanted to suggest out loud that maybe it was not too late, that I could return to immersing myself in plants and animals, that I could just as well teach science to middle school students as teach them the form of the short story by way of Edgar Allan Poe. I wanted to talk.

Instead, I let myself drift along, taking in the colors of a river that flowed as ineluctably as fate, its course determined long ago. Matte orange bromeliads. Lustrous orange butterflies. Look how the bromeliads tied themselves to the trees, but didn't live off them; they weren't parasites. Rather they lived from the dying leaves and other vegetable matter that floated into their petals, soft pastel cups which cradled rainwater and condensation. Insects died there and were digested. I remembered.

A commotion in the bush, maybe a jaguarundi, sent small birds fluttering out of the canopy. White spider lilies grew in clusters along the bank, slender tentacles reaching out—for what?—from the heart of each flower.

Henry's traveling kit didn't include shoes, but did include rum. It was dark, and tasty.

"Do we want to take a swim?" he asked.

Later, we lay on the shore. Because Henry wore no shirt, it was difficult not to stare at his left nipple, pierced with a shape wrought in gold. It was meant to be noticed, and he looked pleased when I asked. A marijuana leaf, he said.

"I thought it was a bird," I said.

"Well, it make me feel like a bird."

He would not be a mere boatman forever, Henry said, but surely manage his own fleet of half a dozen canoes someday.

He knew the plants and animals on the river, taking seriously his job as a guide. "And I read," he said.

About those things he didn't know for certain, he said, he had "informed" opinions. The sudden and mysterious fall of the great pre-Columbian Maya Empire, the question archaeologists and epigraphers have debated for decades?

"No one know where the Maya disappear to," he said. "One day they just pick up they bags an' say, 'I'm goin' home.'"

I curled my toes into soft sand. All around us, wild purple bougainvillea emerged from the bush, circling the trunks of huge trees. This was bougainvillea at the Creation, I thought, lush and brazen, embracing giants, not dwarfing itself to accommodate a tame trellis as it might at home. I felt Henry's hand on my bare shoulder and followed his gaze to a pair of dragonflies with pearly blue necks. The sun shone on their black filigree wings as their bodies moved and went still, moved and went still, copulating on the bow of the boat. It was full midday, but there under the jungle canopy, on a beach practically hidden from the river, the searing air only warmed, like the temperature that opens a bloom.

I drew myself up on one elbow, and reaching over, fingered the gold leaf on Henry's chest. "Does that hurt?" I asked.

"I do feel it," he said.

I dropped my hand, but Henry stretched his arms above his head and closed his eyes. "You keep doin' that," he said.

It was natural we would make love, I suppose, as natural as the possibility that the river journey would pull me back into imagining a different present for myself.

We motored all the way on the return, to beat the dark, and spoke only twice.

"I can come to da hotel," Henry said. "My uncle own it."

"Maybe not," I said.

Some time later, I heard tinkling sounds, as if from small bells. I searched both sides of the river for what it might be but did not turn around in the boat.

"Da goats," Henry finally said to my back, and I could tell he had a knowing, contented look on that fine face. I didn't understand why speakers in these parts said "goats" for sheep, but I didn't ask.

Journalist and documentary filmmaker Mary Jo McConahay is the author of Maya Roads: One Woman's Journey Among the People of the Rainforest. *Visit her website at www. mayaroads.com.*

෨෨ ෨෨ ෨෨

Holiday Camp

Two young Texans find work in England—
and discover a whole new world.

*G*inny tore open the envelope, postmarked from London,
a few months before we were to leave.

"Butlin's Bognor Regis welcomes you to your place of
employment," she read. "Assignment: Retail catering."

The name looked regal enough, with "Butlin's Ltd. of
London" embossed in gold across the top of the stationery.
Elated, she continued: "Listed below is a brief description of
the facilities enjoyed by our staff during off-duty hours. These
include use of the indoor and outdoor pool, dancing in the
large ballrooms, variety shows, plays and films in the numer-
ous theatres, outdoor and indoor sports."

"Wow! It must be a fantastic hotel!" I said. "Retail catering?" I repeated, imagining the possibilities. "We'll need a
cocktail dress. Lots of cocktail dresses!"

It was the spring of 1969. The Beatles were about to record
Abbey Road, John and Yoko were planning a "bed-in" for
peace, and the British rock invasion was in full force. Screaming and jumping up and down on the pastel floral bedspread
my Mom had recently sewn for my room, we bounced with
our arms in the air and our hips making rock-and-roll moves

as we realized that our summer would be spent in the land of Mick Jagger, Twiggy, and the Queen.

I was born extremely inland, in Texas, surrounded by open plains and shopping malls. The farthest I'd ever been was across the border to Mexico, which had opened my eyes to other places, but not yet my mind. So, at twenty, I decided to spend the summer in Europe with my best friend Ginny. We paid $25 to a student travel agency that promised to find us work abroad.

Ginny and I arrived in London's Gatwick Airport at 2 A.M. on a June morning, each of us lugging two enormous bags stuffed with matching outfits, several evening dresses with accessories, dozens of shoes, and enough of our favorite hairspray to last three months. Pouring out of the airplane along with the rest of the packed-in college students assigned to the bargain flight, we fell behind as we dragged our bags through the nearly deserted airport. We immediately set out in search of a payphone to look up the address in a phonebook—because the work assignment, we had discovered on the plane, said only "Butlin's Bognor Regis," with no street number or location. We scoured the phone listings. It wasn't under hotels, motels, or even hostels.

"Come on. Let's ask someone," I finally said, and we found an official-looking counter.

"We want to go to the Butlin's Bognor Regis Hotel," said Ginny.

"Don't know it," came the dismissive answer. We asked a few other travelers and shopkeepers, but no one recognized the name. An airline attendant shook her head. We were too tired from the long flight to panic but were also at a complete loss. Finally, a nearby janitorial attendant overheard us.

"Butlin's is a holiday camp, dearies," she offered in an accent so thick we could barely understand her, "and Bognor

Regis is a town on the South Coast." A holiday what? Not London? But an hour later we had found the train that would take us the three-hour ride to the southern coastal town of Bognor Regis, and once again all seemed well.

We arrived to watch the rising fog reveal a village full of smoke stacks beside a grey sea.

"You must be staying for quite a while," the taxi driver remarked as he tried to stuff all four bags into his trunk. "Where to, luvvies?" He resigned himself to sharing his front seat with two of the bags and squeezed the passenger-side door shut.

"Butlin's!" we said at once, now confident in our destination.

"Butlin's?" He gave us the once-over. "Whadd'ya want to go to that dump for?"

We looked at each other, then back at him.

"We're working there," Ginny said, already defensive and not sure why.

He let out an involuntary guffaw and didn't stop chuckling the entire length of the ride.

Fifteen minutes later, after passing dozens of red-bricked industrial buildings and following a narrow street with a sea wall on one side and dark brown cottages on the other, he stopped the cab. We lined up our bags in front of a compound of low-lying buildings cloaked in mist and surrounded by a high barbed-wire fence. The cabbie wished us luck and drove off, leaving us in the hands of a uniformed guard who stood at the entrance and glumly inspected our papers.

Ginny introduced herself. "We're from Texas," she said, trying to be friendly.

The guard stared at our belongings, then picked up two of the bags with a gruff "hmmpf." We followed him through rows of two-story concrete buildings until he pointed to our room number. We opened the door to a small rectangular space with peeling green paint and just enough room for a bunk bed, a pole for our clothes, a sink, and a foreboding-looking intercom mounted on one corner of the ceiling. Were we in prison? We fell onto our bunks and submerged into sleep. After what seemed like mere seconds, the intercom started blaring a song:

"Do your singing in the chalet
As you start this happy day
While you're singing in the chalet
Think of all the fun you'll get the Butlin's way."

Neither of us stirred. But there it was half an hour later, another loud and zany song. When it blasted a third cheery song announcing breakfast, Ginny lunged toward it, looking desperately for the on-off switch. There wasn't one. We would come to find out that all Butlin's rooms, even the guestrooms, were subject to these intrusions, alerting everyone to their mealtimes and daily schedule of activities.

It was all part of the master plan.

Butlin's Holiday Camps were the inspired creation of a former carnival worker who, shortly before WWII, saw British working-class families bored, isolated, and unhappy during their brief, hard-earned vacations. He decided folks just weren't having enough fun. After the war, Sir Billy Butlin (he was knighted for his efforts) slowly began to buy up former army bases and motels in village towns across England. He hired small-time singers, dancers, and comedians and called them "Redcoats," the glamorous stars and entertainment ambassadors for the camps. It was absolutely mandatory at Butlin's to have a good time. The visitors were kept busy day and night with games, dancing, contests, and Redcoat-led fun. It was inexpensive and predictable, and countless British families flocked to the easy refuge of one week's pay for a week of regimented play.

Butlin's directors wore bright green jackets; supervisors wore blue, managers wore maroon, and we, as service-hands, were issued a drab brown uniform that suggested we were on the bottom rung of our new hierarchy. "Welcome to the Brit-ish class system," the young Icelandic girl said cheerfully as she handed us our uniforms.

"Better raise that hem six inches if you don't want the blokes to laugh," advised the rough-looking girl with dark curly hair who walked us to our new job. Her skirt showed almost all of her considerable thighs.

It was sound advice. The miniskirt ruled the day, and Nora, our new Irish friend, had worked here for several summers and knew the ropes. Nora showed us the massive cauldrons where we were to steam milk for morning tea and demonstrated how to position our heads as far away as pos-sible to clean the rancid-smelling crust left on the sides each night. She warned us not to be late for our early shift serving tea, never to be caught talking to the Redcoats, and to stu-diously avoid dates with the guys from Poland. Ginny and I were assigned a split shift from 5:30 to 8:30 A.M. and then 4 to 10 P.M., six days a week for the equivalent of $12.50 per week.

That night after our evening shift ended, Ginny and I decided to check out the camp. The campers' rooms, called "chalets," were shockingly similar to our own quarters: long straight lines of concrete buildings with rooms of barebones furnishings. Even the yellow, pink, and green paint couldn't hide the resemblance to military barracks. In the evenings, parents were allowed to leave children in their rooms and go out for the evening. Roaming nannies rode bicycles up and down the rows of chalets to listen for crying babies or out-of-bed children and if need be, locate the parents, who were usually enjoying a show at one of the pubs.

After inspecting the guestrooms, we slipped into the back of one such pub, arriving just in time to see a Redcoat plac-ing tiny chairs in a small circle on the stage. He called for volunteers. Multiple hands went up, but he was only inter-ested in the largest and heaviest members of the crowd, and

he wasn't afraid to point them out (even if they hadn't volunteered) and coerce them to the stage. A game of musical
chairs began, always with one chair too few, and we watched
as the guests competed for the tiny chairs and fell awkwardly
on the floor, their corpulent bodies like overturned tops struggling to get up. The crowd loved every pratfall, and no one
seemed embarrassed. I watched them enjoying themselves
and remembered something my Mom used to tell me: "Get
off your high horse."

At 5:30 the next morning, Ginny and I found the workers'
mess hall, smelling it blocks before we arrived. Kippers—
dried and salted fish—were the first things to greet us in the
dark. Luckily, we did have other choices: eggs swimming in
grease, sliced white bread smeared with yellow margarine,
bacon submerged in even more grease, and tea with milk. We
forced down a few eggs and arrived at our posts behind the
counter of a tea station.

"I must have my tea boiling hot," the first customer insisted.

"Mine must have one-quarter milk with tea to the brim,
medium hot," said the next.

I leaned in and listened hard, struggling to understand
the thick British slang as each customer specified the precise
temperature they needed their tea. It seemed this was the
one department in which they were particular, though. I was
continually astonished by their utter acceptance of medio-
cre service, rigid schedules, bland food, and intrusions of the
ubiquitous intercom offerings.

Sir Billy's taste clearly informed the décor of the camp. The
walls were orange, green, and purple, and plastic flowers were
everywhere. Virtually all the tables were covered with garish
paper-mache decorations, and large objects hung from the ceilings: painted chairs, buckets, and big glittery stars. One coffee shop even offered an underwater view of the glass-bottom

swimming pool so diners could enjoy their tea and watercress sandwiches while watching the bottom half of kids treading water across the glass, occasionally submerging to make faces at them. Contests were also immensely popular at Butlin's, and Ginny and I eventually witnessed the crowning of "Snorer of the Week," "Baldest Man," and "Miss Knobby Knees."

After a few days, the four other American workers showed up at our chalet door with their backpacks. "We're getting out of here tomorrow," one announced. "This place is too weird, too much work, and it's just not worth the money. You two should come with us."

Our chance to escape! That night, I wrote plaintively to my mother about the "inexcusable" conditions of the camp: miserable working shifts, terrible food, the carnival-like atmosphere. Ginny and I pondered our options, but we'd been raised to finish our commitments like good Southern girls, and the next morning, we watched as the last link to our American lives packed up and disappeared out the front gate. We stayed on.

"How far is Texas from the United States?" a plain-faced woman asked me as I lined up bread across the counter. Her hairnet was pulled tight over her unruly hair.

I was on special assignment now, working in a small back room with the "sandwich ladies," helping spread thick margarine over the hundreds of slices of white bread they used to prepare sandwiches each day for picnics and lunches.

"Texas is a part of the United States, Dorothy," one of the women corrected her.

Undeterred, Dorothy persisted, curious about the cowboys I knew, the wild saloons I must have frequented, and the horses I surely owned. I was amazed by their ignorance— though not yet by my own—but in the end, I loved being with these rumpled, silver-haired, gregarious ladies. They spent six days a week in this back room, perched on high stools around a big square table, talking nonstop as they buttered the bread, laid out mystery meats, cheese, tomatoes, and lettuce, and finally wrapped the finished sandwiches carefully in cellophane for campers on-the-go.

I sat quietly during most of the chatter: Dorothy's daughter had become pregnant at fifteen and was now living at home again. Glenda's husband worked at a nearby factory and stayed drunk at the pubs most nights. Amanda lived in a boarding house and had met an imperfect suitor at her dance lesson on Saturday night. All had dropped out of high school. They got only one day off a week from this repetitive work, yet they seemed strangely content—happy, even. They didn't yearn to be American, as I had previously assumed the entirety of humanity did. In fact, they might not have yearned for anything more than what they already had.

It was in that room, with morning light coming in through the dark wooden shutters around a big table with the Sandwich Ladies, that my mind finally cracked open to life's diverse riches. The simple activity of making sandwiches for hours on end while savoring what the present circumstances had to offer was my entry to other customs and ways of living. I felt completely at ease at this table, in a place I hadn't known existed, with friends I could never before have imagined. From then on, whenever I was invited into unusual or foreign situations that might previously have provoked fear in me, my answer was always: yes.

Back home, Ginny had been my only "political" friend. Her boyfriend's draft number had come up just before we left, so he had conceded and joined the Navy. And suddenly war became very personal. But in long conversations with our young multi-national coworkers, all of whom were outraged by the U.S. war on Vietnam, she couldn't win an argument.

"How do they know more about us than us?" she complained.

"America sends your brothers to kill thousands of people in a place you know nothing about to prevent Communism from spreading?" Ali from Afghanistan would pin us in. With each night spent out in the company of "the servants of the working class," we grew more distant from the paper–thin perceptions we'd held so close.

"I luv ya, ya big Yanks ya," the short, red-haired Scottish boy greeted us every morning at 5:30 as we began our first shift. Ginny and I settled into our daily chores and started making plans. We shipped the overstuffed suitcases home at considerable expense and bought train passes to travel during our last few weeks. I was promoted to a maroon uniform, much to Ginny's dismay. We both knew it was only because our blue-coated supervisor was after me, but that bump in class was still a sweet, guilty pleasure.

Late one night halfway through the summer, Ginny and I walked to a community staff room that housed a small black-and-white television set, mostly cabinet with a many-framed small screen in the middle. We sat on the floor with a few dozen coworkers, half-asleep, with sweaters and blankets around us as the evening chill set in. We could barely see the ghostlike figure that stepped off the spaceship and onto the moon, but there was silence among the small group of people from at least ten different countries. A sense of human pride seemed shared, beyond our cultural divide, and I felt all of humanity sitting there with me. And later, when the moon was visible, I could picture someone up there, right then, and imagine millions of people around the world also staring up at this white, round, mystical moon, all seeing a different part of the exact same, wonderful thing.

It was my richest souvenir from Sir Billy's holiday camp: knowing that we all are, in dissimilar conditions, simply seeing a different side of the same place, while striving to relish our small distinct lives.

In the end, Ginny and I did make it to London. We shopped at Carnaby Street for the latest androgynous fashions not far from where Twiggy had made her start, and we toured Buckingham Palace where the Queen was in residence. We even saw Mick Jagger, after spending an evening with a couple of animated young French guys who spoke no English but were comical company, making us goofy pointed hats out of newspapers to protect us from the next day's sun. Sharing blankets, cold tea, and baguettes throughout the long summer night, we staked out a place in the front row for a free concert in Hyde Park the next day. The Rolling Stones performed for 250,000 fans a month before Woodstock, letting three thousand white butterflies loose into the London sky in honor of their dead overdosed guitarist.

We left Butlin's shortly thereafter, bound for the European rails with two small backpacks. We rode up and down the Eurail lines, sleeping nights on the trains, waking up many mornings in a country different from the one in which we'd gone to sleep. I met my first New Yorker in Amsterdam, an attractive, sarcastic young guy as foreign to me as the Italians. We held long conversations in bohemian cafés with fellow backpackers, and Ginny became increasingly able to defend—and adjust—her political positions. We feigned nonchalance as we befriended a striking black man in Paris who spoke impeccable English in addition to his native French. We three walked the Champs Elysées together at midnight, newly minted friends.

Returning home weeks later, I peeled the "America: Love it or Leave It" banner from my bulletin board and replaced it with a group shot of the Butlin's crew. Ginny impulsively married her boyfriend the day before he shipped out to

Saigon. We stopped wearing dresses and started wearing jeans, every single day. The revolution had arrived.

Martha Ezell has worked as an educator, social worker, mortgage broker, apple picker, artist's assistant, and short-form documentary maker. Her films include "Taking Up Space: Socrates Sculpture Park," "Elephant Seals of Ano Nuevo," and "Szechuan Summer." She's addicted to the ocean and has recently learned to surf near her home in Sonoma County. This is her first published writing.

❧ ❧ ❧

Tongues and Arrows

"As people are walking all the time, in the same spot, a path appears." — *John Locke*

*I*n a courtyard shadowed green where twilight streams through feathering branches, everyone wants to know why everyone else is here.

We are sitting at long tables before steaming bowls of onion soup, dark and salty and pungent. Four hours ago I had no reservation and nowhere to spend the night, which means my literal reason for being here is that I followed a Dutch political science student in orange socks from the bus station to the Pilgrim Office, and then walked across the street and begged a hostelier named Jacques for a spare bed. That my backpack is now sitting upstairs next to a clean bunk, and that I am sitting down to soup and wine and a plate of pasta puddled in melted cheese, seems a small miracle. Which is the only kind of miracle I expect to encounter, now or later, and meanwhile the question is batted back and forth across the table with the speed of thought, or faith: why are you here?

The question is meant to get at motivation, not at method or intention. Our intentions, after all, are the same. We all plan to walk westward in the morning, and to keep walking westward on subsequent mornings, until we have arrived in Santiago, in northwestern Spain, nearly eight hundred kilometers away from this small town on France's southwest border. We aren't the first to do it and we won't be the last. St. Jean has been a pilgrims' town as long as there have been pilgrims on the Camino de Santiago, and there have been pilgrims here for over a thousand years.

For the story is this: that in the early years of the ninth century, a shepherd named Pelayo followed a peculiarly bright star to a field in Libredón. There, buried beneath the wild grass, he found the bones of a saint. On that spot an altar was built, and a cathedral around it, and they named the cathedral for *Santiago de Compostela:* Saint James of the Field of the Stars.

And the people came. They walked, or they rode on horses or donkeys. Later, they would ride bicycles, too. There would be hundreds of them, and then thousands, and then hundreds of thousands, streaming across Europe in rivulets converging over the dead saint's bones. In some centuries the streams would be thin, and in others they would flood the countryside in a desperate torrent; but the people would always come. They would be poor or not-so-poor. They would be penitent or convicted or curious. Some would want to suffer. Some would want to see the world. They would come for healing or solace or adventure, for spiritual pardon or legal pardon or epiphany. They came so the dross of their workaday lives would turn to alchemical miracle. They came so that something would change.

And so tonight, here in St. Jean Pied de Port, we are gathered at the beginning of things; and this is dinner but it is also reconnaissance, a preliminary casting session, and we inspect each other keenly, sussing out friends and allies and people to be avoided, trying to identify who will be central to the story we are about to tell ourselves, and who peripheral.

It's a luminous Polish redhead's turn to speak. Dressed in virgin blue, she smiles, hands fluttering to her hair to smooth it.

She opens her mouth, but before her words reach the air there is an "Excuse me, everybody," and then Jacques is standing, proposing a toast to "beautiful journeys." We raise our glasses. Jacques calls for a round of applause for each of the eight nationalities represented at the tables. We applaud eight times. The Polish redhead starts again: she is walking the Camino as penance for her sins, of which, she says, she has many.

The girl with the orange socks, which she packed specifically to show her support for the Dutch national soccer team, this being a World Cup year, is walking because she "likes trekkings" and doesn't know what else to do.

The Australian computer programmer, who is thirty-eight and looks ten years younger, is walking for the same reason.

Ditto the tall Irish girl.

I don't hear what the Austrian guy in the HARDCORE CHRISTIAN t-shirt says, but I can guess.

When the expectant silence reaches me I am swept with an unfamiliar shyness. I watch my fingers fiddle with the stem of my wineglass.

I came to walk, I say, because I like to walk, and because I am interested in long walks, and why people take them, and what they are looking for, and whether they find it. And because I went on a different long walk once and I got hurt and had to stop.

I say I have an academic interest in failure.

Certainly I am not looking for redemption.

I don't believe in redemption.

There are things I do not explain.

"Do you want more wine?" the Aussie asks. I hesitate.

"When a woman hesitates," says the redhead, "that means yes."

"Will that hold up in a court of law?" the Aussie asks.

I let him fill my glass.

There are things I do not explain because I cannot even explain them to myself. The facts are tired: how five summers ago I'd planned a different walk on a different continent, two thousand miles, south to north, a walk four times as long as this Camino, through ever-unfolding ranges of green American mountains, running parallel to the sea.

"I would like," says Jacques, tapping a fork against a wineglass, "to give you each some gifts." Two tables of fetal pilgrims look up from dinner plates and cast eyes in his direction. He holds up what looks like a length of yellow police tape, emblazoned with arrows, scallop shells, and, in enormous lettering, the hostel logo: *L'Esprit du Chemin.* The spirit of the way.

The ribbon, Jacques tells us, is a symbol of the spirit and shared purpose of all pilgrims on the Camino. "We'd like you to tie it on your packs," he adds, "and then you will all know you have all been here. If you want an extra one that is O.K. too!"

Because Jacques is the kind of hostelier who answers "Might you have any beds available for this evening?" with a tranquil "Cucumber water?" and because, as he has told me, he is not in fact the hostelier at all, but rather a friend of the owners, taking care of business while they are on vacation, I suspect him of an unimpeachable sincerity even as he waxes poetic about the transformative bliss of providing free advertising.

"Our next gift," says Jacques, "is energy pearls."

He holds up a small glass bead, pinched between thumb and forefinger. It's blue, but, he assures us, the energy pearls are available in a variety of colors. Jacques himself always carries one in his left pocket. "We are," he says, "ninety-seven seventy-nine percent positive energy, and three percent negative, and we spend all our time thinking about the three percent. So the pearl is to remind you of all that is good, all the good energy in the world and yourself."

I am halfway through the third glass of wine, and I find this kind of beautiful.

With my fork, I poke a pearl onion stained scarlet with marinated beets, and it pops out of its skin, slides across the plate. I do not explain that on that earlier walk, I shredded a footful of ligaments and had to stop walking a thousand miles short of my destination. Or that in the years since leaving those other mountains, I've held onto their memory with a voraciousness that embarrasses me. I don't explain that it took three years before the foot pain began to subside, and that I have a nauseating worry the damage is permanent. I do not say: if I cannot walk across Spain now, if my body fails me again, then I will have lost a dream whose largeness I do not want to think about. All the words sound treacly and precious. *Stop being such a drama queen.* And now I've flown across the sea to walk into a country where even mawkish words will be beyond my reach.

"No, no, *no,*" in peevish tones floats up from the foot of the table, where a middle-aged Dutch woman is roundly castigating two English girls. The girls' university term starts in exactly four weeks, which means that if they want to get to Santiago, they'll need to walk very long days. They are runners and believe their bodies are up to the task. I eyeball them. They're disgustingly fit and they're probably right. But this is the wrong thing to tell Dutch Mary. Apparently it is entirely the wrong way to go about walking the Camino, and represents a desecration of the spirit of the affair. "You must give up the plans and the forcing," she instructs. "You must let go of this idea that there is a right way to walk. You must walk slowly. You must feel the essence of the Way. You will not have time for the whole thing." Her voice is rising, her gestures untamed. "You must go home before you reach Santiago," she says, and she is nearly spitting. "You can finish later."

"I think we'll be fine, thank you," says one of the girls, coolly.

I think we'll be fine. Verbal salt over carnal shoulder, a desperate kind of charm. Something to mutter in the choked roads of St. Jean. This afternoon, walking, we all spilled over throat-narrow sidewalks and into the streets, backpacks bobbing. Each of us, in order to get to the hostel, dodged snub-nosed cars careening over cobblestones, churning through puddled pilgrims. We rippled and receded. *I think we'll be fine.* A pilgrim's first labor: to get out of St. Jean alive. Say it: *be fine.*

This town feels unreal, has since the moment I stepped off the bus, and did all through an afternoon of wandering the streets. I'm trying to pinpoint the source of the alienness now, and I don't think it's Jacques or his energy pearls. There's a different, older and vaguely fabricated quality to this unreality, as though a generic medieval flavor had been poured over the town to support its claims to history: Napoleon, the Romans, centuries of pilgrims. Outside the courtyard where we are sitting, the Rue de la Citadelle threads between whitewashed brick buildings taller than the street is wide. Do places carry layered ghosts of their pasts, auras laid over old streets? I couldn't feel them, but I'd have been willing to blame my imperceptions on some absence located within me.

It's a funny club to be in, this *pilgrim* corps, I'd thought then, as my eyes trailed away from the wooden placard and over the foot-travelers spattering the streets: each of us instantly recognizable to the others (those backpacks! those quick-dri t-shirts and sunhats! the beaming incompetence of outsiders!) before we'd exchanged so much as a *buen Camino,* a *bonne route,* a *safe travels,* nor even enough words to ascertain, if there were one, a common language. There was an unmistakable *we*, and I still didn't know who *we* were. But *we* put euro coins in the donation box at the Pilgrim Office, collected accordioned oaktag booklets—our *credencials*, to entitle us to stay in pilgrim hostels each night—and pocketed them. We tied bleached scallop shells with holes drilled through them to our bags. The shells, symbol of St. James, swung across the fabric as we walked, soft zipping noises preceding syncopated clanks against metal water bottles. When we began to look, we found shells everywhere: cast in bronze, etched in stone, painted in yellow on square blue signs, expectant hieroglyphs implicating us in some silent, coded pact whose terms I didn't understand. The best I could offer was a map in one hand, and I held it like a talisman. And now, here, in the courtyard, Jacques is standing again, tapping that glass again, because a late pilgrim has straggled in, the first Dane of the evening, and we've got to applaud for Denmark.

After dinner I go up to the women's bunkroom and trip on the uneven stairs for the third consecutive time. I pick myself up with a threadbare dignity and glower at the wall above the staircase landing, which is plastered with motivational sayings from the Buddha. "Do not look for happiness; happiness is the Way," the wall advises me serenely, and then again in French to be sure I've understood: *Le chemin c'est le bonheur*. The wall makes a fitting counterpart to the guidebook I've brought, a slim, orange-spined volume subtitled *A Practical and Mystical Manual for the Modern Day Pilgrim*. The *Mystical Manual* is one of the best-selling English-language books about the Camino, alongside memoirs with titles like *Walk in a Relaxed Manner, The Power of Now,* and *Pilgrim in Aquarius*. It is full of inspirational quotations and blank, lined pages on which to write daily "reflections" about my spiritual progress. It has good maps.

Before I fall asleep I page through the *Mystical Manual*. I want to get a look at the terrain for tomorrow's walk, which will be through the Pyrenees and over the Spanish border. The terrain, as the *Manual* shows me, can be best described as "up." The *Manual* also advises me, before I begin walking, to fill out a *Self-Assessment Questionnaire: Inner Waymarks*, in which I am to score myself on a scale of 1-10 on my awareness of such personal attributes as *clarity on what inspires you, confidence to follow your intuitive sense of direction,* and *ability to recognize your patterns of defence*. A single, giant, misty, purple question mark floats helpfully behind the text, an exercise in thematically appropriate typography. I can download extra copies from the *Mystical Manual*'s website if I like, in order to repeat the exercise on my return.

I do not fill out the questionnaire.

What I know is this: I want something from this walk I don't believe it can give me.

At the end of town, beyond a stone bridge that caps the river in a neat curve, the yellow arrows begin. They begin without fanfare, recommencing after an in-town hiatus. St. Jean is only one of a thousand places to start walking the Camino, which despite its name is really a network of paths lacing over Europe, all meeting in the cathedral in Santiago just as the grooves in a scallop shell come to a single point at its base. The Camino has no beginning: only an end. Somehow, still, we begin.

The first arrow points to a second arrow which points to a third and they all point up. The entire Camino will be marked with yellow arrows, here to Santiago, painted on road signs and guardrails and rocks. So we drift, all of us, like seeds clumped and floating in the wind, through woods and along switchbacking roads that would be wide enough for cars to pass if there were any cars. The woods and the roads open at last into a vast and rolling expanse of sheep-scattered fields, under a hill-hemmed sky all shot with light.

I shade my eyes and squint and try to see. I tell an Austrian carrying devil's sticks that the dark patches far up a distant hilltop are sheep. He disagrees. He thinks they are rocks. We make a bet, but neither of us is willing to walk up the hill to settle it, so instead we sit companionably on the side of the road near a pile of boots and eat the omelet sandwiches Jacques's wife packed us this morning. The sandwiches are good, soft egg and chewy bread, and there is the simple pleasure of using a body and then nourishing it. The pile of boots is also a pile of socks and trinkets, offerings heaped at the feet of a statue of Mary, the Virgin of Orisson. She is blue and white and crowned and holding Jesus, and she stands at the far end of a rock outcropping, silhouetted against the valley below.

The vista is uncanny. Cypress-studded peaks and sweeping fields beneath a brilliant sky. All the clustered roofs of the small farms tiled red, each curving shingle like a flowerpot sliced lengthwise. We might as well have walked up the road and into a Chagall painting. In its way, it feels as imaginary as St. Jean. "My priest says to me that when I fly to St. Jean, my soul would take a few days to catch up," says the Austrian, and as we sit and eat and talk in this borderland, the brown winter woods of Georgia ebb at last for a space of time. My camera case is affixed to the front of one shoulder strap. I let my fingers trail over it like water. There comes upon me a weird peace I do not wholly trust, though it occurs to me fleetingly that, rather, I might not wholly trust myself.

"Yesterday is history, tomorrow a mystery, and today a gift—that is why it is called the present!" chirps the *Mystical Manual*.

I sigh and stuff the *Manual* in a side pocket.

I am trying to pretend I haven't been fighting memory all morning.

There is a place in Georgia where another trail begins. A mountaintop where a metal plaque is set into stone "for those who seek fellowship with the wilderness." Near it, a small swipe of white paint adorns a boulder. The first white blaze or the last, depending on your bearings or desires; one end of a long line of blazes inked onto stone, soaked into creviced bark, stretching from here to a mountain in Maine. Each end is as arbitrary as the other, the status of both mountains merely the byproduct of years of civic squabbling. Nevertheless, between them a seam of painted beacons lights the way, sending travelers up a root-stubbled trail narrow as shoulders, winding brown and bare through barer trees.

Behind every yellow arrow, this is what I see.

The open blueness of the summer sky turns branch-latticed and dark.

Over these undulating hills false summits spread like nesting dolls un-nested.

June is part March.

Northern Georgia is here in southern France, and no one knows it but me.

We rise, and walk, and pass a wayside cross, and the track turns to rough grass. Another set of footsteps falls in beside me. Another pilgrim, a blond Lithuanian who's already been walking for weeks. Hello hello yes and where are you from and when did you start and why and nice to meet you.

"I like scary things," says the Lithuanian.

"Oh?" I say.

"It's easy to scare people," he says.

"Ah," I say.

"Do you believe in ghosts?" he says.

"Probably not," I say.

"You should," he says, sanguine.

"Oh?" *Why* isn't the Austrian saying anything.

"If you believe in ghosts, you won't be scared of them," he says.

I decide a logical analysis is best skirted at this juncture.

"If you believe in ghosts, people will be scared of you and leave you alone," he says.

That *would* provide incentive.

"My ex-wife, she sleep with me, she go to mental hospital," says the Lithuanian. Apropos of nothing. "All women, they sleep with me, they go to mental hospital."

The Austrian is looking straight ahead. I school my expression placid.

"You don't believe me, you can try," the Lithuanian adds, a smirk playing on his lips.

"I'll keep that in mind," I say.

I reach the Spanish border ten or fifteen minutes later.

In this moment, as I stand on the dividing line between what has happened and what has not yet happened, the things I do not know are legion.

I do not know that I'll see neither Dutch Mary nor the redhead again after today.

Nor do I know that the tall Irish girl from last night, whom I haven't been thinking much about, will turn out to be a central character.

I don't know that my old injury will flare five days from now, nor that for the rest of the journey the only way I will be able to walk without intense pain will be to hire a taxi each day to drive my bag up the road, and I will feel like I am cheating.

I don't truly understand how many people I will talk to. I will see them walk, and I will see them invest their walks with meaning. They will be seeking some kind of clarity or epiphany or inspiration. They will be trying to get over deaths, betrayals, losses, addictions, neuroses, impossible standards, immeasurable sadness.

In six weeks' time I will reach the Praza do Obradoiro in Santiago.

I will find no epiphanies waiting for me there.

Yet I will have a momentary wave of a wholly unexpected sadness, not at the square itself but a moment earlier, as I am rounding the corner and I get my first glimpse of the cathedral, that ancient worn stone building with moss growing up its spires and its carvings weather-worn, that building so many people have spent so much time over so many centuries trying to reach. Something bittersweet.

Perhaps this will be because first love always has a certain irreplicable quality. More likely, it will be because I will have come to question the entire notion of epiphany; or, at least, of imputing transformative capacities to particular places. I will have come to believe that to move on from our griefs, we've got no one to look to but ourselves. That miracles are always of our own making. Which will give me a spare and windy feeling, like some great northern wasteland, stones and snow and empty space. Something freeing, but lonely. And so I will be moved watching a young Italian couple walk into the square together holding hands, and knowing that whatever meaning their journeys held for them, they took those journeys together.

This trip will not give me what I want of it, but it will give me something else.

In this moment I know none of this.

It's the problem of inheriting a script but no cast list or stage directions. We're left guessing at our costars, at the contours of our set. We never know where our attention should be focused. Or how to wrestle all the lurking ghosts of our former selves and our persistent loves. All of it: the problem and the blessing of the present tense.

In this moment I am only standing on the border, which might better be called the *frontière* or the *frontera* depending on the direction you are facing and the landscape you are leaving behind, but 778 kilometers from Santiago regardless, distance being distance, howsoever named.

In St. Jean half the signs were in Basque, full of Zs and Xes and Ks, so that merely reading them made the tongue tingle, as if with a mouthful of bees. When you do not speak Basque, to see all these signs written in a language isolate, a tongue with no familial connections, might lull you into false security: thinking that in your own idiom, you are never so alone. This comfort is illusory. Keep staring at the signs and they will, without changing, change before you. They will turn wry. As if we didn't each in our way already speak a private isolate; as if we weren't all forever failing to comprehend one another anyway. As if this failure weren't the deepest source of a dream of uncommon understanding.

Fall to silence, then, as you walk up through the mountains and out of France. Watch, instead, your own body. Your knees as they flex, your calves as they tighten. Your shoulders and hips where they bear the load of an unfamiliar and turtling weight. Adjust your gait to a newly centered gravity. Stop to tape the red beginnings of a blistered heel, that peculiar heated sting. Swallow water in long icy draughts, and feel the measured contractions of its cold slide from throat to belly. When you begin to walk again, notice the stretch of your stride. Try to re-inhabit yourself, muscle and shell and sinew, quick and red and alive.

What is easily forgotten: that speech, too, is of the body. The rhythm of hard breath changes all the sounds on your lips. This is not so different from the moment when you move your body past a carved stone marker and Ronceveaux turns to Roncesvalles. Once, long ago, a *roi* and a *rey* drew lines on a map and said: here is where one land will become another. And a long line of barbed wire. And now *basque* turns to *el basco*. When the language you speak fades into the language you do not speak, even the words for what is strange are strange.

El basco itself, however, lies calm across this bright high borderland, a changeless strangeness no matter on which side of the line your body falls. This is still Basque country. Zs and Xes and Ks will still buzz and swish and clack across shop signs for days, before they begin to fade.

Who is to say where one story ends and another begins?

Jessica Wilson is a native Northeasterner currently living in the Midwest while scheming ways to travel to the opposite side of the globe. She holds an MFA in nonfiction from the University of Iowa and is working on a memoir about landscape, performance, and long-distance walking trails. Her work has appeared in Alligator Juniper, *the* Daily Palette, Glimpse Magazine, the Seneca Review Online, *and* New Fairy Tales. *Between St. Jean Pied de Port and Santiago, she also managed to a) accidentally flood a Spanish pilgrim hostel; b) become an unintentional model for a persistent Portuguese guy intent on photographing her feet; and c) meet a man on a horse who believed himself to be the last surviving Knight Templar.*

ACKNOWLEDGMENTS

Every book is a cooperative effort, but an anthology takes this premise to the next level. I *literally* couldn't have done it alone. First and foremost, thanks to the several hundred women who submitted stories this year—you are truly the reason this book exists. My heartfelt gratitude goes to the Travelers' Tales' dream team: James O'Reilly, Larry Habegger, and Sean O'Reilly, for steadfast encouragement, guidance, perspicacity, and good humor. Natalie Baszile: you are uncommonly patient, infinitely supportive, and utterly marvelous, and I feel privileged to know you and work with you. For generous amounts of feedback and support, my love and gratitude go to Dan Prothero, Dolly Spalding, Erica Hilton, Lynn Bruni, Kimberley Lovato, Jen Castle, Elizabeth Barrett, and Anthony Weller. Thank you also to Stephanie Elizondo Griest, Don George, Phil Cousineau, Jim Benning, Rolf Potts, Jeffrey Tayler, Laura Deutsch, Lucy McCauley, and Jaime Clarke for spreading the word and recommending travel stories. Finally, thanks to all you readers out there. You mean the world to us.

"Lost and Liberated" by Kimberley Lovato first appeared on *Gadling.com*, May 27, 2011. Published with permission from the author. Copyright © 2011 by Kimberley Lovato.

"The Runaway" by Ann Hood first appeared in *MORE Magazine* August 2011. Published with permission from the author. Copyright © 2011 by Ann Hood.

"Bridge on the Border" by Molly Beer published with permission from the author. Copyright © 2012 by Molly Beer.

"Our Own Apocalypse Now" by Haley Sweetland Edwards first appeared on *Wrold Hun,* March 7, 2011. Published with permission from the author. Copyright © 2011 by Haley Sweetland Edwards.

"I Think I Must Be Beautiful" by Blair Braverman published with permission from the author. Copyright © 2012 by Blair Braverman.

"Passion and Pizza" from the forthcoming title *Driving Hungry*, by Layne Mosler. Used by permission of Vintage Books, a division of Random House, Inc.

"Bones Surfacing in the Dirt" by Lauren Quinn first appeared on *Matador.com,* August 2, 2011. Published with permission from the author. Copyright © 2012 by Lauren Quinn.

"Mare's Milk, Mountain Bikes, Meteors & Mammaries" by Kirsten Koza published with permission from the author. Copyright © 2012 by Kirsten Koza.

"Letting Go on the Ganges" by Kristin Zibell published with permission from the author. Copyright © 2012 by Kristin Zibell.

"Birthright" by Emily Matchar first appeared in *Perceptive Travel*, February 2011. Published with permission from the author. Copyright © 2011 by Emily Matchar.

"Spiral-Bound" by Kate McCahill first appeared on *Numero Cinq* 2010. Published with permission from the author. Copyright © 2010 by Kate McCahill.

"Meat and Greet" by Abbie Kozolchyk published with permission from the author. Copyright © 2012 by Abbie Kozolchyk.

"Death and Love in Kenya" by Anena Hansen published with permission from the author. Copyright © 2012 by Anena Hansen.

"Dance of the Spider Women," by Laura Fraser first appeared in *AFAR Magazine* July/August 2011. Published with permission from the author. Copyright © 2011 by Laura Fraser

"On the Macal" by Mary Jo McConahay published with permission from the author. Copyright © 2012 by Mary Jo McConahay.

"Holiday Camp" by Martha Ezell published with permission from the author. Copyright © 2012 by Martha Ezell.

"Tongues and Arrows" by Jessica Wilson published with permission from the author. Copyright © 2012 by Jessica Wilson.

ABOUT THE EDITOR

Lavinia Spalding is the author of *Writing Away: A Creative Guide to Awakening the Journal-Writing Traveler*, chosen one of the best travel books of 2009 by the *Los Angeles Times*, and coauthor of *With a Measure of Grace: The Story and Recipes of a Small Town Restaurant*. She also edited *The Best Women's Travel Writing 2011*. A regular contributor to *Yoga Journal*, her work has appeared in a wide variety of literary and travel publications, including *Sunset* magazine, *Gadling*, *World Hum*, *Post Road*, and *Inkwell*.

She lives in San Francisco and can always be found at www.laviniaspalding.com. Visit her there to see more of her work and to read interviews with the authors from The Best Women's Travel Writing series.